Development and Human Rights

Development and Human Rights

Rhetoric and Reality in India

JOEL E. OESTREICH

Oxford University Press is a department of the University of Oxford. It furthers
the University's objective of excellence in research, scholarship, and education
by publishing worldwide. Oxford is a registered trade mark of Oxford University
Press in the UK and certain other countries.

Published in the United States of America by Oxford University Press
198 Madison Avenue, New York, NY 10016, United States of America.

© Oxford University Press 2017

First issued as an Oxford University Press paperback, 2020

All rights reserved. No part of this publication may be reproduced, stored in
a retrieval system, or transmitted, in any form or by any means, without the
prior permission in writing of Oxford University Press, or as expressly permitted
by law, by license, or under terms agreed with the appropriate reproduction
rights organization. Inquiries concerning reproduction outside the scope of the
above should be sent to the Rights Department, Oxford University Press, at the
address above.

You must not circulate this work in any other form
and you must impose this same condition on any acquirer.

Library of Congress Cataloging-in-Publication Data
Names: Oestreich, Joel E., author.
Title: Development and human rights : rhetoric and reality in India/Joel E. Oestreich.
Description: New York, NY : Oxford University Press, [2017] |
Includes bibliographical references and index.
Identifiers: LCCN 2016039644 | ISBN 9780190637347 (hardcover : alk. paper) |
ISBN 9780190086855 (paperback : alk. paper)
Subjects: LCSH: Human rights—India. | Economic development—Social aspects—India. |
United Nations—India.
Classification: LCC JC599.I4 O47 2017 | DDC 323.0954—dc23
LC record available at https://lccn.loc.gov/2016039644

Contents

1. Human Rights, Politics, and Development — 1
2. Development and Human Rights in India — 31
3. The United Nations Development Programme — 60
4. The United Nations Children's Fund — 86
5. Other UN Agencies Involved in Rights-based Approaches — 117
6. Strategies and Outcomes of Rights-based Approaches — 149
7. Conclusion: New Ways of Pursuing Human Rights Promotion — 178

Notes — 197

Index — 203

Development and Human Rights

1

Human Rights, Politics, and Development

MAP 1 Contemporary India.

THIS BOOK IS to a great extent the result of an experience I had in 1993. I was working at the time as a consultant for the United Nations Children's Fund (UNICEF) in Dhaka, Bangladesh. While I was there, the country was undergoing a round of complex, sometimes violent, maneuvering between the two main political parties—the Bangladesh National Party, and the Awami League—and this resulted in regular *hartals*, or general strikes. I had an opportunity to discuss the political situation with the head of the UNICEF office in Dhaka, an inspiring leader, Rolf Carriere. It seemed to me that he must be sorely tempted to use his influence to affect the upcoming elections. After all, UNICEF was helping millions of people directly or indirectly through its various programs: if the Resident Representative (as his title was at the time) of UNICEF made it known that UNICEF thought one candidate was better than another for the children of Bangladesh, his opinion could potentially sway an election. Of course, this suggestion horrified him: if the UN were to interfere that way in the political affairs of a host state, it would be thrown out the next day. Such a blatantly political action was simply unthinkable. In a world of sovereign states, UNICEF and all other intergovernmental and nongovernmental agencies operate only with the permission of their host state. They are invited in by those host states, and states retain full sovereignty and control over their territory; no government would stand for an unaccountable international agency interfering with its domestic politics.

At that time—now more than 20 years ago—this attitude made a great deal of sense and did not seem inconsistent with the mission of the UN and its agencies. UNICEF, for example, was then almost entirely interested in promoting a handful of high-impact child survival strategies that were shown to be very successful, such as hand-washing, micronutrient supplements, proper sanitation, breastfeeding, and girls' education (Black, 1986). The Convention on the Rights of the Child (CRC), which contained a long list of child rights, was a new document and of uncertain significance (Smyke, 1990). Indeed the head of UNICEF, James P. Grant, had consigned his child rights advisors to primarily a public relations rather than operational roles, for fear that the CRC would prove "overly political" (Oestreich, 2007, p. 48). Other agencies also devoted their work to entirely nonpolitical fields where they could provide governments with technical support through programs of cooperation. There was no desire to get involved in politics, and, indeed, they studiously avoided it. The only exceptions might have been the work of international financial institutions—the World Bank and the International Monetary Fund (IMF)—UN-affiliated institutions whose "structural adjustment" programs with debtor countries could have clear and often significant political implications

(Berg & Betchelder, 1985; Haggard & Kaufman, 1992; Mosley, Harrigan, & Toye, 1991).

Today, in India as elsewhere, UN agencies have taken on a remarkable set of development priorities. They may not be quite so extreme as intervening in an election, but they certainly seem far more intrusive in a state's internal affairs than most anyone would have considered in the past. Currently, in the ancient city of Varanasi (the former Benares), for example, UNDP and its partners are helping women run for local political office and training them on how to be politically effective; around India, UNDP is engaged in activities like teaching ordinary citizens how to file right-to-information requests with the government and training members of the transgender community how to protest job discrimination. UNICEF is helping organize local communities to manage schools and demand services from government agencies. World Bank staff, when planning projects, considers issues like whether members of untouchable castes are being excluded from local governance and takes steps to guarantee their inclusion, even when that means making enemies among the local elite. UN Women is working with government agents to change the way laws are enforced (for example, laws regarding the use of mobile sonogram equipment to determine the gender of unborn children) and challenging local government officials who still condone forced sterilization.

These are not minor changes in the way the UN (and UN-family agencies like the World Bank) defines its role. They open tremendous potential for development assistance to become more effective by working more directly on the political and social structures that truly impede progress for many millions. And they have equally tremendous potential for advancing the cause of human rights by allowing development agencies to work directly to promote people's rights. They also say something about the ability of the UN and its agencies to adapt to new circumstances and take on some autonomy in defining their role—there has been no international mandate from states to make these changes. Yet very little has been said about what all this means for world politics. It is no small thing that a branch of the UN feels it has the ability to involve itself in inherently domestic, political matters. Indeed, theories of international relations are still catching up with the independence that these agencies seem to show. Thus, the implications of these changes are important and wide-ranging, yet little studied.

To advance our understanding of these issues, this book presents an investigation into how UN agencies, in the name of a "rights-based approach to development" (RBA), have been pushing the boundaries of political involvement in developing-country politics in a way once thought impossible.

(I have chosen to write it in the first person, since this investigation is so substantially based on my observations and interview research while living in India on a Fulbright fellowship. To write in the third person would introduce too many awkward phrases.) This book will argue that the work of UN agencies in RBA represents a new, potentially more effective way of promoting and protecting human rights than traditional mechanisms—one that is not just a "rhetorical" commitment to rights, but real and important. One goal of this book is in the policy realm: to present a complex, careful case study of how rights can be promoted through development assistance. But to make this case, I argue, it is important to demonstrate two further points. The *first* is that UN agencies are grappling explicitly with civil and political (C&P) rights and not just economic, social, and cultural (ES&C) rights. While there is a growing consensus that these sets of rights are closely intertwined and interdependent (Donnelly & Whelan, 2007; Nickel, 2008; Whelan, 2010), the fact remains that UN development agencies have largely limited themselves to promoting ES&C rights and left C&P rights to the bodies directly charged with their promotion, such as the Committee on Human Rights, and the Human Rights Council. Promotion of C&P rights is much more politically sensitive. It is surprising that UN agencies do this, and even more surprising that they take steps to do so while almost hiding the fact that they do! Yet their inclusion in the development project is a good sign of a move from rhetorical to real commitment to the human rights project. As will be discussed in more detail, the very fact that they try to hide their work on rights shows that this work is real and meaningful; there would be no need for covering it up if it were merely a public relations exercise. A focus on C&P rights can highlight where UN agencies are taking on the most controversial rights issues and not avoiding the implications of RBA in difficult areas.

The *second* point is that when UN agencies advocate for politically sensitive rights they are showing a high degree of independence from states. They are forced to develop strategies to exercise that independence. Analysis of international organizations (IOs) by international relations scholars has shown that IOs exhibit much more independence, under certain circumstances, than traditional "realist" theory would predict. The reluctance of development IOs to promote rights—and, more to the point, to get involved in political matters—has slowly been dissolving. It is important to understand how IOs are asserting this independence and how they are pushing back against state resistance. This is vital from a practical perspective—seeing what strategies will help in the pursuit of human rights—but it also sheds more light on the ability of IOs to act independently.

If UN development agencies are pursuing C&P rights, and are doing so in ways that overcome or go around the resistance of host states, it leads to the larger conclusion: a commitment to RBA, and the language of human rights, is transforming UN agencies into potentially important actors in the human rights field. And not actors with a weak, mainly rhetorical commitment to rights, but ones with important new tools in rights promotion. These processes are almost entirely unremarked on, yet they represent a vital, almost groundbreaking shift in how UN agencies go about their work. They move rights promotion away from traditional "naming and shaming" strategies and promise a more cooperative, hands-on approach to improving rights worldwide. This opens tremendous new possibilities in the struggle for the respect of international human rights.

Two Key Questions

Shifting the Focus: Civil and Political Rights in Economic Development

The focus of this work will be on civil and political rights and how they are being promoted through a rights-based approach to development. This requires some explanation. It is most certainly not my intention to privilege one set of rights over another. Indeed, as will be discussed below, in RBA properly understood, there is no easy or meaningful division between the two categories. But UN agencies have traditionally emphasized ES&C rights, disregarding their close dependence on C&P rights. This both ignores the interdependence of these sets of rights and elides the political difficulties of rights promotion properly done. Essentially, any state can and will claim that they want to promote ES&C rights, such as nutrition, housing, or health care. And when they fail to do so, they simply argue that these rights take time to implement or are dependent on economic resources. It also allows states to simply focus on providing goods rather than tackling the *root causes* of deprivation. Similarly, UN agencies have always been working to promote health care, food security, shelter, and the like because these are uncontroversial; no states oppose health care and food security! (Not openly, anyway.) Simply using the term "rights" does not necessarily change much about the specifics of their work; using rights language can be, and too often is, a purely rhetorical exercise. So the political problems that frighten many UN agencies away from promoting human rights are much less intense—and perhaps entirely eliminated—when the discussion is primarily about ES&C rights. But promoting the right to freedom of speech, freedom of religion, even the rights to life and liberty, seemed a very different matter; as does tackling the political inequities that lead to deprivation of food, shelter, education, and so forth. Indeed, promoting C&P rights is central to a "true" understanding of what it means to promote ES&C rights and is central to the concept of a rights-based approach. It makes the rights-based approach different from a model where agencies simply *provide* social goods—goods that might not be provided in the future. A nonrhetorical approach to ES&C rights *requires* an approach to C&P rights and the political issues that come with them.

Thus the practical goal of this project is to bring civil and political rights—so-called negative rights—to the foreground of research on the rights-based approach to development. Properly understood, RBA must grapple with the political side of development. As Hans-Peter Schmitz puts it, "from a [RBA] perspective, poverty is not primarily due to a lack of resources, but a result of discrimination and political decisions of those holding power" (Schmitz, 2012, p. 525). Varun Gauri "define HRBAs as principles that justify demands against privileged actors, made by the poor or those speaking on their behalf, for using national and international resources and rules to protect the crucial human interests of the globally or locally disadvantaged" (Gauri & Gloppen, 2012, p. 3). Nearly all work on RBA emphasizes that the approach is not just about alleviating poverty or helping in other development metrics but also about attending to the root causes of poverty and deprivation—discrimination, lack of voice and input into development programs, ineffective governance, and other measures of powerlessness. RBA is ultimately about giving power to those who lacked it before, thus allowing them to be "empowered" to provide for their own welfare and improve their social and economic situation. Power is always a political process, and thus RBA is inherently about politics at some level. For too long, UN agencies had largely ignored the political implications of both sets of rights, but this is changing with the implementation of rights-based approaches to development.

Given the emphasis on political empowerment and changing structures, however, surprisingly little attention has been paid in the RBA literature to the promotion of civil and political rights. Rather, the focus is on economic, social, and cultural rights—the so-called positive rights. Brigitte Hamm, in a seminal 2001 work, notes that "while a human rights approach to development refers to all rights and thus emphasizes the interrelation and interdependence of human rights, it pays special attention to economic and social rights as the authentic concern of development policy" (2001, p. 1006). Hans-Otto Sano (2000), in another early work, focuses on "entitlements" as the key element of RBA, with "empowerment" as a step toward getting "duty-holders" to live up to their responsibilities. Thus empowerment—often poorly defined as some sort of participatory process to be worked out later—becomes a tool for claiming economic, social, and cultural rights and making sure they are provided by a state that feels obligated to do so. Gready and Vandenhole, for example, note in a paper on how rights promote development that "'freedoms to' are as important as the classic liberal 'freedoms from'" and that "a human rights based approach . . . has motivated development agencies to become more involved in advocacy, and many are now involved in both service delivery and capacity building *as well as* advocacy . . . work on economic and social rights has encouraged more constructive engagement with states around policy development and service delivery, to complement more adversarial engagements" (2014, pp. 6–7; emphasis in original). Similarly, Langford, Sumner, and Yamin (2013, p. 22) note the importance that Amartya Sen places on the indivisibility of human rights, and then they note that "of particular relevance to development is the growing prominence and acceptance of ESC rights" and consider how human rights impact state commitments toward the Millennium Development Goals.

The focus on the ES&C side of rights is understandable from a number of perspectives. First, the goal of most modern development projects is to improve people's welfare, and this is best put in terms of ES&C goals. The notion that development *is* freedom (however defined—more on that later), or is the attainment of a broad range of rights that promote human freedom and flourishing, is still not part of the normal development discourse. Second, as this book will discuss in greater detail, C&P rights are more "political," and thus it is more difficult to advocate for them with state representatives than ES&C rights. While it is one thing to pressure states on the right to food (a right that commits states only to "progressive realization"), it is quite another to advocate political freedoms. And, of course, those freedoms are harder to measure or even to tie directly to human development (Hertel & Minkler, 2007). So, where C&P rights are included in most work on RBA, they are included in fairly vague terms: there is talk of "empowerment," "participation," "fighting discrimination," and similar language. When these terms are described in more detail—what does it mean to empower groups or to give them voice?—it is usually in relation to particular projects (Brouwer, Grady,

Traore, & Wordofa, 2005) rather than general principles. What is missing is a general notion of which C&P rights are desirable in and of themselves.

In fact, few development organizations are really dealing with C&P rights promotion beyond the notion that "empowerment" and other such buzzwords constitute a basic element of RBA. As Uvin (2002) has importantly shown, such concepts border on meaninglessness when they are not tied to real, substantive change in how development is done. Talk about people "claiming" their rights, about governments being held "accountable," and other such terms, fade into insignificance if they are not accompanied with real political change. Cornwall and Brock (2005) make a similar point when they show the always-changing meaning of these terms, often to suit the development orthodoxy of the time or the priorities of particular agencies. Caroline Thomas (1998) has accused the financial institutions in particular of using rights talk as a shield for policies of exploitation. Hannah Miller (2010), while generally approving of RBA, points out that "rights-based" approaches can too easily become "rights-framed" and that there is so little consensus on what RBA means that rights language justifies a wide variety of practices, some more rights-oriented than others. In other words, there is a real danger that rights become a mere rhetorical exercise by UN agencies: and as the following research will show, many within these agencies do in fact lack either a commitment to human rights or a poor understanding of what they are.

This book will also show that some UN agencies *are* in many cases considering the importance of human rights, C&P rights in particular, and doing so explicitly. By explicitly, I mean both doing it out in the open (without trying to hide their concern for these rights, out of respect for their political sensitivity) and looking not just at buzzwords but also at specific rights, such as speech, due process, personhood, and others. There is some camouflaging of the work. Indeed, that will be shown as an essential part of what the UN is doing. But that is not the same as hiding it completely or simply refusing to deal with the issues.

Why is this important? First of all, a rights-based approach to development is simply incomplete—if not incoherent—if it does not include a concern for real civil and political rights, beyond easy buzzwords like empowerment and sustainability. And C&P rights must not be seen merely as instruments for the promotion of ES&C rights; understanding RBA properly requires considering equally the promotion of *all* rights as the very definition of development. Second, an explicit C&P rights agenda in development assistance means they can help promote and protect human rights in a way that has the potential to be much more powerful than current methods. These are the work of specific human rights bodies based in Geneva and New York, which mostly just collect reports and expose violations. Understanding the C&P promotion potential of UN development agencies shows a potentially powerful, innovative way of promoting rights on the ground through direct development assistance.

The difficulty of all this is seen in how agencies avoid talk of rights. The operation that needs to be done was summed up well by one UN development official (who was so concerned about government reaction that he asked that not even his agency be identified): "The enigma of the government," he said, "is that the moment you go to the government and say 'right based,' they get their back up." But, he continued, his agency could talk of inclusiveness, the poorest of the poor, the marginalized, and women's rights: "That's where the acceptance of these things is fairly OK." His goal, he said, was to foster demand for services through political empowerment: "The intent is rights, but we don't want to say this is a policy to promote rights"; instead, it is presented as "community-level engagement."[1] In other words, these organizations—UNICEF, the UNDP, even the World Bank—know that talk of rights is upsetting to governments, but they press forward with it anyway, in disguised ways.

As noted, it is not the intention of this book to reify C&P rights as the highest goal of development projects or to suggest that there is a clean line between the two. Each type of right is needed for the promotion and protection of the other, and the interdependence and indivisibility of human rights norms is well established (Hertel & Minkler, 2007; Shue, 1980). There is no bright line between the two, and C&P rights need not be privileged above ES&C rights as priorities for the UN. Indeed, the fact that they are so interdependent makes any such privileging meaningless; you can't have one without the other. Instead, the goal here is to use C&P rights as a way of showing whether *all* rights talk by UN development agencies pursuing RBA is, in fact, just talk; divorcing the two from each other can be the first step toward draining the two concepts of meaning, exactly by ignoring their "interdependence and indivisibility." My intention is to show that C&P rights are being pursued in a way that brings real significance to efforts to pursue all rights standards: without recognizing their connection, efforts to pursue *either* set of rights become more rhetorical than real. But the pursuit of ES&C rights has been loudly trumpeted by UN agencies, while the corresponding, and necessary, work on C&P rights has been kept almost secret—as we will see, many staff simply don't want to talk about it.

The Politics of Rights and Development

So, *why has* this work on C&P rights been kept relatively quiet and secretive? This book will look at how UN agencies navigate the tricky political terrain of rights promotion. Before the advent of RBA, UN staff could (with varying legitimacy) present their work as being purely technical and apolitical in nature (see J. Ferguson, 1990; I. F. I. Shihata, 1991). But clearly this is not really the case anymore. How can staff promote human an expansive and holistic set of rights without alienating their government counterparts? How have UN agencies adapted to the new requirements of their role? What new diplomatic skills have to be developed? "Many times the government said no, you can't do this," one UN staff person told me, in reference to rights-based programming; but instead of bowing to this pressure, "we can be persistent, [and] sometimes they relent."[2] Said another, "The minute you aren't neutral, its trouble,"[3] but there are ways of pushing for human rights without appearing to lose that neutrality.

Some years ago, I was doing research on how UN agencies integrated rights issues into their daily operations. I had a chance to talk with a well-placed official of the World Health Organization (WHO)—as usual, "off the record" and with many caveats about how difficult it was to discuss human rights in a technical organization like the WHO. We were discussing the policy in some countries of putting people who are HIV-positive in quarantine or even in prison (specific, influential countries were named). The WHO considered this a bad policy from both human rights and public health perspectives. It was an obvious rights violation since it meant depriving people of their freedom only because of their health status. And it was poor public health policy, since it meant that people would be afraid to get tested or to seek help if they were HIV-positive. The WHO wanted to see this policy changed: the official I spoke to saw it as much as a moral imperative as a public health one. But, he said, they had to tread very lightly in pressing for a change in policy. If they seemed to be critiquing government policies in terms of how it treats its citizen's rights, they risked being asked to leave or at least being marginalized and ignored. The WHO, he recognized, had a policy of promoting human rights and felt it was a good thing (or many within the organization, but not all, felt that way), but the policy was for many reasons more rhetorical than real.

United Nations agencies and affiliated institutions now speak the language of rights. Yet their implementation of rights remains sketchy: there is a great deal of ambivalence about where rights—with the necessary element of C&P rights—fit into the overall picture of development. Work done on the training and bureaucratic needs of IO staff helps us understand some of this inconsistent application of ideas: in the WHO, for example, one challenge is simply convincing people with scientific, medically based training to consider more "fuzzy" concepts like human rights. Another example is the international financial institutions (IFIs), which continue to be of two minds on human rights; their documents are certainly not shy about mentioning rights, yet the agencies as a whole have no comprehensive human rights policies (Alston, 2005; Horta, 2002; I. Shihata, 1992; Tomasevski, 1989). The reason why the World Bank, for example, is so inconsistent in its use of rights language is illustrative of the larger problem that faces all UN agencies. The World Bank, according to its Articles of Agreement, is severely restricted in its ability to interfere with the politics of a borrower state. The Articles make this point clearly:

> **SECTION 10. Political Activity Prohibited**
> The Bank and its officers shall not interfere in the political affairs of any member; nor shall they be influenced in their decisions by the political character of the member or members concerned. Only economic considerations shall be relevant to their decisions, and these considerations shall be weighed impartially in order to achieve the purposes stated in Article I.

There were good reasons for including this provision in the Bank's Articles. The one usually cited is the start of the Cold War: for the World Bank to seem legitimate, it couldn't look as if it were only going to lend to allies of the US and other capitalist or "Western-leaning" states (Kraske, 1996). More importantly, however, was concern over the Bank's financial soundness: the first Bank officials worried that if they were not insulated from political pressure (e.g., to lend only to American allies), they would not be perceived as operating on a sound financial basis, and their credit rating would suffer accordingly. To only a slightly lesser degree, all UN development agencies (and, for that matter, many development NGOs) face similar pressures. Examples are legion. In addition to the aforementioned cases of the World Bank, UNICEF, and WHO, Alexander Betts has shown the reluctance of the global refugee regime to discuss the human rights of refugees for fear of alienating important actors (Betts, 2009).

On the one hand, they are bound by the terms of the UN Charter, which includes the promotion of human rights as a key purpose of the UN. That is reinforced by documents such as the Universal Declaration of Human Rights, which are part of international law and even the customary law of nations. On the other hand, the UN is an international, intergovernmental body, neutral to political arrangements and operating at the sufferance of member states. It is not supposed to interfere with states' internal political arrangements, a fact made most pointedly by Article 2(7) of the Charter, which states in part, "Nothing contained in the present Charter shall authorize the United Nations to intervene in matters which are essentially within the domestic jurisdiction of any state."

Over the course of years studying the UN and its efforts to integrate rights into development practice, these issues have come up again and again. For example, the CRC is now UNICEF's central programming document, and yet it remains a controversial issue within UNICEF; some staff feel it detracts from their mission, makes it overly political, and is too difficult to quantify in terms of results. These competing pressures have led to an odd dichotomy within UN agencies; in New Delhi, for example, talking with two people in adjoining offices can be like talking with people in different countries. Several midlevel UNDP staff members told me they had never heard of Article 2(7) and were surprised to learn of its existence. A World Bank governance expert would only talk to me about rights as we strolled around Delhi's Lodhi Gardens, to make sure I couldn't record the conversation or take notes. Another must have said "this is off the record" a dozen times in our conversation. One high-level UNDP officer with whom I spoke was quite insistent that "rights are what we do." Rights are part of the mandate of the UN, written into the UN charter, and considered central to how the agencies have been tasked to do their jobs. Yet, at the same time, other staff were much less forthcoming about their work. "We take a soft approach," another UNDP person said, one in a position where they would be expected to work on many rights-related issues: "One treads a very fine line when one runs that campaign," was their response, referring to campaigns for human rights norms.[4] "It is a very, very political process" warned one official,[5] while a UNICEF staff person said, "We have to keep the human rights framework in mind, but we have to sell it to our targets in a way that is culturally sensitive and aware of what will work."[6] Around the world, it is no longer uncommon for UN Country Directors to be asked to leave—essentially declared persona non grata—for speaking too plainly about human rights.

The UN and its agencies have been understandably reluctant to discuss the obvious political implications of its changing development paradigm. Much of this, I will argue, stems from the same reluctance the UNICEF Resident Representative felt 20 years ago: UN development agencies remain deeply uncomfortable with the notion that their work is something other than purely technical in nature. Yet they are also ambivalent about it: RBA is a central directive of UN development planning, and promoting rights is now central to the mission of all UN agencies. It is hard to explain just how profoundly inconsistent and conflicted UN staff could seem when I asked them what their relationship with human rights was, just as they disagreed on the implications of Article 2(7). Some insisted their work had nothing to do with promoting human rights and the rights-based approach to development was essentially apolitical and rhetorical; others said promoting human rights was the *central* mission of all UN agencies. Most common, really, was a little bit of both: staff acknowledged that RBA was, of course, a rights policy, yet seemed uncomfortable actually talking about what the UN was doing to promote rights in practice. The concern remained that as an international agency that answered to all its members, it was not appropriate or wise to say too openly that they were there to promote human rights (which would, of course, imply, that there were human rights problems that needed correcting). It took a bit of pushing to get some to open up about these issues, although certainly this was not always the case, and many staff did speak openly about their desire to promote human rights along with economic development.

So, it was no surprise that the rhetoric and reality of rights did not always match up. It was also no surprise that the lack of agreement sometimes ran both ways. If there were staff who spoke of rights in the context of a "rights-based approach" but were not, in fact, ready to do much about them, there were others who were working in the opposite direction: working diligently to support rights, but trying not to use the language, for the same reason. A typical conversation with staff would start with them insisting that their agency had no human rights policy. Then the rights of women would be brought up or perhaps indigenous peoples. Then the issue of fighting discrimination. Finally, it would be agreed that yes, rights were important but not something to be spoken of in exactly such terms. Rhetoric and reality were kept carefully separate.

International Organizations Independence and Rights Promotion

Why does all this matter? Each of the two questions above—whether UN agencies are prepared to promote true C&P rights in their development work, and how they are able to act independently and in opposition to national pressure to make that happen—are important in themselves. They show something new and important about how rights are being promoted through development assistance. Taken together, they also demonstrate how UN agencies can act as independent agents, promoting controversial, sometimes unexpected, sets of policies. This, too, is important. The process is far from perfect: as the case studies will show, these large bureaucracies are inconsistent in their use of the terminology of RBA, as well as inconsistent in their application of ideas. But individual staff have surprisingly wide latitude to adapt, and they sometimes use that latitude to push for ideas they consider important.

This independence is important because it sheds light on the internal workings of international organizations (IOs) and in particular on their ability to set and act on a new international agenda. Research in this area is not new: my work (Oestreich, 2010, 2012), for example, has examined the ability of international agencies to set their own agenda independently of member states, drawing on groundbreaking work done by Barnett and Finnemore (1999, 2004), Reinalda and Verbeek (2004) and others (E. B. Haas, 1990; Haftel & Thompson, 2006; Ness & Brechin, 1988). This work is increasingly part of the mainstream of IO studies and requires only a limited treatment here. Primarily, it involves defining alternative sources of IO activity than simply the wishes of the states that create IOs and, presumably, control them for their own purposes—the "realist" view of international organizations. This work has taken various directions. One prominent set of ideas looks at principle-agent problems: the difficulty of controlling IO staff from often-distant locations, whether by headquarters personnel or by member states themselves (Hawkins, Lake, Nielson, & Tierney, 2006). This work takes a rational methodology, assuming rational self-interest by both principles and agents. Other work (Sarfaty, 2005; Weaver, 2008) considers international organizations through a more sociological lens, examining the training, desires, and even personalities of IOs; policies, both good and bad, are influenced by the incentives staff face, the way they learn their jobs, and the environment in which they work. Bureaucratic politics is also offered as a source of independent thinking (Barnett & Finnemore, 1999). The literature on "epistemic communities" and regimes (Cross, 2013; Galbreath & McEvoy, 2013; P. Haas, 1992) has developed on the idea that communities of experts—sometimes less formal modes of organization, but sometimes formalized into specific IOs—have scientific knowledge that they can use to influence state behavior and bend it toward specific policies.

Most academic studies of the independence and influence of IOs focus on how they can pursue their preferred policies in the face of resistance of powerful member states. "Resistance" is an important element here: if IOs make policy that is not resisted by states, there is no particular theoretical puzzle. They are just acting as any bureaucratic organization. As Haftel and Thompson (2006) neatly summarize the field, most of the attention is over the relationship between the IO staff, on the one hand, and those charged with its oversight, on the other. Variables such as the power of individual states, the decision-making rules within organizations, how their bureaucratic interests diverge from the desires of member states, and the complexity of issues before the IO can contribute to IO independence. However, nearly all this work assumes that the resistance to be overcome is part of the policy-making process, and that the resistance comes at the level of the oversight bodies or assemblies of states: thus, for example, work tends to focus on the adoption of new agendas by agencies (e.g., the Bank's agenda on the environment; Wade, 1997) or why the WHO and other organizations might appear as "rogue" agents (Cortell & Peterson, 2006).

As will be discussed a bit more below, India has shown some resistance to the concept of a rights-based approach to development; in international fora it has been ambivalent at best to the idea of social conditions tied to foreign aid. However, the focus here is different. What is almost entirely left out of work on IO independence is the process of policy *implementation*, not adoption. This isn't a case of a "rogue" agent or even an agent exercising a level of discretion that might seem beyond its bounds. The agencies studied here are all working within their mandate, which has evolved into rights promotion. The resistance they face is not the official sort, where a state uses an international forum (or their informal levers of power, such as the ability to make staffing decisions) to shape international policy. While there is some pushback (as Chapter 2 will show) at the international level to the idea of promoting rights through development, that is not the focus here. In this case, India does not deny that the rights-based approach to development should be the official policy of agencies like UNICEF or the UNDP, nor does it attempt to "officially" deny the importance of RBA to its development. Yet a basic premise of this work is that there is still resistance to the policy: only it is resistance that is often hidden, and at least as much at the local level as the level of official federal policy. This is an important, but overlooked, issue when we seek to understand IO independence—their independence at the implementation level, not the policy level.

The sociological approach of Weaver, Sarfaty, Barnett and Finnemore, Dijkzeul and Beigbeder (2003), and Barnett and Finnemore (2004), among others, help us understand the internal working of IOs, even in the face of state resistance. Staff have their own ideas, their own training, and often their own set of priorities. It is well established that these are not just dictated by member states but also come from a variety of sources: how they are trained, the environment they live in, and (following principle-agent theory) what actions will advance their careers. As the research in India showed, different staff interpreted the same overall mandate differently. The work of Robert Wade or my own writing (Oestreich, 2007, p. 55), on how staff training can make them resistant to new ideas, is clearly echoed in the difficulty that UNICEF's health team is having in creating a comprehensive human rights–based program. Bureaucratic politics theories make it clear why, for example, some staff in UNDP consider gender issues a top priority, while others are still paying only lip-service to gender mainstreaming (Moser, 1999; Razavi & Miller, 1995). The idea that IO staff might act in ways that are "independent" of member states is now well established, as is the notion that IOs are not unitary actors, but rather, complex bureaucracies that act in unpredictable and sometimes illogical or inconsistent ways.

This more nuanced understanding of IOs, as complex, "open" systems (as defined in Scott, 1992) that draw ideas from their environment and institutional structure and then act according to their own internal dynamics, is not new. This book looks at this dynamic in a novel context: that of how development-related IOs push back against the resistance of host states rather than powerful member states at the transnational level. It shows how this pushback works, why it is necessary, and what strategies staff take in pursuing their own agenda and the agenda of their organization. And it suggests that this pushing back and capacity for independence has important real-world consequences.

In this case, those consequences relate to the promotion of human rights, particularly C&P rights. UN agencies are increasingly becoming part of the overall human rights machinery, yet the attention of most human rights scholars remains fixed on the New York– and Geneva–based institutions. Most literature on promoting human rights still talks of "naming and shaming" strategies or, in the final resort, coercive action by the UN Security Council. But what is the role in human rights promotion for UNICEF, UNDP, WHO, and other such agencies? Just as important, what *should be* their role, since they are not designed to be rights agencies but development ones? Conversations with staff in these organizations suggest that they are struggling with this question every day. It was not unusual, in my interviews, for staff at one point to insist that their agency was fully a part of the UN human rights machinery and that they were not afraid to confront governments on rights issues, and later in the same discussion to insist that their work was entirely apolitical and technical. Similarly, while some staff had a clear idea of what RBA meant for rights promotion, others seemed to fall back on vague platitudes. Sorting out the various implications of RBA for the UN is an ongoing process.

It was also noted above that India has not entirely embraced the concept of a rights-based approach to development. India accepts the work of UN agencies in its borders and makes no overt effort to deny the relevance of rights to development. Internationally, however, it has not supported an aid regime that emphasizes human rights. As Emma Mawdsley puts it, "Indian development cooperation . . . is characteristically not accompanied by policy conditionalities. Southern partners [like India] reject the practice of imposing changes on partner country governance structures . . . critics of this (official) stance of non-interference express concerns that it will undermine efforts to reduce corruption . . . and promote human rights" (2016, p. 153). At the Busan Fourth High Level Forum on Aid Effectiveness, held in South Korea in 2011, India largely sided with China and other southern states to press for a development architecture with less emphasis on conditionality and more on promoting economic growth through enhanced business ties and South-South cooperation (Eyben & Savage, 2013; Mawdsley, 2014). While not directly opposed to the strategies of UN agencies such as UNDP and UNICEF, India, China, and other states have indicated a suspicion of the UN's motives and tactics, perceiving a form of neocolonialist meddling. So, there is some resistance at the global and the operational levels.

The Rhetoric of Rights and United Nations Agencies

There were a number of patterns discernible during my interviews with UN staff in New Delhi and elsewhere over the course of my research. One has been described already; the tendency of staff to first *deny* that they have a "rights policy," and then in a sense confess that, yes, a focus on empowering women, providing access to justice, decentralizing government, and promoting democratic participation were issues that involved fairly uncontroversial human rights. Another pattern was the move from vague and uncontroversial rhetoric about a right to development (RTD, discussed later) to, finally, something more concrete. Typically, I would ask staff what a rights-based approach meant to them, and I received answers such as "providing people with their right to development," "holding duty-bearers to account," or perhaps something on the Millennium Development Goals as a "comprehensive list" of rights that needed to be provided. In one example a UNICEF field officer explained to me the importance, for children, of having a sports program at their school as an example of a rights-based approach to development. Since education was a right and having athletic programs in schools (in a conflict-prone region of the country) was a good way to engage students with their school and build their sense of security and self-confidence, providing such programs was a rights-based approach to development. When I asked another staff member what they considered the most pressing human rights issues in India were, they answered "farmers' suicides"—the terrible phenomenon of farmers killing themselves as a result of debt, poor harvests, and other causes. This is certainly a tragic issue, and indeed was mentioned as a rights matter during India's Universal Periodic Review, but it is a human rights violation in a very vague sense; that of defining poverty itself as a rights violation, along with its consequences.

Also, as noted a moment ago, UN staff talked vaguely about "holding government duty-bearers to account" or of passing laws requiring government to provide certain goods and services. This was the pattern among UN staff, and even more so among government officials with whom I spoke: human rights were defined as declarations that the poor were entitled to certain things, and then that it was the obligation of the government to provide those things or set up circumstances where they could be provided.

Why this pattern? To be more than a rhetorical exercise, RBA needs to go beyond the simple notion that development is a right and that therefore promoting development is promoting rights; merely invoking the word "rights" when discussing important development goals is not enough. Human rights properly understood are about more than just repackaging entitlement policies. Many staff members *did* understand this, but there was also hesitation regarding the issue. So, a better way, I found, to get to the heart of the issue was not to ask, "What is a rights-based approach to development?" Rather, I asked, "What *are you doing differently* now that a rights-based approach is being implemented?" If you are a member of, say, the United Nations Population Fund (UNFPA), whose mandate is to promote family planning and healthy motherhood, you will have a set of policies that you think are effective: enhancing access to reproductive health services, promoting girls' education, fighting child marriage, that sort of thing. Simply relabeling these as a rights-based approach by calling them rights is not a real change in how services are provided—or how people provide for themselves. Asking, "What are you doing differently?" gets closer to the heart of the problem. It helps separate how these agencies talk about a topic, from the real changes that do—or don't—represent RBA properly understood.

Rights in Development and the Right to Development

Earlier it was noted that the focus of this book would be on civil and political rights rather than economic, social, and cultural rights. Yet we have seen that RBA, done properly, largely erases this distinction; each set of rights must reinforce the other. Then why insist on making this distinction at all? This requires some justification and explanation. The indivisibility of rights is a basic premise of the UN system and the international human rights system.

One reason is to present a "hard case" of rights promotion. Focusing on ES&C rights is fairly uncontroversial when done by UN agencies and prone to rhetorical sloppiness. No one objects to, say, efforts by the World Food Programme (WFP) to feed people. If this were the extent of promoting a "right to food," there would be no issue to examine. Even if (as is the case) the WFP insisted there was far more to the right to food than that, it would be easy enough for states to avoid its political implications if they wished and for IOs to do the same if convenient. But avoiding the implications of C&P rights is more difficult, and thus presents a clearer case of challenging states to live up to their obligations. And the issue runs even deeper than that. Since ES&C rights are, in a sense, "aspirational" (Wiles, 2006)—that is, many states are not able to provide them (e.g., some states simply lack the resources to adequately house and educate all their citizens)—it is easy for states to say they are trying to provide ES&C rights or working with the UN for their provision, while protesting that they merely need more time. But C&P rights are (all things being equal) easier to provide and thus harder to explain away when they are violated.

To be sure, there are ways to take exception to what I have written thus far. Many ES&C rights are not truly aspirational, rightly considered. For example, many states of the Global South *could* guarantee most ES&C rights with available resources if they had the will to do so. Nor, as Henry Shue shows us, are C&P rights quite so readily guaranteed, divorced from other considerations: protecting civil liberties requires, in fact, quite a bit more from governments than passive respect. Instead, governments must establish police forces and judicial systems, educate citizens on their obligations, provide opportunities to be heard, and so on (Shue, 1980). Still, the point here is that UN agencies approach ES&C rights differently, and states react to them differently. Tell a government you are there to help with implementation of a right to shelter, and they will rarely object; tell them you are there to implement a citizen's right to free speech or freedom of religion, and they might well tell you that it is none of your business. This is particularly true if you are a development agency, not an agency specifically charged with human rights promotion.

There is an irony here. It is traditionally developing countries—roughly speaking, members of the G-77 group in the UN—who have pushed most for seeing positive and negative rights as being connected. Much of the distinction between the two is a relic of Cold War political realities; the Western, capitalist nations insisted that civil and political rights (not well respected among the Soviet Union and its allies) were the only "true" human rights, while the Soviet-aligned states argued that economic, social, and (to a lesser extent) cultural rights were more important to advance human welfare (Nickel, 2008; Whelan, 2010). At the Tehran World Conference on Human Rights in 1968, the indivisibility of ES&C rights and C&P rights was established and made part of the general human rights discourse (Burke, 2008); but, at the same time, it presented an opportunity for many developing countries, linking human rights to the broader agenda of decolonization, to suggest that ES&C rights had to *come before* C&P rights to make the latter rights possible. So declaring the indivisibility of rights could provide another way to shield states from criticism that they were not doing enough to promote civil and political rights. The Vienna Declaration of 1993, coming after the end of the Cold War, reinforced and reaffirmed the indivisibility of these categories of rights, declaring the Cold War division at an end. Yet the practical effect of this declaration was minor. It represented a consensus on goals, but little in terms of implementation (Boyle, 1995).

Another problem separating rhetoric and reality here is the sometimes murky, always confusing, connection between RBA and the idea of a right *to* development. These are distinct concepts, although they are often intermingled. Both inside and outside the UN, the two ideas are often used as if they were the same thing, or, at any rate, more closely related than they actually are. Peter Uvin (2007) and Jack Donnelly (1999), among others, warn against a simplistic connection between the two and even suggest that there are serious dangers in a lazy effort to see the connections. To understand the rhetoric of rights in India as used by the UN agencies active there, it is important to examine both their connections and their differences.

The idea of a "right to development" is generally traced to a proposal by Keba M'baye in 1972 (Barsh, 1991, p. 322), although its antecedents go back substantially (UN, 2013, pp. 17–35). The notion that development itself is a right can strike some observers as an odd concept, difficult to define and impossible to implement in an intellectually coherent way. It "emerged from the prevailing political climate" of its time (UN, 2013, p. 3); in particular, developing economies pressed for it along with a New International Economic Order that would correct perceived imbalances in the global economy that worked against their economic advancement. Promoting a right to development was a political decision intended to impose obligations on wealthy states of the Global North, who were held responsible for the poverty of the South and thus should help fight that poverty (H. Ferguson, 2011, p. 6). It also presented a reaffirmation, on the part of developing countries, of the importance of economic, social, and cultural rights as opposed to civil and political rights. For this reason, among others, the United States, in particular, was opposed to the Declaration on the Right to Development, and other wealthy states remained ambivalent, despite the fact that it was only a declaration and not something with the force of international law.

Development as a right is not the same as a rights-based approach to development; there is no *necessary* connection between the two. It is entirely possible to think of development as something that is advanced through people's human rights or even as defined as implementing those rights, without making development itself a right. Both the right to development and economic, social, and cultural rights suffer from the same intellectual problems: since they require active government efforts and sufficient economic resources and political will, they can both be put off as things that would be nice, but can't be guaranteed in current circumstances.

Still, there are connections between the right to development and the rights-based approach to development that are important if we are to understand how the UN approaches RBA. First, the Declaration on the Right to Development stipulates that development is a right of peoples and states. As Sengupta puts it, there are four main propositions of the declaration:

1. The right to development is a human right;
2. The human right to development is a right to a *particular process of development* in which all human rights and fundamental freedoms can be fully realized—which means that it combines all the rights enshrined in both the covenants and each of the rights has to be exercised with freedom;

3. The meaning of exercising these rights consistently with freedom implies *free, effective, and full participation* of all the individuals concerned in the decision-making and the implementation of the process. Therefore, the process must be *transparent and accountable*, individuals must have equal opportunity of access to the resources for development and receive fair distribution of the benefits of development (and income). And finally;
4. The right confers unequivocal obligations on duty-holders: individuals in the community, states at the national level, and states at the international level. (Sengupta, 2001, p. 2527; emphasis added)

As we will see in Chapter 2, the right to development uses some concepts that have found their way into rights-based approaches as well. In particular, a central role for "participation" of people in the process of development (Barsh, 1991, pp. 329–330), equity (World Bank, 2006), and an emphasis on holding governments (both one's own and those of other states) to account for aiding in the realization of rights, both civil and political rights and economic, social, and cultural rights. As we will see in the following chapters, UN staff views these elements of the right to development as central to what a rights-based approach means and refers to them as having the force, not of law, but of settled UN strategy when approaching the process of development.

Second, the very idea of a rights-based approach is to some extent a result of dissatisfaction with the right to development and a desire to reshape the rights-development link in a more intellectually serious and meaningful way (Sengupta, 2013, pp. 81–82). RBA has the virtue of dealing with *specifics* about the rights-development link and making policy suggestions. It provides a plausible picture of how the two are causally related, while avoiding the trap of defining development as a right and thus implying that anything promoting development is also promoting rights. It was noted above that the push for a rights-based approach resulted from dissatisfaction with older efforts at development promotion which seemed to violate not just people's rights but also basic notions of human dignity. Development agencies have often been viewed as working against what development ought to *actually be doing*; for example, promoting structural adjustment policies that, however theoretically necessary they might have seemed, actually undermined human welfare. The general intellectual argument of the 1990s was over how to restructure development assistance to meaningfully address the plight of the world's poor and to have a development system that directly address their needs (H. Ferguson, 2011, p. 10).

Thus, intellectually, the right to development and RBA can be distinguished and dealt with as entirely separate concepts. However, as they are currently defined the two find themselves merged, albeit uneasily. The danger of rights becoming a mere rhetorical exercise stems partly from the tension between a right to development—itself primarily a rhetorical concept—and the rights-based approach to development—ideally a set of policies designed to promote development, defined as not just economic advancement but also as a step toward some sort of social justice. At its worst, the notion of RBA allows development to be defined as a right; thus anything that promotes that right becomes a rights-based approach to development. This can be harmful since it has the potential to alienate governments that are suspicious of development agencies—government development bodies, UN agencies, or NGOs—that seem to be too insistent on the language of human rights.

It says a lot about how rights language was avoided in traditional development work, that (as Chapter 2 will discuss) UN development agencies had to be directed to do so in the 1990s by UN Secretary-General Kofi Annan. After all, these agencies are expected to adhere to the principles of the UN charter, yet rights language and ideas has never been easy to integrate into their work. It might well be that *any* development agenda is going to impact human rights, positively or negatively. But agencies such as UNDP, UNICEF, WFP, and others have usually used neutral, technical, economic language to describe their work rather than language with clear normative implications like "rights" or "empowerment" or "mobilization." RBA potentially represents a tremendous leap forward in operationalizing the indivisibility of positive and negative rights. And undeniably, the end of the Cold War, and the political debate around rights it sustained, has made this possible (Roth, 2004, p. 64). It is the argument of this work—and of many works on the topic—that a true rights-based approach *must* integrate a concern for civil and political rights with one for economic, social, and cultural rights.

A focus on C&P rights, then, is not intended to deny the important interrelationship between the two sets of rights. Indeed, the goal is the opposite: to show that development rights properly understood are in fact incorporating all forms of social protection and empowerment. As we have seen, development agencies have mostly emphasized development rights and de-emphasized C&P rights since that made their work more politically palatable: yet a rights-based approach, and indeed the right to development as a whole, requires that the indivisibility of rights be taken entirely seriously. Thus the focus is on C&P rights not because they are somehow "prior" to development rights, but because they have traditionally been elided in the name of political expediency by UN agencies outside the traditional rights-promoting ones, such as the Human Rights Council, the various Committees, and the High Commissioner for Human Rights.

India as a Case Study of Rights Implementation

What does the political side of RBA look like in practice? To answer that question, this book represents an in-depth case study of a single country. There are plusses and minuses of using this method to explore the questions of rights-based approaches. Examining in depth a single country allowed me to look at the strategies of RBA, and the types of problems which occur in its implementation, that a larger, transnational study would not. These are not questions about statistics; rather, they are about the day-to-day challenges faced by staff as they try to implement a new policy. Looking at many countries or focusing on themes would have diluted the study and would also leave me vulnerable to the accusation that I was selectively choosing anecdotes that were "interesting" or that fit my preconceived notions. I wanted to see both the good and the bad, without having to choose specific cases that fit my preconceived notions of what RBA was or should be.

I selected India for a few reasons. It is a huge country that hosts the UN's largest developing-country presence; thus, the widest possible range of issues to study are available. India has a well-developed legal system, which means that rights issues would be raised, debated, and acted on by the national government, as well as by local governments: there would be things happening in the legal sector that translated into real change. I note that I attempted to examine *everything* that the UN agencies I study are doing in India, the good and the bad, to avoid the appearance of being selective in my study. I recognize, to be sure, the limitations of the case-study format; I try not to draw conclusions that can't be supported through this particular method.

There are plenty of academic and practical works describing what RBA is in the global context, and plenty more short case studies of how it is being applied in this or that particular situation (a women's empowerment project in Zambia; child rights in Ecuador; etc.). What I wanted to do was be both more comprehensive and more specific. What does it mean to look at a single country through the lens of RBA? How well is it applied in a meaningful, rather than just rhetorical, way? How does it color the way development is understood in a particular context? Is it applied in a way where all projects fit logically together, or is it haphazard and poorly thought out? Does the approach work—not just this or that project, but the approach as a whole—and how is "working" defined? Answers to these questions seemed lacking in the literature. Along with the two basic questions that frame this book—and that form its essential question, that is, the role of UN agencies as real rather than rhetorical human rights promoters—this book provides a useful examination of what RBA looks like in a national context. Rather than cherry-picking the best projects as exemplars, it is the only project I know of that considers the good and the bad, the real and rhetorical, of RBA as applied at the national level.

This book is largely the result of interviews done while living in India on a nine-month Fulbright fellowship in 2012 and 2013, as well as sabbatical funding from Drexel University, plus later follow-up interviews in India and New York. It is based on interviews with approximately 50 different UN staff from the United Nations Development Program (UNDP), the UN Children's Fund (UNICEF), the UN Entity for Gender Equality and the Empowerment of Women (UN Women), the UN Population Fund (UNFPA), the World Bank, and other agencies. I spoke with people ranging from temporary consultants to the UN Resident Representative. (The Resident Representative in 2012 did not ask for anonymity, and so he is identified in this work; for other interview subjects, the UN asked that I not name them and avoid providing enough information for them to be identified by the reader. This in itself speaks to the sensitivity of the topic!). All UN staff spoke in their personal capacity, and their observations do not necessarily reflect the views of the UN or specific agencies and organizations. Only one major body—the World Health Organization (WHO)—proved difficult to get information from. I also spoke with a variety of staff at various Indian- and foreign-based nongovernmental agencies, and approximately ten government representatives from the local to national level. This is a smaller number than I had hoped for, but arranging such conversations was not easy. Government officials often did not want to talk, and when they did, they usually stuck to platitudes; unsurprising, given the nature of their jobs, but not especially helpful to my research. This work also draws on UN and other documents about programming in India; the intention is to supplement that with a more nuanced view of how UN staff perceives the pursuit of human rights.

Plan of This Book

Obviously, this book is a very personal work. As mentioned, I chose to write it in the first person partly to avoid clumsy language, partly to be honest about how much of it comes from my observations, and partly because it is based on a collection of experiences and anecdotal evidence regarding what UN staff think and do.

The next chapter will briefly review some of the key human rights issues facing development agencies in India. It will look at the issue of human rights and development from two perspectives: one from the viewpoint of human rights agencies themselves, the other from the viewpoint of the UN development apparatus. Chapter 2 asks, to what extent do the development agencies approach the key rights issues identified by the more traditional human rights mechanisms? How much of the talk of rights from these development agencies is mere rhetoric, and how much does it really address the important rights matters that India is grappling with? The focus will be particularly on civil and political rights, not economic, social, and cultural rights, for the reasons spelled out earlier in this chapter.

Chapters 3, 4, and 5 consist of case studies. Chapter 3 looks at the United Nations Development Programme (UNDP); Chapter 4, at the UN Children's Fund (UNICEF); Chapter 5 is shorter case studies of the World Bank, UN Women, and the United Nations Population Fund (UNFPA). These chapters focus in particular on the matter of rights diplomacy in UN agencies. My overall premise is that if UN agencies are *meaningfully* moving into areas of rights promotion that were once out of bounds for political reasons, and that remain sensitive, we would expect to see resistance from the Indian government to these new policies. I focus on what form that resistance takes, how the agencies being studied try to get around that resistance, and what we can learn both about the policies being pursued and the new skills required of UN staff.

Chapter 6 reviews two important themes from the three case studies. The first part of Chapter 6 distills some of the key lessons about what kind of new diplomatic skills UN development officials have learned as they shift to the rights-based agenda. A few clear themes about how to overcome government obstruction were repeated again and again in interviews, as I asked staff what they did in the face of this resistance. Chapter 6 also reviews how *effective* various policies have been. It reviews the assessments of various policies undertaken by UN agencies. There is not much point in discussing what RBA means to UN agencies without considering whether it works. Interestingly, most agencies don't make much effort to determine if their policies are actually effective in terms of promoting "development," however defined. Partly this is because the desired outcomes are extremely difficult to quantify; partly because it is almost impossible to attribute changes in a country as large as India to any particular program or policy; and partly because the policies themselves are considered to be good and desirable, regardless of what is achieved. Chapter 7 reviews some of the key themes and also considers the plusses and minuses of using the UN development machinery as an addition to the regular human rights mechanisms.

References

Alston, P. (2005). Ships Passing in the Night: The Current State of the Human Rights and Development Debate Seen Through the Lens of the Millennium Development Goals. *Human Rights Quarterly, 27*(3), 755–829.

Barnett, M. N., & Finnemore, M. (1999). The Politics, Power, and Pathologies of International Organizations. *International Organization, 53*(4), 699–732.

Barnett, M. N., & Finnemore, M. (2004). *Rules for the World: International Organizations and Global Politics*. Ithaca, NY: Cornell University Press.

Barsh, R. L. (1991). The Right to Development as a Human Right: Results of the Global Consultation. *Human Rights Quarterly, 13*(August), 322–338.

Berg, E., & Betchelder, A. (1985). *Structural Adjustment Lending: A Critical View* (1985-21). Washington, DC: The World Bank.

Betts, A. (2009). *Protection by Persuasion: International Cooperation in the Refugee Regie*. Ithaca, NY: Cornell University Press.

Black, M. (1986). *The Children and the Nations: The Story of UNICEF*. New York: UNICEF.

Boyle, K. (1995). Stock-Taking on Human Rights: The World Conference on Human Rights, Vienna, 1993. *Political Studies, 43*(1), 79–95.

Brouwer, M., Grady, H., Traore, V., & Wordofa, D. (2005). The Experiences of Oxfam International and Its Affiliates in Rights-Based Programming and Campaigning. In P. Gready & J. Ensor (Eds.), *Reinventing Development? Translating Rights-based Approaches From Theory Into Practice* (pp. 63–78). New York: St. Martin's.

Burke, R. (2008). From Individual Rights to National Development: The First UN International Conference on Human Rights, Tehran, 1968. *Journal of World History, 19*(3), 275–296.

Cornwall, A., & Brock, K. (2005). *Beyond Buzzwords: "Poverty Reduction," "Participation," and "Empowerment" in Development Policy*. Geneva: United Nations Research Institute for Social Development.

Cortell, A. P., & Peterson, S. (2006). Dutiful Agents, Rogue Actors, or Both? Staffing, Voting Rules, and Slack in the WHO and WTO. In D. G. Hawkins, D. A. Lake, D. L. Nielson, & M. Tierney (Eds.), *Delegation and Agency in International Organizations* (pp. 255–280). New York: Cambridge University Press.

Cross, M. K. D. (2013). Rethinking Epistemic Communities Twenty Years Later. *Review of International Studies, 39*(1), 137–160.

Dijkzeul, D., & Beigbeder, Y. (Eds.). (2003). *Rethinking International Organizations: Pathology and Promise*. New York: Berghahn Books.

Donnelly, J. (1999). Human Rights, Democracy, and Development. *Human Rights Quarterly*, *21*(3), 608–632.

Donnelly, J., & Whelan, D. J. (2007). The West, Economic and Social Rights, and the Global Human Rights Regime: Setting the Record Straight. *Human Rights Quarterly*, *29*(4), 908–949.

Eyben, R., & Savage, L. (2013). Emerging and Submerging Powers: Imagined Geographies in the New Development Partnership at the Busan Fourth High Level Forum. *Journal of Development Studies*, *49*(4), 457–469.

Ferguson, H. (2011). *The Right to Developmenet and the Rights-Based Approach to Development: A Review of Basic Concepts and Debates*. New Delhi: Center for Development and Human Rights.

Ferguson, J. (1990). *The Anti-Politics Machine: "Development," Depoliticization, and Bureaucratic Power in Lesotho*. New York: Cambridge University Press.

Galbreath, D. J., & McEvoy, J. (2013). How Epistemic Communities Drive International Regimes: The Case of Minority Rights in Europe. *Journal of European Integration*, *35*(2), 169–186.

Gauri, V., & Gloppen, S. (2012). *Human Rights Based Approaches to Development: Concepts, Evidence, Policy*. Washington, DC: World Bank Development Research Group.

Gready, P., & Vandenhole, W. (2014). What Are We Trying to Change? Theories of Change in Development and Human Rights. In P. Gready & W. Vandenhole (Eds.), *Human Rights and Development in the New Millennium* (pp. 1–26). New York: Routledge.

Haas, E. B. (1990). *When Knowledge Is Power: Three Models of Change in International Organizations*. Los Angeles: University of California Press.

Haas, P. (1992). Introduction: Epistemic Communities and International Policy Coordination. *International Organization*, *46*(1), 1–35.

Haftel, Y. Z., & Thompson, A. (2006). The Independence of International Organizations: Concept and Applications. *Journal of Conflict Resolutoin*, *50*(2), 253–275.

Haggard, S., & Kaufman, R. R. (Eds.). (1992). *The Politics of Economic Adjustment*. Princeton, NJ: Princeton University Press.

Hamm, B. I. (2001). A Human Rights Approach to Development. *Human Rights Quarterly*, *23*(4), 1005–1031.

Hawkins, D. G., Lake, D. A., Nielson, D. L., & Tierney, M. J. (Eds.). (2006). *Delegation and Agency in International Organizations*. New York: Cambridge University Press.

Hertel, S., & Minkler, L. (Eds.). (2007). *Economic Rights: Conceptual, Measurement, and Policy Issues*. New York: Cambridge University Press.

Horta, K. (2002). Rhetoric and Reality: Human Rights and the World Bank. *Harvard Human Rights Law Journal*, *15*(1), 227–243.

Kraske, J. (1996). *Bankers With a Mission: The Presidents of the World Bank, 1946–91*. New York: Oxford University Press.

Langford, M., Sumner, A., & Yamin, A. E. (2013). Introduction. In M. Langford, A. Sumner, & A. E. Yamin (Eds.), *The Millennium Development Goals and Human Rights: Past, Present, and Future* (pp. 1–34). New York: Cambridge University Press.

Mawdsley, E. (2014). Human Rights and South-South Development Cooperation: Reflections on the "Rising Powers" as International Development Actors. *Human Rights Quarterly, 36*(3), 630–652.

Mawdsley, E. (2016). India's Role as an International Developent Actor. In K. A. Jacobsen (Ed.), *Routledge Handbook of Contemporary India* (pp. 146–158). New York: Routledge.

Miller, H. (2010). From "Rights-based" to "Rights-framed" Approaches: A Social Constuctionist View of Human Rights Practice. *International Journal of Human Rights, 14*(6), 915–931.

Moser, C. O. N. (1999). *Mainstreaming Gender and Development in the World Bank: Progress and Recommendations.* Washington, DC: World Bank.

Mosley, P., Harrigan, J., & Toye, J. (1991). *Aid and Power: The World Bank and Policy-Based Lending* (Vol. 1). New York: Routledge.

Ness, G. D., & Brechin, S. R. (1988). Bridging the Gap: International Organizations as Organizations. *International Organization, 42*(2), 245–273.

Nickel, J. W. (2008). Rethinking Indivisibility: Towards a Theory of Supporting Relations Between Human Rights. *Human Rights Quarterly, 30*(4), 984–1001.

Oestreich, J. (2007). *Power and Principle: Human Rights Programming in International Organizations.* Washington, DC: Georgetown University Press.

Oestreich, J. (2010). UNICEF: A Human Rights Agency? In D. P. Forsythe (Ed.), *Encyclopedia of Human Rights* (pp. 121–129). New York: Oxford University Press.

Oestreich, J. (2012). *International Organizations as Self-Directed Actors: A Framework for Analysis.* New York: Routledge.

Razavi, S., & Miller, C. (1995). *Gender Mainstreaming: A Study of Efforts by the UNDP, the World Bank and the ILO to Institutionalize Gender Issues* (Occasional Paper 4). Geneva: United Nations Research Institute for Social Development.

Reinalda, B., & Verbeek, B. (Eds.). (2004). *Decision Making Within International Organizations.* New York: Routledge.

Roth, K. (2004). Defending Economic, Social and Cultural Rights: Practical Issues Faced by an International Human Rights Organization. *Human Rights Quarterly, 26*(1), 63–73.

Sano, H.-O. (2000). Development and Human Rights: The Necessary, but Partial Integration of Human Rights and Development. *Human Rights Quarterly, 22*(3), 734–752.

Sarfaty, G. A. (2005). The World Bank and the Internalization of Indigenous Rights Norms. *Yale Law Journal, 114*(7), 1792–1818.

Schmitz, H. P. (2012). A Human Rights-based Approach (HRBA) in Practice: Evaluating NGO Development Efforts. *Polity, 44*(4), 523–541.

Scott, R. (1992). *Organizations: Rational, Natural, and Open Systems*. Englewood Cliffs, NJ: Prentice Hall.

Sengupta, A. (2001). Right to Development as a Human Right. *Economic and Political Weekly*, *36*(27), 2527–2536.

Sengupta, A. (2013). Conceptualizing the Right to Development for the Twenty-First Century. In United Nations (Ed.), *Realizing the Right to Development* (pp. 67–87). New York: United Nations.

Shihata, I. (1992). *Human Rights, Development, and International Financial Institutions*. Presentation at the American University, January 24, 1992. World Bank.

Shihata, I. F. I. (1991). *The World Bank in a Changing World*. Boston: Martinus Nijhoff.

Shue, H. (1980). *Basic Rights: Subsistence, Affluence, and U.S. Foreign Policy*. Princeton, NJ: Princeton University Press.

Smyke, P. (1990). *UNICEF and the Convention on the Rights of the Child*. Unpublished manuscript of the UNICEF History Project. New York.

Thomas, C. (1998). International Financial Institutions and Social and Economic Human Rights: An Exploration. In T. Evans (Ed.), *Human Rights Fifty Years On: A Reappraisal* (pp. 161–187). New York: Manchester University Press.

Tomasevski, K. (1989). *Development Aid and Human Rights*. New York: St. Martin's Press.

United Nations. (2013). *Realizing the Right to Development*. New York: United Nations.

Uvin, P. (2002). On High Moral Ground: The Incorporation of Human Rights by the Development Enterprise. *Praxis*, *XVII*, 1–11.

Uvin, P. (2007). From the Right to Development to the Rights-Based Approach: How "Human Rights" Entered Development. *Development in Practice*, *17*(4–5), 597–606.

Wade, R. (1997). Greening the Bank: The Struggle Over the Environment 1970–1995. In D. Kapur, J. P. Lewis, & R. Webb (Eds.), *The World Bank: Its First Half-Century* (Vol. 2, pp. 611–734). Washington, DC: Brookings Institutions Press.

Weaver, C. (2008). *Hypocrisy Trap: The World Bank and the Poverty of Reform*. Princeton, NJ: Princeton University Press.

Whelan, D. J. (2010). *Indivisible Human Rights: A History*. Philadelphia: University of Pennsylvania Press.

Wiles, E. (2006). Aspirational Principles or Enforceable Rights? The Future for Socio-Economic Rights in National Law. *American University International Law Review*, *22*(1), 35–64.

World Bank. (2006). *World Development Report 2006: Equity and Development*. Washington, DC: World Bank.

2

Development and Human Rights in India

CHAPTER 1 INTRODUCED THE overall concept of this volume and its intention to examine what a well-conceived rights-based approach to development looks like to UN agencies. It raised two key questions, posed in the context of development in India. First, how has a rights-based approach to development helped the UN more directly engage the development machinery in rights promotion and particularly the promotion of civil and political rights? Second, to what extent are UN agencies able to pursue these goals despite the resistance they will inevitably face from the government (as well as other sectors of society)? What new diplomatic and political skills will they have to develop, and how can they use these skills? This chapter will bring further focus to the first question that frames the theme of this book: the integration of civil and political rights in the work of UN development agencies, with India as an example. After briefly reviewing what a rights-based approach to development is, Chapter 2 looks at the central human rights issues confronting the UN in India. If we are to understand whether, and how, UN agencies confront and try to mitigate human rights violations, it is, of course, vital to know what those violations are. How are they framed by the UN, and how do they relate to the central themes of RBA?

Chapters 3, 4, and 5, which include case studies looking at a variety of development organizations in India, will show in more detail how these rights are translated into action on the ground; and, more importantly for the argument of this book, the type of government and social resistance they produce, and how UN development experts work overtly and covertly to overcome this resistance. The overall goal of the present chapter and the case studies is to demonstrate that UN agencies do have specific policies on civil and political rights, that they are able to independently pursue these policies at times, and that the policies are making a difference (as explained in Chapter 6) in the promotion and protection of human rights in India.

What Is the Rights-based Approach to Development?

First, we must consider what a rights-based approach to development *is*, and how it connects two separate, although closely related, issues: human rights and development. There is no single concept of rights-based approach to development, but rather a wide variety of development concepts grouped under that phrase; sometimes they are quite different and even contradictory. Instead, the idea of an RBA encompasses several parallel, often intersecting, trends in development thinking, going back at least to the 1990s. To see where the important questions are in terms of the connection between RBA and human rights as the UN defines them, a short description of RBA is needed.

The connection between rights and development is long-standing. And surely they are inseparable: development will always be a political process, guided by the powerful, changing social structures, helping some, and harming others. However, the UN's current definition of a rights-based approach to development began with Secretary-General Kofi Annan, who in the 1994 document "An Agenda For Development" (A/48/935) explicitly linked democracy, human rights, and development (see also Uvin, 2004, p. 125). By 1997, Secretary-General Annan's program for UN reform included a directive that all UN agencies include human rights into their programming. He advocated viewing rights as a "cross-cutting issue" to be integrated into all UN activities. Annan felt strongly that human rights were central to the mission of the United Nations. They are an important expression of the ideals that the UN is based on and should be promoting. The United Nations Development Fund (UNDP) issued guidelines on "Integrating Human Rights with Sustainable Development" (UNDP, 1998) by 1998, and dedicated the 2000 *Human Development Report* to human rights. The United Nation Children's Fund (UNICEF) in the 1990s had already indicated its interest in using the Convention on the Rights of the Child (CRC) as a programming document. While at first this was mainly a public relations move rather than a real programming change, by the early 2000s it began to think seriously about the CRC as a way to change and expand its work (Oestreich, 2007).

Perhaps the most basic, and widely cited, description of the rights-based approach to development as understood by UN agencies is the "UN Common Understanding of the Human Rights-based Approach to Development Cooperation" (UN Development Group, 2003), which arose from an inter-agency UN workshop in 2003. The statement summarizes the rights-based approach in three points:

1. All programmes of development co-operation, policies and technical assistance should further the realization of human rights as laid down in the Universal Declaration of Human Rights and other international human rights instruments.
2. Human rights standards contained in, and principles derived from, the Universal Declaration of Human Rights and other international human rights instruments guide all development cooperation and programming in all sectors and in all phases of the programming process.
3. Programmes of development cooperation contribute to the development of the capacities of duty-bearers to meet their obligations and of "rights-holders" to claim their rights.

The first two points work in opposite (albeit reinforcing) directions: the first says that development should further rights, the second that rights should further development. The third point is more wide-reaching, saying in effect that since now development is being explicitly linked to a "political" concept (that of rights), political agents must be engaged in the development process in a particular way—as the duty-bearers on whom rights place obligations. This section will briefly examine the three concepts in turn.

Development Should Promote Rights

Building from concepts of "human development" (Streeten, 1994) and development "with a human face" (Cornia, Jolly, & Steward, 1987), there is nothing especially new in the idea that development must be thought of as more than mere economic growth. Still, linking development directly with rights is a further step in redefining development away from simple economic growth, adding overtly political and moral elements that were not part of the UN's programming before. While it is true that development always has a political component—even economic growth in its most basic form can't be separated from its political context—RBA makes this component far more explicit and wide-ranging.

In one sense, the idea that "development should promote rights" simply means that development programs should focus on those development goals that are seen as basic human rights—largely on the "positive" rights of food, shelter, the highest available standard of medical care, and so forth. Policy documents on rights-based programming do discuss lack of food, education, or resources in general as "rights violations" that need to be addressed. A report of the United Nations University, for example, presents hunger as a rights violation, with an implicit reference to Article 25 of the Universal Declaration of Human Rights (Guha-Khasnobis & Vivek, 2007). The Office of the United Nations High Commissioner for Human Rights (OHCHR) references not just poverty as a rights violation but also the right to shelter, work, food, nutrition, and a variety of other rights, and it frames development as the fulfillment of these rights (OHCHR, 2006).

Peter Uvin (2004) has usefully and rightly noted that this can lead to a very simplistic and self-serving notion of development and rights by simply redefining development as rights promotion. This is all too true in many cases, as he documents, but such simple equivalencies can be avoided. For example, the OHCHR report states that health is a human right and defines it appropriately not as the right to be healthy, but "the right to the enjoyment of a variety of facilities, goods, services and conditions necessary for the realization of the *highest attainable* standard of health" (OHCHR, 2006, p. 12; emphasis added). This emphasizes not just the provision of goods and services but also the political dynamic that allows for the realization of those goods and services—within the limits of the local context. "The focus ... is on the relationships, institutions and processes, which determine development outcomes or change" (Brocklesby & Crawford, 2004, p. 13). In other words, RBA looks not only at whether people are experiencing improved material conditions but also whether the social and political forces that prevented improvement in the past are being addressed and remedied.

A key element of this process (that is to say, one that calls for changes in legal rules, government structures, and social policy) is the empowerment of people to provide for themselves. There is no single definition of empowerment, despite (or perhaps because of) the fact that it is so central to the discourse of development and rights. And we must be very careful not to use it too freely and carelessly. Chapter 5 will examine this term more closely. But we can begin here with the World Bank's statement: "In its broadest sense, empowerment is the expansion of freedom of choice and action. It means increasing one's authority and control over the resources and decisions that affect one's life. As people exercise real choice, they gain increased control over their lives." The Bank statement suggests four elements of empowerment:

- Access to information
- Inclusion and participation
- Accountability
- Local organizational capacity (World Bank, 2002, pp. 14–18)

Empowering people, particularly the poor, is a self-reinforcing process: development should be designed to give people control over their lives and the decisions that affect them, and empowerment is a key factor in promoting development. Development, UNDP and others argue, must enable citizens to take control of their own lives and to effectively use the resources available to them. Development projects should aim to politically, economically, and socially empower people, both as a good in itself and as a self-reinforcing step in the development process. Development is thus explicitly defined in political and moral terms, as well as economic (Hill, 2003).

Perhaps most importantly, the inclusion of rights into development planning also means paying attention to key rights issues such as exclusion, discrimination, and even political repression. Here, the focus is as much on such "negative" rights as racial or gender discrimination, as on the "positive" rights mentioned above. For example, a well-designed development project ought to ensure that previously underserved populations—girls, racial and ethnic minorities, the extremely poor, the physically disabled—are being incorporated into project design and implementation. It is not good enough, the thinking goes, to increase overall coverage (of, say, immunization) if that increase does not equally cover the most vulnerable groups. Careful analysis, therefore, is required before development projects begin, so that such groups can be identified and built into plans. Furthermore, helping such groups is to be an *explicit* part of any UN project or country plan of action. It is not enough, say, to ensure that girls receive the same educational opportunities as boys; an education program is supposed to directly address the problem of discrimination both by making sure that underserved girls are found and brought into the educational system, and by addressing the legal and social impediments to girls' education. This might include changes to existing legal structures, public information campaigns, training for teachers and local politicians, or a host of other interventions.

Development and rights are thus seen as intimately linked, and proper development promotes people's rights and political status. Too many development projects in the past focused only on providing services, or fostering growth, with little attention to how those affected the larger picture of people's interaction with society. Yet if, as Sen (1999) says, development is the promotion of rights, then development projects have to be designed to do more than just provide a higher level of material welfare; they have to also attend to the overall condition of the people they are supposed to help and address inequality, powerlessness, and patters of oppression and exclusion.

Rights Can and Should Promote Development

The other side of the equation is the assumption that promoting rights will, and should, promote better development outcomes. It is not easy to show a direct cause and effect between greater human rights and increased economic development (Grugel & Piper, 2008). Even so, a central precept of RBA is that respect for rights does, in fact, promote development in its various definitions.

Some causal mechanisms are posited—although it should be noted that some of these concepts define "rights" fairly loosely. "Participation" as a development strategy is one central feature. People have the right to participate in the decisions that affect their lives, including development planning—as stated in Article 25 of the Covenant on Civil and Political Rights, as well as in the Universal Declaration of Human Rights. Assuring this right, through projects designed to hear local voices, is expected to improve development work in several ways. A rights-based approach, by listening to local voices, presumably helps development experts provide what local people actually want and makes them able to learn from their experiences, rather than using a "cookie cutter" approach that ignores local conditions. "It emphasizes the importance of ensuring the active and informed *participation* by the poor in the formulation, implementation and monitoring of poverty reduction strategies" (OHCHR, 2006, p. 5; emphasis in original). Further, participation aids in "accountability," that is, holding political officials responsible for the success or failure of policies and execution. "Decentralization and democratization of local-level governance will . . . be necessary to enable the people, especially the poor, to monitor the activities of the Government" (OHCHR, 2006, p. 18).

RBA also assumes that as people are empowered politically and socially, this in turn allows them to take greater advantage of opportunities and to use their abilities and resources in the most effective way. Recognizing a right to education, for example, and making sure it is implemented, has obvious development implications: not only because educated citizens are more productive and able to pursue economic opportunities, but also because a literate and informed citizenry can demand more from its government in terms of rights and development. Education of girls, in particular, is seen as vital, as so many are excluded from economic activity outside the home (UNDP, 2006). "Access to Justice" programs, which aim to reform judiciaries and generally give people the ability to redress wrongs, also are thought to lead to greater development; people who have no faith in the legal system are less likely to start businesses or trust their neighbors and strangers, and this, of course, affects their ability to be economically productive (UNDP, 2010b). More generally, the respect for human rights gives citizens greater control over their own lives and allows them to be the stewards of their own development and resources; rights move states from "service delivery" to true bottom-up development.

Also, civil liberties seem to make people more productive. However, a direct connection between civil liberties and economic progress is not easy to establish. Daniel Kaufmann for example has found a *"large direct causal effect from better governance to improved development outcomes"* (Kaufmann, 2004, p. 15; emphasis in original). In saying this, Kaufmann directly ties improved governance to improved human rights (although he also notes that "governance factors such as corruption and rule of law are not, however, necessarily fundamental determinants of socio-economic development," 2004, p. 18). The debate over whether democracy and respect for political and civil rights is in fact conducive to economic growth—or whether authoritarian or "semi-authoritarian" (Ottaway, 2003) regimes have better growth outcomes—has been debated in many forums, with no certain results (see, for example, Knutsen, 2012; Narayan, Narayan, & Smyth, 2011). But even if authoritarian states do show impressive economic growth, the *definition* of development in RBA includes respect for rights, including civil rights, and thus is part of a rights-based approach as a moral imperative. Respect for *all* rights is, by dint of RBA, a UN-wide imperative, and therefore the link is taken for granted even if such a link is not so easy to demonstrate (and if it leads to the conclusion that some fairly wealthy countries are not "developed" since their respect for rights is lagging).

Rights Hold Duty-Bearers Accountable to Meet Their Development Obligations

A rights-based approach to development, finally, places emphasis on the responsibility of governments to fulfill the rights, both positive and negative, of their citizens. It is seen as a way to "hold governments to account" for their actions in development and development-related actions. We have seen in Chapter 1 that this concept—of "holding governments to account"— gets tossed around far too easily in the development field, but it can have specific meaning, and it is something that *good* development work can promote. Rights create duties, whether enforceable or not: in most cases the duty-bearers are government entities, and rights-holders can and must hold duty-bearers accountable when rights are not respected (Nickel, 1993). Duty-bearers must respect rights or provide for their fulfillment. Not all rights generate similar types of duties, but as Shue (1980) and others convincingly show, even C&P rights generate positive duties on states, for example, to provide a legal system that protects civil liberties.

Literature on RBA makes clear that a rights-based approach relies on generating duties and making sure those duties are fulfilled. But it is important to see that there is more involved than merely *asserting* people have rights or even codifying those rights in a legal system. India, for example, has many rights codified in law, but the implementation of those rights is lacking, and often citizens lack the ability to hold government accountable, even in a country that is democratic and has a well-developed legal system. As one World Bank reports asks, "Many governments in developing countries see service provision as an act of benevolence rather than of responsive and accountable governance.... How do we ensure that citizens in developing countries have the right to be served by their governments rather than to be (ruthlessly) rules upon?" (Shah, 2008, p. 2). Another document, from the UN High Commissioner for Human Rights, states, "Perhaps the most important source of added value in the human rights approach is the emphasis it places on the *accountability* of policy-makers and other actors whose actions have an impact on the rights of people. Rights imply duties, and duties demand accountability" (quoted in Cornwall & Nyamu-Musembi, 2004, p. 1417; emphasis in original).

What states are held accountable for will cover a wide range. Services demanded largely include economic and social rights, but political rights are also included. Are governments providing courts and access to justice, information, and opportunities for voice? Are they creating mechanisms of accountability? In some ways this aspect of a rights-based approach is more about the politics of pressuring governments into action rather than a programming tool in itself. As a key UNDP document puts it, "the global legitimacy of human rights provides an objective starting point for dialogue and discussions with government, the people, and external partners"; however, the same document also notes that "[the policy] helps policy-makers and citizens recognize the power dynamics of the development process ... [and] facilitates the development of quantitative benchmarks and indicators for measuring progress in development planning and delivery" (UNDP, 2006, p. 8). In other words, while there is a rhetorical component to this (using the power of the concept of rights to push states to provide social services) there is also a programming aspect, in so far as it directs attention to the political side of development decision-making. These policies are all highly political, and development agencies understand they must be careful not to hurt relationships with host governments.

Human Rights and Development in India

If we begin with the premise that rights-based approaches to development mean that UN agencies are now active in the promotion of human rights, it is important to see *which* rights are being promoted, and *how* that promotion is happening. RBA, as discussed in Chapter 1, is a well-known set of ideas at this point, and there are any number of case studies about how this type of development practice helps people in particular situations (e.g. Crawford, 2008; Guha-Khasnobis & Vivek, 2007; Nyamu-Musembi & Cornwall, 2004; UNDP, 2012). Less examined is how the *overall* picture of rights is addressed—how the UN development assistance framework looks at all the rights issues a state faces and incorporates them into its programming. This will give some idea of the potential and limitations of RBA as a way of promoting rights, as well as some sense of how UN staff understand their jobs in relation to the challenges faced by specific countries in which they work.

The importance of the connection between positive and negative rights in theory, and the difficulty of implementing that connection in practice, is evident when looking at the Constitution India and the various other legal rights that have been enacted by the Indian Parliament since the Constitution was written. The Indian Constitution, drawing on its British legacy, is progressive and well-developed (Khosla, 2012). Adopted in 1949 (and taking effect in 1950), it was written for an emerging state that was instituting a new democracy, concerned with economic development and poverty alleviation, and trying to knit together a diverse society with various regions, ethnic and religious minorities, indigenous peoples, and castes that faced historical discrimination (Mohanty, 2009, pp. 136–140). Part III of the Indian Constitution lays out a comprehensive set of justiciable rights, primarily civil and political rights, although others, such as a right to education, are also included. Significantly for this project, Part III also includes a right to "equality" that encompasses caste, race, gender, religion, and other categories (Vaidyanathan, 2005). Part IV contains "directive principles" of the Constitution, nonjusticiable "active obligations" of the Indian state (Deol, 2011, pp. 106–108). These include promoting economic equity, child welfare, equal pay for equal work, the elimination of caste discrimination, and other positive obligations of the state to promote mostly ES&C rights. Added to this is a system of public interest litigation (PIL) that has substantially advanced the ability of Indian courts to intervene when rights are being violated. PIL, as it has developed, allows parties other than those whose rights have been violated (including NGOs and the court itself) to file suit contesting human rights violations and other violations of the public interest (Craig & Deshpande, 1989).

Along with these constitutional provisions are a number of other important legal rights. These include a Right to Information act, passed nationally in 2005; a right to education act, passed in 2009; and right to work legislation, the Mahatma Gandhi National Rural Employment Guarantee Act of 2005. These will be discussed in subsequent chapters, as various UN agencies work toward their implementation in India. As we will see in this chapter, both constitutional provisions and legislation guaranteeing various rights is one thing: effective implementation of these rights and their enjoyment by citizens is another. A rights-based approach to development must be more than simply passing legislation that says people have rights: it is the social, legal, and cultural structure that allows those rights to be enjoyed, including holding government accountable but also in many cases changing a social structure that blocks equality and freedom. Neither positive nor negative rights can be fully enjoyed without the other: yet agencies have shied away from promoting such a holistic view, preferring to focus on the ES&C rights that fall more easily within their mandate.

Human Rights Issues in India

So, what are the key rights issues to address? India is, as most everyone knows, a rapidly developing country and a very large one. The population is greater than 1.2 billion. The gross domestic product of India, according to the World Bank, was US$1.84 billion in 2012 and averaged about 7.3% annual growth in the years 2003–2012 (World Bank, 2013, p. 13), slowing down a bit after that. The growth in India's economy is largely attributed to a large series of economic reforms begun in the early 1990s, which moved India away from a more socialist and state-controlled economic model and toward one that loosened government control over the economy, encouraged foreign investment, devalued the currency (and allowed it to float), and generally integrated India into the world economy (Joshi & Little, 1996). The Indian economy is now the within the top ten globally in terms of absolute size, according to the World Bank, and third overall by purchasing power parity. And it continues to grow.

India is not generally on the list of the world's serious human rights abusers—far from it—and a conversation about rights with UN staff of *any* organization in New Delhi normally includes a disclaimer to this effect. Most UN staff are aware—sometimes acutely so—that the primary rights they deal with are those related to their development mission as opposed to gross rights abuses. Only sometimes do these development-related rights overlap with the traditional human rights machinery based in New York and Geneva. The Indian legal system is certainly flawed (more on that in the case studies), but it also presents many opportunities for truly progressive work on human rights. UN staff recognizes (as do I) that the well-entrenched democratic system and functioning legal system make India a particular sort of case in terms of human rights.

A full treatment of the human rights situation in India is, of course, well beyond the scope of this project. The purpose of this short section is simply to highlight how those agencies and organizations tasked specifically with human rights promotion see the key issues; these will then be contrasted with how the UN development apparatus defines human rights in India. The point is to see where the "rhetoric" of development and human rights does or does not match up with how a more traditional set of actors define the issues.

A good starting point is the 2013 report (issued around the same time as my fieldwork) for India of Human Rights Watch, which annually assesses the rights situation in India (as in other countries) and flags issues of concern. The 2013 report begins by noting, "the country has a thriving civil society, free media, and an independent judiciary," but it goes on to assert that "longstanding abusive practices, corruption, and lack of accountability for perpetrators foster human rights violations" (Human Rights Watch, 2013). (More recent reports note concern about the government of Narendra Modi and its commitment to freedom of speech and an active civil society.) Among the most serious issues, the 2013 report lists:

- Impunity of security forces from prosecution for "serious rights abuses."
- Violence committed by Maoist insurgents (Naxalites), particularly in targeting schools, and violence by security forces battling the insurgencies.

- The situation in Jammu and Kashmir, where security forces have committed serious rights violations, including extrajudicial killings.
- Violence in the state of Assam, where there has been an outbreak of communal violence involving tribal groups and the government.
- Threats to freedom of expression, including restrictions on Internet use, and the use of a colonial-era sedition law to silence protestors, despite a Supreme Court ruling that such use of the law was invalid.
- Children's rights (particularly forced labor, sexually trafficked children, and other children in particularly dangerous or abusive circumstances).
- Women's rights.
- Abuses in the extractive industries, for example, the destruction of the environment near mining operations and the effects this has on local residents.
- Access to palliative care for the sick and dying.
- Death penalty cases.
- India's role in human rights abuses in other countries, for example, its role on the Human Rights Council regarding abuses in Sri Lanka or Syria.

These concerns are reflected in various reports issued both before and after 2013.

The National Human Rights Commission of India lists a number of issues they are dealing with. These are (in the order presented on their website):

- Abolition of bonded labor
- Reform of certain mental health hospitals, and women's protective homes
- The right to food
- Abolition of child labor
- Rehabilitation of marginalized and destitute women
- Combating sexual harassment of women in the workplace
- Harassment of women on passenger trains
- Abolition of manual scavenging
- Dalit issues ("untouchables")
- Problems faced by nomadic tribes
- Rights of the disabled
- The right to health
- HIV/AIDS issues
- Relief work for victims of the 1999 Orissa cyclone
- Monitoring of relief measures after the 2001 Gujarat earthquake
- Possible creation of "district complaints authorities" to monitor police-community relations

- Population policy (including development-related population policies)
- Human trafficking

India submitted a report to the United Nations Human Rights Council in 2008 as part of the process of Universal Periodic Review (UPR) and a follow-up report in 2012. These reports mentioned much the same set of issues. It is possible to group the issues into a few categories after looking at the UPR documents. One, clearly, has to do with accusations of abuse of civil rights by government agencies. Most notably this includes India's fight against terrorism in Jammu and Kashmir in particular: use of the Armed Forces (Special Powers) Act of 1958 (Kikon, 2009; McDuie-Ra, 2008) was highlighted, as it gives security forces sweeping powers to arrest and detain people in areas of civil unrest and to suspend various parts of due process. Other abuses by the police and criminal justice system—for example, accusations of abuse of people held in custody, of people held in prison for excessively long periods of time while waiting for a hearing (a *very* commonly heard complaint in India), and of failure to protect minority communities—were raised. In particular, UNICEF and other agencies have also brought up the problem of violence against women and children in violence-prone areas. The failure of police to prosecute many cases of rape and other crimes against women has also been strongly noted by the international community.

A second set of issues centers on discrimination, particularly toward Scheduled Castes, Scheduled Tribes, and women. Scheduled Castes, representing about 15% of the Indian population, are castes who have special protection in the Indian Constitution due to historical discrimination and marginalization; Scheduled Tribes, about 9% of the population, are indigenous populations who also receive special legal protection due to a history of discrimination and worse. While discrimination against each group is illegal in India and banned under the Indian Constitution—and while there is no doubt that progress has been made toward greater equality—there is clear data that members of both groups are poorer than the population in general, more marginalized from services, and still discriminated against by many people in the larger population, as well as by various arms of the government (Deshpande, 2011). Fighting caste and tribal discrimination has been a long struggle of the Indian government and Indian society as a whole. The report of the UPR also noted discrimination against "the urban poor, informal sector workers, internally displaced persons, religious minorities, such as the Muslim population, persons with disabilities and persons living with HIV/AIDS." Similarly, a number of agencies note the prevalence of unequal treatment and status of women. This expresses itself in various ways, ranging from property laws to sexual harassment and rape, to sex-selective abortion, and even to "dowry murders" (the estimated 8,000 or so women murdered each year so that their husbands are free to marry someone with a larger dowry or because the family was unable to pay the agreed-upon amount) (Panda & Agarwal, 2005).

A third set of issues is grouped as the "right to work and to just and favorable conditions of work." These include such issues as bonded labor, scavenging, sweatshop labor, child labor, and other very difficult work conditions. Such conditions continue to be depressingly common in India, despite efforts to abolish them, and violate many international labor and other rights documents. Indian labor conditions are all too often extremely severe, and pay is extremely low even for those with regular employment. A fourth set includes restrictions on the religious practices of minority religions.

Although less relevant here, there are, of course, important violations of more specific economic, social, and cultural rights. These have been raised, for example, in the context of UPR, although Human Rights Watch and other agencies (e.g., Amnesty International) have paid less attention to them, as they prefer to focus more on civil and political rights. Questions about guaranteeing the right to health (or health care), the right to education, and the right to "social security and an adequate standard of living" continue to be of central concern in India. Some of these, of course, are closely related to other rights: discrimination against women, naturally, deeply affects women's ability to pursue an education or even to have an adequate standard of living; and children's rights, protected under the CRC. Other issues include the lack of effective housing policies, poor maternal and neonatal health care, and inadequate resources spent on education. There is overlap with other issues; for example, in the UPR report the "right to health" is related to people, such as ship-breakers, working in conditions that damage their health; the right to education is often denied, particularly to the children of Scheduled Castes and Tribes; and inadequate housing is related, in part, to the denial of due process under the law to people being evicted from their land for various reasons.

Human Rights Issues Incorporated in Key UN Development Strategies

How, then, are these rights issues incorporated into the programming documents and plans of the various UN agencies tasked with following a rights-based approach to development? The 2013–2017 United Nations

Development Assistance Framework (UNDAF) for India lists six broad, general goals for the current planning period. These are:

- Inclusive growth
- Food and nutrition security
- Gender equality
- Equitable access to quality basic services
- Governance
- Sustainable development

Only some of these "outcomes" have some obvious connection with the pursuit of human rights. Fostering "inclusive growth," for example, certainly means that economic growth is important, but also that those who have not benefited from India's economic rise should be able to do so. The benefits of growth should be more equitably distributed. Inclusiveness informs a great deal of what each of the UN agencies in India are trying to accomplish; it is a term that gets used frequently by UN staff when explaining the meaning of RBA. Equity as a concept is discussed in depth in Chapter 5, in the section on the World Bank. It is a complex topic, and one that is extremely important to UN development efforts, but difficult to define satisfactorily. Equity does not necessarily mean the same as "equality"; while rights are to be equal, equity requires that the distribution of resources and growth is implemented fairly, not equally. It means that all should benefit from economic growth: in India, the failure of growth to benefit the poorest classes is particularly stark and troubling.

How does local staff translate equity into a rights issue? One respondent in India, working for UNICEF, noted the importance of equity for his unit: he described equity as "a lens to achieve better results, better numbers, more cost effective."[1] This staff member meant it primarily as a way to look at data to find underserved areas, where the most cost-effective interventions could be attempted. On the other hand, a person in another unit used equity as part of a public knowledge campaign to promote attitudes about equal rights (among girls versus boys, lower castes versus upper castes, etc.).[2] Most significantly, another UNICEF staff member specifically said that "equity" was often used as a term to imply *political inclusion*: New York, this staff person said (referring to UNICEF headquarters), likes the term equity. The language seems to be considered less controversial than political empowerment or inclusion, with their implication of disturbing the status quo.[3]

Improved governance is also cited as an important UNDAF outcome: the goal is "governance systems [that are] more inclusive, accountable, decentralized" and that help make "programme implementation more effective for the realization of rights of marginalized groups, especially women and children" (UN-Government of India, 2013, p. 23). The UNDAF leaves these rights fairly open, although presumably these include both C&P right and ES&C rights. Political reform that leads to more accountable government and empowered citizens will facilitate achievement of enhanced respect for rights. The nature of this process is captured in a 2010 document that stated, "In contrast to the focus on duty bearers in the majority of projects, the Access to Justice component is working with [women] . . . to empower them with legal literacy and create a demand for justice at the grassroots" (Menon-Sen & Shiva Kumar, 2010, p. 19).

Like the UNDAF, the UNICEF 2013–2017 planning document (UNICEF-India, 2013) also says surprisingly little specifically about rights, considering the importance of RBA and particularly the status of the CRC in UNICEF programming. Scheduled Castes and Scheduled Tribes are mentioned, certainly, as are the rights of women and girls. But nothing is said about the connection between civil and political rights and achievement of UNICEF plans. The World Bank's 2013 strategy document uses the word "rights" three times in its 163 pages (although, to be fair, a lot of those pages are tables and graphs rather than text).

Asking UN staff in India how they define "rights," and in particular what C&P rights they most want to promote, results in a surprising range of answers, some seemingly on target, some less so. Some staff, again, fell back on the rhetorical notion that services had to be "made a right" that people could "demand" and governments would "be held accountable for providing." This was the most common notion expressed, and it suggests thinking stuck in the older "service provider" paradigm of development, where services are provided by the government. One UNDP staff member—highly placed in a position that dealt with many highly politicized issues—listed farmer suicides and death from starvation as the key human rights issues for her. Again, these issues may in the broadest sense be rights related, but only broadly so. And even here, she said, "You can't talk to the government about these issues" because of their political sensitivity. UNICEF staff, not surprisingly, mentioned various elements of the CRC as their key human rights concerns. Another staff person, working on education issues, mentioned sports for children in conflict zones as a key part of how they envisioned a rights-based approach: the thinking was that sports built self-confidence and helped children overcome the mental stress of being in a conflict zone, and that this was a right of children. Now, there is nothing wrong with wanting to help children in conflict zones to receive a good education, and such an education is a right, but answers like this often suggested, to this interviewer at least, that the notion of how rights factored into RBA were fairly vague. "I do talk about rights," said another UNICEF staff person: "[adequate nutrition] is a fundamental right of children."[4] But what translated nutrition from a matter of service delivery to one of helping children seize their rights was left unsaid. As we will see in Chapter 4, there *is* some good thinking about what this means; the late Urban Jonsson (2003), for example, has written extensively about this with particular reference to UNICEF, and the right to nutrition is well laid out in the CRC. Yet translating that into policy, which is beyond a rhetorical commitment to providing children with food, is a greater challenge.

Beyond that, matters of equity and discrimination dominated the question of "What human rights issues are most important to you?" Caste and tribal status arose frequently. Most often this was tied to disaggregating data to look for underserved groups. In a crude form this was just about changing *outcomes*—that is, making sure that lower caste people had the same access to education or social welfare programs. More sophisticated answers included changing attitudes toward Scheduled Castes, Scheduled Tribes, girls, institutionalized children, and other disadvantaged groups. In areas where there were large numbers of Scheduled Tribes, issues of land and forest rights were brought up. Most of all, perhaps, when discussion of RBA went beyond securing ES&C rights, it was about *participation*: forming school committees, helping people (particularly women) run for office, and informing people of their entitlements under various social welfare schemes.

It is important to note that one cluster of human rights issues is not dealt with by UN agencies in India, nor any other NGOs with the exception of the International Committee of the Red Cross. That is the situation in Jammu and Kashmir, and any issues associated with fighting terrorism stemming from that conflict. UN agencies do not operate in Jammu and Kashmir, and I have no recollection of anyone mentioning the situation there or any rights issue related to the ongoing threat of terrorism in India. This clearly seemed to be off the table for anyone in the development side of the United Nations.

Specific Civil and Political Rights Promoted by the UN in India

Interviews with UN staff often began with them denying that they had any policy to promote civil and political rights. As the conversation went on, I would mention various policies as having clear rights implications, and often the same person would say something along the lines of "Well, yes, I guess that is a rights policy." The number of times that this happened pointed to both the reluctance of UN staff to openly discuss that they were promoting C&P rights and that there is yet no general consensus on exactly what a rights-based approach means. The concern over state resistance will be discussed in greater detail below. In this section, I list some of the key civil and political rights being promoted by UN agencies at the operational level. This is different from the overall strategy documents listed above, and many of these are not necessarily referred to as rights policies, although they have clear rights implications.

Decentralization

Decentralization is a key development strategy for UN agencies as well as bilateral donors, NGOs, and others involved in the development enterprise. It is almost an article of faith among development practitioners that moving decision-making closer to the people who are supposed to be helped—the poor and disenfranchised—through the decentralization of government will lead to more responsive, better-planned development policies (Jayal, Prakash, & Sharma, 2006). Lack of citizen participation, bloated bureaucracies, and unaccountable bureaucrats are identified as serious problems in creating effective development policy (Bardhan & Mookherjee, 2006).

Over-centralization of governmental power and a lack of democratic accountability lead to more than just poor development planning; it also denies people their democratic rights (Crook & Manor, 2000). Many countries centralize power to maintain control of the population by overly controlling central authorities, and many assume that decentralization will give people more voice in the political process—not only a boon to good development policies, but also a key element of the right to political participation. The idea that democracy is a human right is controversial and, in any case, not implementable, but both the Universal Declaration of Human Rights (Article 21) and the Covenant on Civil and Political Rights (Article 25) recognize rights to political participation and equal access to social services.

Decentralization of political power has been a central strategy of the Indian government at least since 1992. India had a long tradition of local government through Panchayats (local governing bodies). Mahatma Gandhi famously idealized the role of local Panchayats as small republics, to which power could be devolved; although it should be noted that others were less enthusiastic, they considered the village level to be the home of caste and other biases (Jodhka, 2002). In 1992, the 73rd and 74th amendments to the Indian Constitution strengthened the Panchayati Raj Institution (PRI) system and instructed states to more effectively devolve power to the local level. As Vineet Kapoor explains, there were many reasons for wanting to strengthen the Panchayat system (Kapoor, 2006). There was the above-mentioned argument that local development would benefit from increasing local voices and participation. Strengthening the Panchayats, it was hoped, would reinvigorate democracy in general in India, where grave concerns exist about "elite capture" and other problems that block true citizen participation. This was also intended to create a higher level of political accountability, both to help the poor and to generally make the system more genuinely democratic.

A key strategy of all UN development agencies in India, as well as the World Bank, is to strengthen the system of PRIs and provide capacity development for their operations. This works on a number of different levels. Capacity development of Panchayats and the speeding of decentralization are expected to make development projects more participatory and to empower people at the local level by giving them a voice in development decision-making. For example, the UNDP is providing technical support for decentralization to state- and district-level officials, as well as to Panchayat members themselves, on how to effectively express a voice in policy decisions (UNDP, 2008a). Decentralization is also expected to increase transparency and help fight corruption as well as make officials more accountable. The World Bank has funded a number of programs to strengthen Panchayats, streamline their finances, and provide technical support. Yet more than one World Bank staff member refused to allow me to take notes during our meeting, such was their sensitivity to the idea that they had a rights policy.

Panchayat support is not the only mode of decentralization in India. For example, UNICEF has been supporting the creation of school-management committees at the local level to involve people in running schools and give them the tools to demand that schools be open, accountable, and of high quality (Jayal, Prakash, & Sharma, 2006; Mullen, 2012). UNDP and other agencies support local self-help groups that empower women to make decisions about issues ranging from sanitation arrangements to health care. The

UN-Government of India Joint Programme on Convergence, to use another example, is a comprehensive project to enable "elected representatives and local functionaries [in] performing their role in formulation, execution, and monitoring of integrated district development plans," through a comprehensive set of capacity-building projects at the state and local government level (UNDP, 2010a). This includes training district facilitators, improving local budgeting, and training local government officials. Government decentralization is a key element of all UN programming. While it is defended as a key step in creating more effective and responsive development initiatives, political participation—as a human right—is promoted by UN programs, embraced by the government, and given a central role in development policy.

Nondiscrimination

Nondiscrimination is an important human rights goal, and some form of it is included in nearly every international human rights document. Article 2 of the Universal Declaration of Human Rights mentions "race, colour, sex, language, religion, political or other opinion, national or social origin, property, birth or other status." Caste discrimination and discrimination against indigenous peoples are also important issues in India, and nondiscrimination against these categories is enshrined in the Indian Constitution and in Indian law. Nevertheless, they remain important problems, and economic data shows that there are grave inequalities as a result (Deshpande, 2011).

Nondiscrimination is a central component to rights-based development and pervades all the UN's work in India. A number of discriminated-against groups are specifically targeted by UN programming. As mentioned, most notable are Scheduled Castes (people in castes that are historically marginalized in Indian life and are targeted by the government for special assistance), Scheduled Tribes (marginalized indigenous groups), and women and girls. Other marginalized groups were also mentioned both in numerous official documents and in my interviews with UN staff. These include working children, migrant workers, people with disabilities, "third gender" (transgender) people, and various others. It is important to be clear that UN staff sees the goal of ending discrimination as a good in and of itself, not only as a tool for promoting other rights.

Fighting discrimination is central to the very concept of RBA—discrimination means disempowerment of entire communities and, thus, a denial of freedom to its members. The United Nations Population Fund (UNFPA), for example, argues that fighting discrimination against women and girls is among its highest priorities and aims at nothing less than changing societal norms about the value of girls and women (UNFPA, 2012). UNICEF strives for similar societal changes through its Communication for Development (C4D) program. UNDP makes reaching underserved groups and fighting discrimination central to nearly all its programming. To bring up one example from many, UNDP has a major project under way to build government capacity around India's important Mahatma Gandhi National Rural Employment Guarantee Act, which guarantees the rural poor 100 days of paid employment per year but often is implemented in a way that discriminates against various groups, from lower castes to migrant laborers. The Joint UN Programme on HIV/AIDS (UNAIDS) makes fighting discrimination against high-risk groups a central strategy of its work, as do all other agencies working to fight the spread of HIV/AIDS—which is to say, essentially all UN agencies.

It bears repeating that while UNAIDS and the WHO, for example, will argue that fighting discrimination is an important development tool (because it has instrumental value in fighting the spread of HIV), and UNICEF will certainly argue that fighting discrimination against girls also has vital instrumental value, these agencies do not shy away from declaring that nondiscrimination has value in and of itself. So, the UNDP project Pathways for an Inclusive Indian Administration indicates that better management of Indian administrative services "is key to helping realize the Government objective of greater inclusion through enhancing service delivery to the marginalized and vulnerable (UNDP, 2011–2012)." Yet it does not reference any further goals—helping the marginalized and vulnerable is assumed to be the definition of development, not a tool to promote it. Interviews with UN staff showed that they, too, considered fighting discrimination an end in itself; a human rights goal that is now incorporated into the development process.

Access to Justice

Under the heading "access to justice," UN agencies have taken on a number of rights-promoting projects aimed at creating a more just, equitable, and efficient legal system in India, as well as creating an environment that promotes the goals mentioned above: effective political participation and nondiscrimination. Access to justice includes such rights as a fair trial, citizenship (a serious problem in India where many births go unrecorded), legal literacy, training of judges, and training of lawyers and legal aid workers (UNDP, 2008b).

Access to Justice programs are wide-ranging, and it would be impossible to completely summarize them here. For an example, UNDP is working to "develop legal and representational capacity of [civil society organizations] and networks providing access to justice services to women and men belonging to disadvantaged groups" (UNDP, 2011). UNDP trains local legal aid workers to inform such groups of their rights and help them petition the legal system to redress wrongs. The program also seeks to increase legal awareness in all sectors of society of rights, particularly their right to political participation through their elected representatives. Programs sponsored by UNDP and other agencies also include training of judges, government bureaucrats, lawyers, and others on judicial reform and proper procedure, as well as capacity building of the legal system in general.

Here, one can see a direct connection: it is clear that access to a fair, well-functioning legal system leads to improved development outcomes in terms of increased economic performance, greater transparency, and more government accountability (Sage & Woolcock, 2008). But the entire Access to Justice portfolio can hardly be captured in these terms. Again, to use just one example (witnessed firsthand), the UNDP in Chhattisgarh state sponsored a local NGO to conduct training on legal rights for the *hijra* (transgender) community. After identifying potential *hijra* leaders, the NGO organized a lengthy training session on issues ranging from how to approach the police when they have been the victim of a crime, to effective ways to change local legislation, to self-esteem and job-finding skills. The NGO has also been working with local employers to find jobs for *hijra*, who have traditionally faced severe discrimination that relegated them to begging, sex work, and other extremely marginal activities. Other marginalized communities have also been helped to gain access to the legal system and legal redress. UNICEF, for example, through its Child Protection program, focuses on children who are trafficked, on the children of migrant workers, and on those caught up in the criminal justice system or are institutionalized to help them in their interactions with the government through legal assistance.

Interviews with involved UN staff show that they did not shy away from the rights implications of this work. In the case of the *hijra* community, they readily admitted that their goal is advancing civil and political rights, not encouraging economic development (although it is assumed to follow). Similarly, UNDP staff members working in Orissa state are developing projects to foster indigenous and forest rights, again within the belief that the *definition* of development is the promotion and protection of civil and political rights. They believe that economic development will follow but see no need to justify it on those grounds.

Right to Information

In 2005 the Indian Parliament passed right to information (RTI) legislation, effective at the state, local, and national levels. This act states that citizens have a right to request and receive information from the government and to have their requests fulfilled in a timely manner. It also requires government bodies to maintain information in a way that is accessible to citizens and mandates the creation of public information officers to field requests from citizens. Is information a "human right?" In 1946, General Assembly Resolution 59(1) stated: "Freedom of information is a fundamental human right and is the touch-stone of all the freedoms to which the United Nations is consecrated." The Covenant on Civil and Political Rights, in Article 19, noted that the "freedom to seek, receive and impart information and ideas of all kinds" was a vital part of freedom of expression; a later (1995) report by the UN Special Rapporteur on Freedom of Opinion and Expression expanded on this, noting that "freedom will be bereft of all effectiveness if the people have no access to information" (quoted in UNDP, 2004, p. 8). Of course, only the wording in the Covenant has the status of international law (and then binding only on states party to the Covenant), and it remains somewhat ambiguous, as it says nothing specifically about the obligations of governments to respond to citizen requests. Still, there is strong support both for the notion that the "right to know" is an important human right in itself and that it gains extra status from its importance in helping assure other civil and political rights. The Indian Supreme Court has also held that people's right to receive information from the government is fundamental to their right to freedom of expression.

Both UNDP and the World Bank actively support implementation of the Right to Information Act. This support has included building capacity of Indian government officials to respond to RTI requests; campaigns to make citizens aware of their rights and how to access information; support with computers and other technical services to speed up processing requests; and a variety of other efforts. UNDP in particular makes a straightforward rights-based argument for RTI. The World Bank, on the other hand, sticks to the more development-oriented argument that access to information improves accountability and transparency and, thus, development outcomes. Either way, however, a right to information movement is now well entrenched in India, where officials proudly point out that they have greater rights in this area than the citizens of many fully industrialized economies (including the United States). UN agencies continue to support RTI on the grounds that it empowers citizens and makes them better able to pursue a broad range of other rights as well.

Women's Rights

Gender and development, of course, is a widely accepted and practiced field of development cooperation. The incorporation of women's rights into development practice requires little explication here. While it might be considered a subset of nondiscrimination, concern for women's equality and participation in governance is such a sweeping part of development practice that it deserves separate mention.

Efforts to promote the C&P rights of women in India are wide-ranging and important. These include capacity building of government institutions to consider women's place in society, extend benefits to women, and to make sure they participate in government programs. Beyond trying to guarantee that women receive the economic and social rights they are entitled to, UN agencies also consider women's *political* rights to be important. In India, seats in the PRIs are set aside for women, and the UNDP is working with corporate partners in the city of Varanasi (the former Benares) to help women run in PRI elections. UN Women is involved in Bihar in a similar campaign, in partnership with the Government of India. UN Women is also working to prevent violence against women in New Delhi and other places, to guarantee access to family planning for women, to promote education for girls, and a host of other initiatives. UNFPA is working to provide a more basic human right, that of the right to life, by being actively involved in working against sex selection among pregnant women and their families. UNICEF is involved in many similar programs as well as working with law enforcement against trafficking in girls and women.

The Convention on the Elimination of All Forms of Discrimination Against Women (CEDAW) and the CRC, in particular, single out women and girls and provide specific legal guidelines. UNICEF, for example, works strongly to promote the interests of girls and their mothers but, more importantly, it is concerned with the overall status of women and girls within society, not the provision of particular services. UNICEF C4D programs, again, aim to change basic attitudes, not just stop particular practices; UNDP, UNFPA, and other agencies take the same approach. Interviews with UNICEF staff and other communications experts revealed an extensive, holistic set of programs.

They simply were not concerned with the philosophical issues around cultural norms or the appropriateness of challenging political institutions; promoting women's rights, including civil and political rights, was taken as an obvious part of the UN mandate. Women's rights are not just about overall legal equality, but also the very place of women within society.

Conclusion

As we saw above, the overall UN strategy as represented by the UNDAF and other central documents in India makes fairly scant and oblique reference to human rights promotion. Terms like equity and (of course) empowerment are used, but few references to specific rights. UN agencies are, certainly, expected to uphold human rights norms, and documents like the CRC and the Convention on the Elimination of All Forms of Discrimination Against Women lay out some specifics, but how those translate into *strategy* is not explicit in the key planning documents. This is not surprising, given the political and controversial nature of the rights agenda. UNICEF might see the CRC as central to its work, but it treads carefully when signing joint agreements with host governments. When this happens, RBA can be seen as a largely rhetorical exercise.

On the other hand, looking at how UNICEF, UNDP, the World Bank, and other agencies *actually implement* RBA presents a different, more nuanced picture. Here, a variety of C&P rights are raised and addressed, not always in the most direct fashion, but clearly in a way that is meaningful. And not just as a *strategy* of development (that is, looking at rights as a way to promote better development outcomes), but also as a goal of development itself; promotion of rights becomes the definition of what UN agencies are trying to do. This is no small thing; as the next three chapters will show, the politics of pursuing these goals is complex, and UN agencies have to develop new strategies to be able to actively engage in rights promotion. In particular, the following case studies will focus on how rights promotion is translated into specific policies and on the strategies related to those policies.

Again, there are a few different goals involved with these case studies. One is simply to illustrate the importance of translating RBA into real, significant policy on the promotion of human rights. As the studies will show, this is happening. UN agencies like UNICEF, UNDP, and UN Women have thought carefully about how to promote human rights through development aid. Often—too often, really—this thinking has happened at the level of individual staff and the individual country office, rather than through directives from headquarters in New York, Geneva, or elsewhere. Still, it is happening, and it is left up to national staff to figure out exactly how to do it. Secondly, this is leading to resistance of exactly the type that most UN agencies worried about: national, state, and local government officials—and, not uncommonly, citizens outside the government, but part of the larger social power structure—dislike UN efforts to meddle in their country's internal affairs. Chapters 3, 4, and 5 will chart this dynamic, showing the interaction between resistance, development policy, and rights promotion. This will help us better understand this dynamic and see how resistance is being overcome by individual bureaucratic action and initiative. Then Chapter 6 will, in part, sum up how resistance is being overcome and what strategies have been developed to do so.

References

Bardhan, P., & Mookherjee, D. (Eds.). (2006). *Decentralization and Local Governance in Developing Countries: A Comparative Perspective*. Cambridge, MA: MIT Press.

Brocklesby, M. A., & Crawford, S. (2004). *Operationalising the Rights Agenda: DFID's Participatory Rights Assessment Methodologies (PRAMs) Project*. London: Department for International Development (UK). Retrieved from http://www.gsdrc.org/document-library/operationalising-the-rights-agenda-dfids-participatory-rights-assessment-methodologies-prams-project/

Cornia, G. A., Jolly, R., & Steward, F. (Eds.). (1987). *Adjustment With a Human Face*. Oxford: Clarendon Press.

Cornwall, A., & Nyamu-Musembi, C. (2004). Putting the "Rights-based Approach" to Development Into Perspective. *Third World Quarterly*, 25(8), 1415–1437.

Craig, P. P., & Deshpande, S. L. (1989). Rights, Autonomy, and Process: Public Interest Litigation in India. *Oxford Journal of Legal Studies*, 9(3), 356–373.

Crawford, S. (2008). *The Impact of Rights-based Approaches to Development*. London: UK Interagency Group on Human Rights Based Approaches.

Crook, R., & Manor, J. (2000). *Democratic Decentralization*. Washington, DC: World Bank Operations Evaluation Department.

Deol, S. S. (2011). *Human Rights in India: Theory and Practice*. New Delhi: Serials Publications.

Deshpande, A. (2011). *The Grammar of Caste: Economic Discrimination in Contemporary India*. New York: Oxford University Press.

Grugel, J., & Piper, N. (2008). Do Rights Promote Development? *Global Social Policy*, 9(1), 79–98.

Guha-Khasnobis, B., & Vivek, S. (2007). *Rights-Based Approach to Development: Lessons From the Right to Food Movement in India*. New York: United Nations University—WIDER.

Hill, M. (2003). Development as Empowerment. *Feminist Economics, 9*(3), 117–135.
Human Rights Watch. (2013). *World Report 2013: India*. Retrieved from http://www.hrw.org/world-report/2013/country-chapters/india.
Jayal, N., Prakash, A., & Sharma, P. (Eds.). (2006). *Local Governance in India: Decentralization and Beyond*. New York: Oxford University Press.
Jodhka, S. (2002). Nation and Village: Images of Rural India in Gandhi, Nehru and Ambedkar. *Economics and Politics Weekly, 37*(32), 3343–3353.
Jonsson, U. (2003). *Human Rights Approach to Development Programming*. New York: UNICEF.
Joshi, V., & Little, I. M. D. (1996). *India's Economic Reforms 1991–2001*. New York: Oxford University Press.
Kapoor, V. (2006). *Human Rights Based Approach to Development and People's Empowerment Through Participatory Governance: An Examination of Panchayati Raj Institutions in India*. Essex, UK: University of Essex.
Kaufmann, D. (2004). *Human Rights and Governance: The Empirical Challenge*. Paper prepared for a conference co-sponsored by the Ethical Globalization Initiative and the NYU Center for Human Rights and Global Justice, New York. Retrieved from http://siteresources.worldbank.org/INTWBIGOVANTCOR/Resources/humanrights.pdf.
Khosla, M. (2012). *The Indian Constitution*. New York: Oxford University Press.
Kikon, D. (2009). The Predicament of Justice: Fifty Years of Armed Forces Special Powers Act. *Contemporary South Asia, 17*(3), 271–282.
Knutsen, C. H. (2012). Democracy, State Capacity, and Economic Growth. *World Development, 43*(1), 1–18.
McDuie-Ra, D. (2008). Fifty-Year Disturbance: The Armed Fores Special Powers Act and Exceptionalism in a South Asian Periphery. *Contemporary South Asia, 17*(3), 255–270.
Menon-Sen, K., & Shiva Kumar, A. (2010). *UNDP India Mid Term Review of the Country Programme Action Plan 2008–2012*. New Delhi: United Nations Development Programme.
Mohanty, B. (2009). *Constitution, Government and Politics in India: Evolution and Present Structure*. New Delhi: New Century.
Mullen, R. (2012). *Decentralization, Local Governance, and Social Wellbeing in India*. New York: Routledge.
Narayan, P. K., Narayan, S., & Smyth, R. (2011). Does Democracy Facilitate Economic Growth or Does Economic Growth Facilitate Democracy? *Economic Modelling, 28*(3), 900–910.
Nickel, J. W. (1993). How Human Rights Generate Duties to Protect and Provide. *Human Rights Quarterly, 15*(1), 77–86.
Nyamu-Musembi, C., & Cornwall, A. (2004). *What Is the "Rights Based Approach" All About: Perspectives From International Development Agencies*. Brighton, UK; Insitute for Development Studies.

Oestreich, J. (2007). *Power and Principle: Human Rights Programming in International Organizations*. Washington, DC: Georgetown University Press.

Office of the United Nations High Commissioner for Human Rights. (2006). *Principles and Guidelines for a Human Rights Approach to Poverty Reduction Strategies*. Geneva: OHCHR. Retrieved from http://www.ohchr.org/Documents/Publications/PovertyStrategiesen.pdf.

Ottaway, M. (2003). *Democracy Challenged: The Rise of Semi-Authoritarianism*. Washington, DC: Carnegie Endowment for International Peace.

Panda, P., & Agarwal, B. (2005). Marital Violene, Human Development, and Women's Property Status in India. *World Development, 33*(5), 823–850.

Sage, C., & Woolcock, M. (2008). Breaking Legal Inequality Traps: New Approaches to Building Justice Systems for the Poor in Developing Countries. In A. A. Dani & A. de Haan (Eds.), *Inclusive States: Social Policy and Structural Inequalities* (pp. 369–394). Washington, DC: World Bank.

Sen, A. (1999). *Development as Freedom*. New York: Random House.

Shah, A. (2008). *Demanding to Be Served: Holding Governments to Account for Improved Access*. New York: World Bank Institute.

Shue, H. (1980). *Basic Rights: Subsistence, Affluence, and U.S. Foreign Policy*. Princeton, NJ: Princeton University Press.

Streeten, P. (1994). Human Development: Needs and Ends. *American Economic Review, 84*(May), 232–237.

UN Development Group. (2003). *The Human Rights-based Approach to Development Cooperation Towards a Common Understanding among UN Agencies*.

UNDP. (1998). *Integrating Human Rights with Sustainable Development*. New York: UNDP.

UNDP. (2004). *The Right to Information*. New York: UNDP.

UNDP. (2006). *Applying A Human Rights-based Approach to Development Cooperation and Programming: A UNDP Capacity Development Resource*. New York: UNDP.

UNDP. (2008a). *Capacity Development for Local Governance: Factsheet*. New York: UNDP.

UNDP. (2008b). *Fact Sheet: Strengthened Access to Justice in India*. New Delhi, India: UNDP.

UNDP. (2010a). *GOI-India Joint Program on Convergence 2010 Annual Work Plan*. New Delhi: UNDP.

UNDP. (2010b). *Integrating Legal Empowerment of the Poor in UNDP's Work: A Guidance Note*. New York: UNDP.

UNDP. (2011). *Letter of Agreement Between UNDP and the Government for the Provision of Support Services to the Project "Access to Justice for Marginalized People."* New Delhi, India: UNDP.

UNDP. (2011–2012). *Pathways for an Inclusive Indian Administration (PIIA)*.

UNDP. (2012). *Mainstreaming Human Rights in Development Policies and Programming: UNDP Experiences*. New York: UNDP.

UNFPA. (2012). *Country Programme Action Plan 2008–2012*. New Delhi, India.
UN-Government of India. (2013). *India UNDAF: United Nations Development Action Framework 2013–2017*. New Delhi: Governmenet of India and United Nations.
UNICEF-India. (2013). *India Country Programme Document 2013–2017*. New Delhi: UNICEF India.
Uvin, P. (2004). *Human Rights and Development*. New York: Kumarian Press.
Vaidyanathan, A. (2005). The Pursuit of Social Justice. In Z. Hasan, E. Sridharan, & R. Sudarshan (Eds.), *India's Living Constitution: Ideas, Practices, Controversies* (pp. 284–305). London: Anthem Press.
World Bank. (2002). *Empowerment and Poverty Reduction Sourcebook*. Washington, DC: The World Bank.
World Bank. (2013). *Country Partnership Strategy for India For the Period FY2013–2017*. Washington, DC: The World Bank.

3

The United Nations Development Programme

THIS CHAPTER WILL look specifically at the work of the United Nations Development Programme in India. UNDP acts as "lead agency" for the UN in development programming, so it is an appropriate place to start. It is not possible to cover all the program areas where UNDP is active, and certainly not every initiative with which they are involved (for good overviews see Browne, 2012; Murphy, 2006). I will focus on four programming areas in particular: Access to Justice, Right to Information, Democratic Governance, and Government Capacity Building. These are the programming most relevant to the argument of this book. To prevent this chapter from becoming unmanageably long, some other programming areas will be only quickly covered.

To give the chapter further coherence, it will focus particularly on the civil and political rights issues being addressed by UNDP. The next chapter, on UNICEF, will concentrate more on the issue of how UNICEF programming has *changed* or stayed the same under a RBA paradigm. One key issue that will be looked at in the current chapter is the matter of national and local *resistance* to UNDP involvement with C&P rights. It is a premise of this book that promoting C&P rights—real, not just rhetorical, promotion—is bound to provoke resistance from host governments, which do not like UN agencies interfering in these very political areas. The presence of political resistance is a strong indication that UN agencies are starting to push the limits of what kinds of issues they can raise (Oestreich, 2011). States will not concern themselves with weak rhetoric about empowerment or local ownership when these hide the usual service-delivery model of development aid, but they will act differently when real political change is threatened. So when we see resistance we can assume something is happening and learn from the form that resistance takes. Also, recall the argument, made earlier, that it is the fear of government resistance that has held back a fuller implementation of a rights-based policy. How this resistance is overcome or not overcome will also teach us about the independence of UN agencies and how they assert their will in the face of other priorities.

Keep in mind that UNDP programming (and, for that matter, all other programming) is jointly arrived at through agreement with host governments. India, like all states where UN agencies operate, must agree to programs of cooperation. The results of the Second High Level Forum on Aid Effectiveness of 2005, which was to set a new tone and direction for UN aid efforts, also emphasized national "ownership" of and "alignment" with development efforts (DAC OECD, 2005). While straightforward in concept, the practice of promoting national ownership is complex and often political (for discussions see Booth, 2012; Hyden, 2008). As we will see, it does not always mean that the national government is supporting agreed-to efforts, and more often that local governments also resist some aspects of the development program. This tension is understudied in the literature on international organizations, yet it is vital to seeing how UN agencies promote norms and change state behavior.

UNDP Key Programming Goals

The United Nations Development Programme has operated in India since 1951. Like most UN agencies it is headquartered in New Delhi and operates field offices in various parts of the country. The UNDP does not work directly in all Indian states; rather, because of its relatively small budget, it works in states targeted due to their particularly low scores on the Human Development Index—Assam, Bihar, Chhattisgarh, Jharkhand, Madhya Pradesh, Maharashtra, Odisha (or Orissa), Rajasthan, and Uttar Pradesh (Mukherjee, Chakraborty, & Sikdar, 2014). Given the vast size of India, UNDP and other agencies have nothing like the resources necessary to operate throughout the country. Contributions to UNDP-India vary from year to year and come from a number of sources, including the UN regular budget, contributions from specific UN member states, the Joint United Nations Programme on HIV/AIDS (UNAIDS), and the Ikea Foundation, among others. These typically total in the neighborhood of US$30–40 million, but with considerable variation. Although the number of UNDP staff obviously varies as people come and go, in 2013 they reported a full-time staff of 72 people, mostly Indian personnel (the India office has a fairly high proportion of domestic rather than international staff).

During the project period under study, UNDP-India listed five priority programming areas. These were:

1. Poverty Reduction
2. Democratic Governance
3. Energy and Environment
4. HIV and AIDS
5. Crisis Prevention and Recovery and Social Groups (Government of India-UNDP, 2008, p. 6).

The situation analysis of the UNDP in its 2013–2017 Country Programme Action Plan (CPAP) (much like earlier, 2008–2012 CPAP) in particular emphasizes not poverty per se, nor India's score on the Human Development Index and progress toward the Millennium Development Goals (MDGs), but *disparities* within India. "Conditions are hardest for marginalized groups," according to the CPAP, "including scheduled castes and tribes. Forty-seven percent of the rural tribal population lives below the poverty line and there is growing concern about persistently inadequate conditions in districts which are now affected by left-wing extremism. Many structural factors account for underdevelopment in these districts and among marginalized groups" (Government of India-UNDP, 2013, p. 6). The previous CPAP, for the period under study, noted, "Poverty levels vary between states, from 14% to 46%, and are increasingly concentrated among certain regions and social groups" (Government of India-UNDP, 2007, p. 6). The UNDP notes substantial gaps within the country—rural-urban, male-female, caste-based, and tribal-based, among others. The situation of India's poor and others who suffer from lack of access to basic services is within the context of a quickly growing economy and an expanding middle class. Both documents mention the need to identify the poor more carefully, to promote planning with an eye toward building the capacity to reach the underserved, and to reach out to excluded groups.

Chapter 6, on the World Bank, will discuss the place of equity in development programming and how it is defined. It is important to point out that equity is not a human right but is contextualized within a rights-based development framework both as a moral necessity and as a necessary condition for the achievement of other rights. Planning documents mention "effective, accountable and participatory decentralization and a rights-based approach to achieving the MDGs, with a focus on the disadvantaged groups (especially women and girls)" (UNDP, 2007, p. 3). Interviews with UNDP staff repeatedly bring up the issue of inclusiveness and references to the UN's "equity agenda." This was a reference to the 2011 *Human Development Report* on "sustainability and equity," as well as a number of World Bank and other publications from the mid-2000s stressing the need for equity as part of the development process. The documents also stress the guiding principles of the United Nations Development Assistance Framework (UNDAF) signed with the Indian government.

It is important to remember that the UNDP works through the process of "national implementation." That is to say, while UNDP provides funding and expertise, and works with many NGOs, it is the government (in this case, the Government of India and various state and local governments) that actually implements projects. UNDP explains national implementation as a "tripartite system" with government making up two legs of the stool; that is, "owner and recipient of development assistance" and as the "manager" of programming. UNDP is the third leg; that is, the "development partner and funding agency" (UNDP, 2011, p. 8). This is described as an *accountability* relationship, specifying who is ultimately responsible for what aspects of programming and its results.

One high-ranking official at UNDP working with access to justice projects noted national implementation as both a resource and a liability. On the one hand, this person said, it would be a benefit to be able to do direct implementation (she cited UNICEF as an example of this) rather than having to work through government. The government could take a lot of time to convince to get involved in civil and political rights in particular, and it could be frustrating to have to spend time convincing them to do what UNDP wanted. On the other hand, it was "better in the long run," this person said, to persuade the government to take controversial steps itself. This meant not just ownership but political cover for controversial projects such as work on transgender rights or local-level governance reform.[1] Another staff member, working on governance issues in a state field office, also likened UNDP to UNICEF. Staying neutral in political issues, they said, was easier for UNDP staff than for UNICEF staff, thanks to national implementation, which gave UNDP a bit more distance from implementation and made them more dependent on direct government cooperation. This person cited targeting the poorest during disaster recovery as an area that required some political finesse.[2] It meant, this person said, that staff had to truly take the time to engage legislators and other decision-makers and to convince them of the importance of certain policies.

Access to Justice Programs

A good place to start with the Access to Justice portfolio of UNDP-India is with transgender rights. During my stay in India, I had an opportunity to attend four days of a UNDP-sponsored transgender-community training program. The training was officially titled "From Margins to the Mainstream: Nurturing Leadership Among Transgender and *Hijra* Communities." The training took place in Raipur, the capital of Chhattisgarh state, in east-central India. It was an extensive program, which ran for a full month. The training was organized by the NGO Jan Jagriti Kendra (JJK), with support from the Access to Justice division of UNDP-India. Its goal was to help some of the most marginalized people in India be aware of their civil and political rights, as well as their economic, social, and cultural ones.

The training was for people who identified themselves as *hijra* in the Raipur area. *Hijra* make up a traditional community of transgender people in South Asia, especially India; born male, they generally identify as neither male nor female but as a "third gender" (Nanda, 2007, p. 237). "*Hijras* are often subject to ridicule, humiliation and exclusion ... they continue to live ... often on the outskirts of cities and in filthy conditions, shunned by family members. Very few have the means to acquire a decent level of education. The few that do are not accepted into the workforce" (Patel, 2010, p. 290). The training event consisted of 28 members of the *hijra* community, screened by a "jury" organized by JJK for aspects such as leadership potential, understanding of community issues, and availability to work as community leaders later on.[3] The primary goal of the program was to "strengthen the capacity of community members to identify, articulate and advocate for their human rights and development needs, and to participate more actively in the development of policies and programs that shape services delivery effectively to the betterment and inclusion in mainstream for their community" (Masih, Singh, & Mishra, 2012, p. 26).

Once identified, potential *hijra* leaders spent their time taking a variety of different training courses. The quality of the overall experience, it must be said, seemed to vary, even in the relatively short period observed. Local government officials gave what seemed very sound advice, for example on how to petition for better police protection against gender-based violence; on the other hand, some group exercises, designed to instill better business and financial sense, struck this observer as rather too simplistic to be very helpful. Overall, the training encompassed a large number of different goals: to inform the trainees of their legal rights, to build their sense of self-esteem, to equip them with job skills, and to give them some control over their futures. JJK was also working with potential employers in Chhattisgarh to convince them to consider hiring *hijra* as employees, although, at the time of the research, with only limited success. Still, this was seen as an integral part of the process of "empowering" the women involved, and others as well, and to help them better integrate into a society that had traditionally shunned them.

Self-identified *hijra* make up an extremely small portion of the Indian population: estimates are hard to come by, but, in any case, certainly no more than 500,000 in India, and likely much less (Nanda, 2007, p. 226), perhaps as few as 50,000 (although they tend to be mainly in northern India and in some cities are fairly visible). Why, then, invest resources in this very small population as a development priority? An interview with the UNDP staff person who initially suggested the project made it clear that a *moral* imperative motivated her: tasked with the role of ensuring access to justice for the "most marginalized," she identified this group as being definitely in that category. It was then her role to "sell" the idea to more senior staff in the Access to Justice unit, using the moral, not economic, argument. In other words, on the grounds that promoting *hijra* rights was the morally correct thing to do, rather than for its benefit to the national economy. The staff person pointed out that the UNDP has no specific policy to work with transgender groups, although it does have connections through its efforts on HIV/AIDS. She initiated the program by saying (in her account), "This is a group we should be interested in!"[4] Another involved staff person said that they take for granted "that empowering for the sake of empowering, or rights for the sake of rights, is a good thing."[5]

JJK, with UNDP support, is involved in other work with the *hijra* community. JJK and other groups have trained paralegal volunteers, whom they termed Justice Equity Empowerment Volunteers (JEEV), to work with *hijra* and other groups and inform them about their legal rights as well as legal entitlements. (The director of the program for JJK was very specific in conversation about the JEEV workers' title, to be very clear exactly what their role was.) JJK produced a short film laying out legal rights of *hijra* and undertook other efforts to inform them of their rights. They also worked with the police department, legal services authorities, the department of health, and other government officials, as well as potential employers. The ultimate goal, he said, was to make the group self-sufficient and give them the ability to organize themselves and "approach authorities and work for their own betterment."[6]

As a human rights policy, the ambition of the program is wide-ranging. It includes both training *hijra* to demand their civil and political rights (e.g., to petition the government, to be safe from harassment and violence, engage in political participation) and their social, economic, and cultural rights (including employment, access to government welfare programs, and to openly be part of their larger community). It is, clearly, premised on the close connection between them. The JJK official recalled being pushed by his UNDP contact to make clear the connection between C&P rights and ES&C rights, and he revised his program at their direction. He recalls that the specific notion advocated by UNDP was that people who are deprived of their political rights are also unable to get jobs, claim benefits due them, and generally take control over their own destinies.[7] The fact that this project was to reach a very small minority within India, and that it was presented by its UNDP interlocutor as a moral imperative rather than as an economically rational project (e.g., one that would help a large number of people in a cost-effective manner) also highlights the element of C&P rights being promoted by UNDP: ultimately the rationale, at least for the staff involved, was one of bringing political equity and empowerment to a discriminated-against group rather than some more economic definition of "development."

The work with transgender rights in India—and there are other projects well beyond the Raipur workshop and accompanying work being done with JJK—is part of the "Democratic Governance" unit in UNDP-India. Under the heading "access to justice for marginalized people" there are many smaller projects. Although there are too many to list here, they include, for example, several projects to train paralegal workers in target areas (e.g., Bihar and Uttar Pradesh, where they "are now closely linked to the District Legal Services Authorities in assisting marginalized communities"); training of "self-help groups," lawyers and "elected women representatives" from Dalit and other minority communities; and radio spots aired to distribute information about legal remedies to discrimination, among many other projects funded or supported by UNDP (UNDP, n.d.-b, p. 2).

The work of the JJK program, while just one relatively small component of the overall Access to Justice portfolio, illustrates just how closely UNDP and its partners are working with grassroots organizations, rather than governments, to push for citizen empowerment, and, just as importantly, how much it is prepared to justify programming from a rights perspective rather than a purely development one. In terms of C&P rights, the overall Access to Justice program in India fits in two ways. First, recall, specific projects are presented as moral imperatives and as a way of helping those whose rights have been violated through discrimination, disempowerment, and physical abuse (as well as through lack of resources) to gain these rights. Rights are presented as good in and of themselves, including civil and political rights, and their achievement by marginalized groups must be the goal of UNDP if it is to achieve development in India. Development becomes defined as rights achievement, as least in this programming area. At the same time, there is the notion that access to legal justice is a tool of economic development in its more "traditional" sense of increased economic activity, increased ranges of choices available to people, and the gaining of capabilities by people (see for example Chatterjee & Chowdhury, 2012; De Langen & Barendrecht, 2009; Meene & Rooij, 2008). "The Millennium Development Declaration," according to UNDP-India, "reaffirmed Member States commitment to the core value of freedom where men and women have the right to live their lives and raise their children in dignity, free from hunger and from the rear of violence, oppression or injustice. Democratic and participatory governance based on the will of the people best assures these rights" (UNDP, n.d.-b, p. 1).

One UNDP staff person, asked about civil and political rights in the overall Access to Justice program, put the rights implications of programs fairly clearly. This person started by saying, "We don't directly get involved in civil and political rights." Yet, they then went on to say that Access to Justice programming was clearly a C&P rights issue. The government, the staffer said, probably would not allow a bilateral aid agency such as the United States Agency for International Development (USAID) to get involved in these issues; but the UN could work here to some extent since their role as "neutral broker" allowed more "extreme" positions. This sort of ambivalence—stating that they do not get involved in C&P rights, but also putting rights front and center of programming—was far from atypical when talking with UN staff, as has been discussed already. "Automatically," the staff person said, UNDP supports those whose civil and political rights are being violated; yet, "we don't call it civil and political rights, but the rights and empowerment thinking and discourse is there in the organization."[8] This person cited, for example, the creation of "self-help groups" among marginalized people as part of the "demand side" of rights promotion, the "first recourse" for those whose civil and political rights were being violated.

A more senior person within the same unit pointed to an even broader array of related rights issues. This person mentioned Section 377 of the Indian penal code (Mawani, 2015, pp. 417–419), which criminalizes homosexual behavior, as something that is now of concern to the UNDP.[9] In this, there was substantial cooperation with UNDP and other efforts to control the spread of HIV/AIDS, through interest in the rights of "men who have sex with men," sex workers, and other high-risk groups. The staff person cited as an example of progress the decision by the Tamil Nadu Chief Justice (not a state where UNDP is active) to recognize the need for sex reassignment surgery as a "right to health" issue coverable by state funds (see UNDP, 2010a, p. 6). UNDP has organized "sensitization" training for judges regarding Section 377 and similar issues; it has also taken an interest in sex workers, who previously had been arrested by police as criminals. Instead, the strategy was to "empower" them and encourage the Ministry of Women and Children to respect their civil rights.

The same interview subject pointed out that this constituted fairly obtrusive interference with domestic politics and required a great deal of caution. To avoid political resistance, UNDP calls the work "building capacity" rather than "pressuring the executive," or as "training" instead of interfering in politics. Another staff member pointed out that judges, for example, ignored their training or "just humored" the UNDP trainers;[10] this was backed up by another outside observer, a consultant to UNICEF, who also suggested that trainings were met with polite indifference.[11] This person, who had long served the government, was quite skeptical about the level of interest that judges truly had in this training or its effectiveness Of course, this isn't a universal sentiment, and some government interview subjects certainly deny this, asserting that the trainings were well received and useful.[12] But it seems universally felt that results are, at any rate, mixed.

Work being done in one state office with a large population of indigenous peoples makes another good example of Access to Justice programming. A state UNDP officer listed, among their top concerns, implementation of the "Scheduled Tribes and Other Traditional Forest Dwellers (Recognition of Forest Rights) Act" (usually abbreviated FRA) of 2006. This legislation is intended to give tribal peoples greater control of the land they have traditionally lived on. This becomes particularly important to protect it from illegal exploitation of its natural resources by outsiders. This UNDP official was specific that they felt implementation of the act—and, in particular, its provisions regarding community (rather than individual) control over land and resources—was not being sufficiently implemented by local government officials; the interview subject blamed "turf battles" among various government agencies. The UNDP state office commissioned a study on implementation failures which it then presented to local officials as a way to press for change; "I would not say we were very successful in getting the government behind us," this person said, although they described a process of constant pressure on officials and an ongoing struggle to protect the rights of indigenous forest-dwellers.[13]

When asked why this particular field office had decided to make implementation of the Forest Rights Act (FRA) a priority, the response was a simple one: the office defined development as reaching the most underserved and needy, and they had decided that indigenous communities fit that category. The entire process of working on FRA implementation was an "experiment," and UNDP at this point was "testing the waters" in terms of pushing government to respect its terms. Still, they intended to continue to push for implementation, even though there had been "no substantive change" in policies or actions due to their efforts.[14]

The Right to Information

Shekhar Singh, a founder of the National Campaign for People's Right to Information in India, tells an amusing and useful anecdote about India's landmark Right to Information Act—legislation discussed briefly in Chapter 2 and expanded on here. A vegetable seller, who had set up his small stall across the street from the home of a District Collector (the chief administrative officer of an Indian district, which is the largest subdivision of a state), filed a request to be shown the records for the purchase of petrol for the Collector's car. Dr. Singh, hearing about the request, tracked down the vegetable seller to ask him why he would want such seemingly random information. The merchant explained that, every day, he would sit at his stall and watch the Collector's car go in and out of the gates of his office compound and eventually wondered where the official was going. Given that it was gasoline purchased with government funds, the vegetable seller thought he had an interest in finding out how far he was going, how much money was being spent, and if it was being used properly or wasted. That someone in his position, Dr. Singh explains, would feel empowered to even ask such questions was the essential point of the India Right to Information Act and an important step in reforming transparency in India.

The specific roots of the Right to Information (RTI) legal regime in India are in 1994. They stem from an effort by protestors to get information about payment of the minimum wage that had been guaranteed workers. When their request was denied, they demanded to see records of work done; this lead the Mazdoor Kisan Shakti Sangathan (MKSS—roughly "organization for the empowerment of workers and peasants") and later the National Campaign for People's Right to Information (formed in 1996) to demand public access to government records (Roy & Dey, 2002, p. 80; Shrivasta, 2009, p. 121). Singh makes it clear that international pressure was not a major factor in the RTI movement; it was an indigenous effort, similar to other rights movements in India (Singh, 2010, p. 12).

After intense campaigning by MKSS and other organizations in favor of a Right to Information bill, legislation was passed by the Indian government in 2005. The Right to Information Act guarantees the right of citizens to request information not only from the central government but state and local governments as well. Each governmental unit, under the law, must appoint a Public Information Officer (PIO); any citizen can submit a request, and the PIO has the responsibility to make sure the information is provided in a timely fashion (Ashraf, 2008, p. 150). The goal of the RTI legislation is clear enough; Roy and Dey make it out as nothing less than a new, important step toward creating democracy and self-government in India (2002, pp. 82–83). Transparency and the free flow of information serve a number of purposes. They make democracy meaningful by ensuring (or trying to ensure) that voters and citizens are informed and can make meaningful choices. Transparency fights corruption by making the dealings of government open to outside scrutiny. Information helps citizens hold their officials accountable. As Shekhar Singh's example demonstrates, it allows any citizen to see what their civil servants are doing with government money. Effective transparency also means that development efforts are, presumably, better planned since citizens are able to see what is planned, comment on it, and provide input that might otherwise have been ignored by officials with their own agendas.

The preamble of the act states its purpose: "The right to information shall ensure transparency and accountability in all public, autonomous, and statutory organizations and in private organizations run on government or foreign funding shall increase, corruption shall decrease and good governance shall be established." Some studies have indicated that there is no direct, necessary correlation between access to information and development success (Banerjee, Rukmini, Duflo, Glennerster, & Khemani, 2010). Not surprisingly, the connection is indirect, and studies show it is not so simple as just providing information to improve development outcomes or even the level of participation by citizens. Still, official UNDP policy is to support access to information, and UNDP supports RTI legislation and capacity building throughout its operations. The justification provided is broad, ranging from the argument that it promotes more effective and accountable democratic systems to a link with "communication for development"—the more general notion of promoting participation by citizens in development projects (UNDP, n.d.-a). A UNDP practice note, interestingly, mentions the various arguments above about fighting corruption and increasing participation for effective results, but also makes a much more *political* argument. "Political tensions, insecurity, threats of violence and crises within a country have a significant impact on access to information.... At the global level, increasing insecurity has in some instances intensified governments' surveillance and censorship activities and their tendency to withhold information under the guise of national security....The underlying governance principles of an access to information approach are transparency, active participation, responsiveness and accountability" (UNDP, 2003, p. 2). This puts a decidedly political spin on RTI and reflects some of the work done by social movements pushing for the legislation in India, who often mentioned both the legacy of colonialism and the struggle against various insurgencies as forces that worked against citizens' right to know. (It is also noteworthy that the RTI legislation excludes Jammu and Kashmir.)

UNDP did play some role in supporting the push for RTI legislation, although again it needs to be stressed that it was very much an indigenous movement; UNDP took an interest in it and supported it, but it would be a serious mistake to overstate how important their involvement was. Nevertheless, it was an example of a UN development agency injecting itself into the political process, albeit in a careful and finely calibrated way. Since then, UNDP has, working through various elements of the Indian government as well as state and local bodies, supported efforts to both strengthen the capacity of government to implement RTI and empower people to demand their rights under the RTI Act.

In the first case, UNDP has supported training and sensitization efforts for government officials to be aware of their obligations under RTI and to make the program more effective at actually providing information to people. UNDP capacity building includes experts funded by UNDP, who have been placed within the Indian government to help with technical issues. UNDP-supported programs have run training seminars for thousands of government officials at various levels to sensitize them to their obligations under RTI; training for Public Information Officers (PIOs); "reviewing and reengineering business processes and information management systems of public authorities to facilitate sharing of information" (UNDP, p. 4); preparing legal pamphlets; and other activities. UNDP has cooperated with NGO partners, such as the Center for Good Governance in Hyderabad and the Yashwantrao Chavan Academy of Development Administration (YASHADA) in the city of Pune, to undertake training of government officers.

In the second, more complex, case, UNDP has been active in efforts to promote public awareness of RTI legislation and to encourage citizens to use their right to information to increase government transparency. Various studies have demonstrated that lack of awareness about RTI has been one of its greatest hindrances: respondents to surveys have also said that officials have been unfriendly or unhelpful, that rules are hard to understand, and that extra rules are sometimes imposed by public officials to deter requests (Roberts, 2010, pp. 8–12). UNDP has supported a large number of projects to increase awareness and access, which include public information campaigns, the training of "paralegal" workers to help citizens formulate and file requests, development of online courses available to help people understand the law, and even the promotion of "video volunteers" who record stories about efforts to empower themselves through legal means.

This sort of work, from above and below, is needed for more reasons than mere capacity development. As Alasdair Roberts points out in his study of RTI, there is real hostility to RTI from many government officials, who view it as a challenge to their power and to existing social structures. Activists for RTI have been threatened, beaten up, and in at least one case—that of Satish Shetty, who was uncovering corruption in Pune—murdered (Roberts, 2010, p. 12). This violence—a form of resistance to rights promotion—underscores the politically charged nature of what UNDP is doing in this area, and its continuing efforts require a careful diplomatic effort at various levels. A UNDP expert working closely with RTI issues offered much the same insight, noting that his efforts to empower people with information were not always welcome by local officials. "The moment we get careful is when we are endangering people," this consultant asserted.[15] The trick, he said, was not just to disseminate information but to also change attitudes and even the political dynamics in individual localities. Not an easy task in a vast country! Attitudinal change was key. Training "leaders" who were able to stand up for the rights of their fellow citizens and disseminate information was also very important.

It was noted in Chapter 2 that RTI is supported by international law and the Indian Constitution as an essential human right, both in itself and as an important way of accessing other civil and political rights, as well as ES&C rights. This notion has been upheld by the Indian Supreme Court. As Shekhar Singh's anecdote (and many others one might hear in India and elsewhere) demonstrates, access to information is a vital element of effective development, anticorruption efforts, and other reforms. RTI also directly challenges entrenched power structures, and stories of local officials resisting RTI are not hard to come by. The resistance encountered by RTI activists, noted above, speaks to the transformative and political power of information. Both UNDP respondents and other people in India regularly report the resistance that RTI engenders from entrenched power interests, who do not want their activities brought to light or simply resist the scrutiny that comes with public access to information; District Collectors and other officials, an interview subject notes, are used to acting with impunity and often resent the idea that "ordinary citizens" are able to probe into their workings. One must, as noted above, be careful and diplomatic while at the same time "empower" people by informing them of their rights.

Democratic Governance

Although both access to information and access to justice are important components of a well-functioning democratic system, Democratic Governance (DG) is a separate category in UNDP programming and has its own set of policies. Democratic Governance is not a simple term. India is a democracy, the world's largest, and thus promotion of DG does not mean making the country a democracy when it already is one. Nor, of course, does the UNDP pitch DG as the promotion of democracy per se, even in countries that have political systems other than democratic ones. Democratic Governance clearly raises some political issues and requires a great deal of finesse on the part of UNDP and other agencies. As one highly placed staffer put it, rather bluntly, the reaction from government tends to be "Why are you talking of this? India's a democracy already!"[16] Another staffer notes that at the higher government levels the notion of supporting local-level democracy is pretty well accepted and not hard to advocate. State and national level politicians, this person said, don't "feel threatened" by efforts to encourage, for example, greater participation in the Panchayats (as mentioned, the most basic and local-level governing bodies, part of the Panchayat Raj system of local governance found throughout India and South Asia) by women, or Scheduled Castes.[17] The problem, though, is largely at lower levels. This staff person notes that UNDP members do sometimes have to "protect ourselves" by working through civil society organizations (CSOs), rather than pushing directly for action in local government, to avoid looking like they are meddling in local politics. The staffer also noted that, for example, upper caste local officials will sometimes resist efforts to help those in Scheduled Castes run for office or even participate in local politics; they will "keep you busy," in this person's words: not resisting in obvious ways, but using administrative roadblocks to wear out local empowerment efforts. This same person was quick to point out that even at the "very local" level where UNDP often works, many are very supportive of its efforts. Still, they stressed that political "savvy" was necessary in situations where years of work could be quickly rendered futile by, say, a mining project paying big dividends but illegally violating land rights. It was also pointed out that other foreign donors shied away from participating in some local-level government reform. These donors felt it was "too political" for them to get involved in promoting democratic governance.

One key UNDP document lays out the argument for supporting decentralization and supporting capacity building among Panchayats. "The argument for greater devolution is based," it says, "on the experience of States such as Kerala, Madhya Pradesh, Karnataka and Uttar Pradesh, which demonstrate that the transfer of funds, functions and functionaries is the key to more successful decentralization.... In brief ... it is imperative to strengthen decentralization from below, *so that the voices of the poor could carry weight in village assemblies and ward council meeting.*" It then notes, "Initiatives that empower the poor, especially women to manage local resources and local institutions, are steps in this direction. The success of the world's largest experiment in deepening democracy ultimately depends upon the success of these initiatives" (Human Development Resource Center, 2001, p. 2; emphasis added).

At the national level, UNDP supports capacity building for the Ministry of Panchayati Raj (the national-level ministry supporting the Panchayats), to "assist in policy and research, strengthening its capacity in policy and programme design, monitoring and evaluation as well as implementation" (UNDP, 2008, p. 2). "Through training, networking and knowledge sharing, elected representatives and officials will be given opportunities to improve their capability to perform their functions more effectively," as well as changing "motivation, joint decision-making, the provision of resources ... and personal empowerment." This means strengthening state training institutions and creating training materials for elected representatives, as well as "project support ... for networks of elected women representatives" (UNDP, 2008, p. 1). Helping women who want to be elected to local bodies, in fact, is an important priority of UNDP; under national and in many cases state law, up to half of Panchayat seats are set aside for women and are intended to help women make their voices heard in local decision-making.

Some of the work regarding women's empowerment through elections to the Panchayats raises the most interesting questions regarding the politicization of UNDP activities, as well as the need for a particular type of subtlety in programming. One common type of anecdote—not just among my interview subjects, but rather current in any discussion of this issue—has to do with helping women resist being overly influenced by their husbands when the women become local officials. It is one thing for a woman to serve in a local governing body, another for her to act according to her own mind rather than to be a controlled by her husband's opinions. Part of the training—never explicitly mentioned but always a consideration—is simply helping women speak their own minds and to vote the way they believe is right from a "woman's perspective" or at least from their *own* perspective.

One key staff person states directly that helping people run for office is among the trickiest things UNDP does. One key piece of advice is that agencies "have to work both sides"; that is, they must make sure that the community and its people know their rights and that elected representatives know their responsibilities.[18] This echoed a lot of talk about working both the "supply" and "demand" sides of rights issues (see Chapter 6 on what this means), focusing on those who demand their rights and those who are the duty-bearers. Another interviewee stressed the use of a "soft approach." Asked if they saw their work with women's empowerment as a matter of civil and political rights, they said they did, and put it into the larger context of RBA. But this, they stressed, required a cautious approach to the matter. If one speaks in terms of "human development" rather than "human rights," they noted, it is easier to bring up these issues—another example of the politics of rights promotion. Their point was *both* that helping women run for office was, in fact, a matter of civil and political rights, and thus controversial for the UNDP; and that there was resistance, requiring careful diplomacy by UNDP in order to help implement the programs they supported. In terms of rights, they advised, it was important to speak from a development perspective, not a strictly rights one; UNDP talks about "development as a whole" and couches citizen participation as "just one component" of that.[19]

The overtly political nature of this work is emphasized in the way respondents viewed the need for caution and diplomacy. Of course, one key element is to not support any political party or position; it has to be clear that the idea is to help *all* women run for office and to give them the capability to effectively compete and serve, rather than support a particular position. "One treads a very fine line when one runs that campaign."[20] A UNDP official in a state office at first maintained that keeping neutral "has never been a problem" but then acknowledged it was an issue he had to be aware of and to integrate into his plans. He suggested it was probably easier for UNICEF than for UNDP since (in his mind) UNICEF was more involved in capacity development and less in project implementation, and thus faced fewer difficult situations.[21]

Panchayat candidates, it should be noted, are technically not running as members of political parties. Still, involving an international organization at this level of politics requires subtlety. The respondent pointed out that other divisions, such as caste, can be a factor. If there is, for example, a village where a UNDP-supported team is working, they must emphasize that neither sex nor caste is a reason to vote for a particular person. One respondent, working in a district office far from New Delhi, also emphasized that some people—mostly those with an interest in existing power structures—resisted efforts to empower women, lower caste people, and members of Scheduled Tribes. "We tell them, if you deliver better services and people get better services, this is a good thing for you too," repeating an oft-mentioned emphasis on convincing people that they too benefit from empowerment of the poor and disenfranchised. Similarly, this UNDP staffer said the people they were trying to train *also* felt threatened and worried about infringing on traditional power structures: "We say you'll better deliver services if you do this and this will make people better support you."[22]

Another respondent related their experiences working with women in Panchayat elections and demonstrated the perils of this work. Working in the Carpet Belt region of Uttar Pradesh (a state in north-central India), an effort to do a "pre-election voter awareness campaign" on behalf of women candidates in 2005 led to over 700 women filing for candidacy to their local PRIs. The UNDP staff person described the results of this as "complete chaos." More important, the respondent described UNDP officials and women candidates accosted and threatened by local "mafia" and other politically powerful people unhappy with the challenges to traditional structure; one particularly vivid anecdote ended with UNDP staff and local candidates forced to flee by car, and UNDP implementing "security protocols" for staff helping with the elections. The person recounting this story was clear: by necessity UNDP took no political stance and supported no particular position. Yet the very fact of being involved in women's empowerment at the PRI level involved it in violence. "None of our posters said men versus women, or scheduled castes versus upper castes"; it was just "good policies or bad policies." Yet this didn't prevent controversy. In the end, of the over 700 women candidates, more than 250 were elected: "*That* is transformational change!" they exulted.[23] Another informant, in a separate interview but bringing up the same issues; over time, the UNDP staff person said, the dynamic could be changed, but it required the UNDP to work carefully and in the long term.[24]

Capacity Building

On the other side of the democratic equation, UNDP works to build the capacity of government officials to support decentralization through the

PRIs and in general to make government more responsive to local needs and voices. An official in a local office complained that too many government agents did not care about the poor—this staff member blamed cozy relationships with business interests,[25] but other interview subjects mentioned traditional attitudes, caste discrimination, and simple official arrogance as factors. As part of the UNDP's decentralization agenda, the development assistance framework includes "strengthening local governance institutions" to "essentially ... develop the capacities of all governance actors at the district level and below to determine the local development priorities and ensure efficient and equitable delivery of public services through a participatory governance process" (Government of India-UNDP, 2007, p. 11). Specific outcomes and outputs include "capacities of elected representatives and district officials in focus states/districts enhanced to perform their roles effectively"; "systems and mechanisms in place to provide vulnerable and excluded groups access to justice"; and "elected representatives and district officials equipped with participatory and gender-sensitive planning, budgeting and monitoring skills" (UNDP, 2007, p. 6).

One UN goal is to help support India's own "National Capability Building Framework" (NCBF), a product of India's Ministry of Panchayati Raj, itself designed to build capacity for local governance. A UNDP official stated their belief that the NCBF was comprehensive but "not realistic" because the government lacked the ability to carry it out—this person pointed to a lack of appropriate institutions to do all the training necessary, and, indeed, the NCBF is being revised. (Government officials participating in the program, however, spoke well of it, with several noting that UNDP brought outside expertise and needed manpower.) There has been a corresponding shift in UNDP priorities, therefore, to helping government institutions build *their* capacity to help members of the PRIs in providing effective governance.[26] The same informant pointed out that with turnover regular in the PRIs, helping individual members was an unsustainable model for capacity building.

Where do human rights play a role in these projects? Both women's issues and caste issues, of course, are factored into capacity building. Helping women run for office has been discussed already, and assisting them to be effective in their new roles is an obvious follow-up and a clear priority. Caste, gender, tribal status, and other modes of discrimination are built into the various training programs, and local elected representatives are trained to be sensitive to those concerns as well as given the tools to raise them at higher levels of government. Discrimination, political participation, and social empowerment are all also included. An interview subject noted, again, that when programs like these threatened existing power structures there was, sometimes, pushback; a District Collector or local landlord might resist what they see as empowering the poor and disenfranchised to the detriment of existing interests. However, they said, this was only "once in a while, when the communities have not been taken into full confidence." So, for example, the staff person noted that it was important to not just build the capacity of women but also of men so that they did not feel threatened by women's empowerment. A project they were involved with would, in its next phase, include "sensitization of male representatives on gender issues" and a "district strategy" to "overcome the fear of men of being disempowered."[27]

Capacity building for local governance also includes building the capacity of nonelected officials, and here too a rights-based approach aims to integrate various concerns over human rights issues into effective governance. Again, a number of projects fit under this umbrella, but a few are worth mentioning to provide insights into the challenge of working in this area. For example, the project "Pathways for an Inclusive Indian Administration" aims to "strengthen both the capacities of civil servants and their enabling environment with a view towards a more effective, efficient, transparent and accountable public administration system at both the national and state levels." Key project documents mention a focus on the "marginalized and vulnerable" specifically as central elements of the program (UNDP, 2011–2012). The ability of civil servants to effectively design and implement projects and provide for the needs of their citizens is central, but making it inclusive—that is, both making civil servants sensitive to the needs of the poor and marginalized and opening them to the voices of civil society—is considered part of the main project goal.

The potential gap between rights rhetoric and reality is brought clearly into focus by another governance capacity project, one supporting India's landmark Mahatma Gandhi National Rural Employment Guarantee Act (MGNREGA). MGNREGA is another piece of landmark rights-based legislation in India, part of a right-to-work initiative, which guarantees 100 days of paid work. MGNREGA is presented as a "rights based" antipoverty initiative as it supposedly guarantees each eligible worker the right to demand work from the government, which then has an obligation to fulfill that right (UNDP, 2010b, p. 10). Support for MGNREGA is a key element of RBA for UNDP and is mentioned often as an important effort in this area. It is, in fact, a central part of the UNDP program and takes up a great deal of UNDP's time and resources.

Even leaving aside the distinction between C&P rights or ES&C rights, the notion that MGNREGA is an example of rights-based programming shows many of the contradictions of how the term is used—and how it can be improved. MGNREGA does provide a "right" to those who qualify, but that right needs to be provided by the government, and it depends on fair, equitable, and effective service delivery—something that cannot be guaranteed under current circumstances. In this respect it differs from a service delivery model only in the sense that it has been legally codified, thus giving an extra (but hardly infallible) recourse to those who feel their service has not been adequately delivered. MGNREGA has, in many ways, been an extremely successful way of transferring money to the rural poor; yet as important as it is, the program has a variety of problems that prevent full and effective implementation. These include the low level of awareness among the rural population that it even exists (hard to quantify, but a serious problem); trouble getting identification cards to eligible workers; corruption; and discrimination against women, Scheduled Castes, and Scheduled Tribes in the distribution of jobs and money (Pellisery & Jalan, 2011; Vij, 2011). The key issues are ensuring that these groups benefit equally from schemes like MGNREGA and that their rights—in particular, to nondiscrimination—are protected.

Building capacity among local government officials—to direct general development projects, provide services, or administer programs like MGNREGA—are important economic development goals; effective governance and administration is, more or less by definition, important in improving people's lives and moving development forward. But there is, naturally, a difference between simply improving systems and processes, and incorporating civil and political rights in program management. At least one well-placed UNDP expert on governance reform sees positive change in people's right to participation, as a result of capacity building. People going to district officials, this person said, were usually ignored, but that has changed for the better in areas where UNDP-sponsored projects are active. Now they are "more willing to hear and respond to people's needs." Similarly the staffer cites a gender sensitizing training in Rajasthan and a process of advising on "gender subplans" within district gender plans that have incorporated women's rights and empowerment into government planning, administration of MGNREGA, and other similar programs.[28]

Another good example of how this comes together is the Peoples Assessment of Health, Education and Livelihood (PAHELI) program, part of UNDP's general effort to help Indian government agencies with effective implementation of development projects. Working with UNICEF and the government as well as UNDP, PAHELI is a method for going into targeted communities and getting ground-level information on human development in the poorest areas of the country. As staff described it, PAHELI provides citizens a forum to discuss whether their needs are being met by government interventions and redefines development as the provision of *needed* services. It collects indicators regarding human development progress and does so in a way intended to empower people to make it clear what realities they face. It looks, for example, to see not just if MGNREGA is being implemented in a particular area but also if the people in that area know their rights under the program and understand how to claim them; or, another example, not just whether there is water provided but also whether it is accessible and drinkable.

PAHELI is particularly useful for providing information that can measure human development across regions and gauge progress toward the Millennium Development Goals, which then can be compared across districts and states. More important here, UNDP staff see PAHELI as a means of citizen empowerment, similar to RTI and other efforts to hold the bureaucracy accountable. A UNDP respondent working closely with PAHELI specifically tied it to the pursuit of greater government and social accountability. In this case, though, the respondent said, it was less about political penalties (although they said there were some issues in Delhi related to removal of officials due to poor performance) than about changing attitudes. The UNDP official contrasted a "punitive" model of accountability with an "attitude change" one, where officials who were not performing were made aware of the need to change. UNDP staff was, importantly, thinking closely about the nature of service delivery, not just its rhetoric, not just service as a right, but also as a rights-based approach to service.

Here, again, the *resistance* often felt against fairly technical matters helps to locate where the real political issues—those challenging existing power structures—are being pushed against. The UNDP staff person quoted in the last paragraph also noted, in regard to bringing even this sort of accountability to government agencies, "It is a very, very political process," particularly at higher levels such as that of the District Collector. District Collectors and other similarly placed officials do resist; they "ask why," and insist sometimes that they have a better grasp on the situation in their district than any group of ordinary people. "We may be rubbing people the wrong way," this UNDP official said.[29] This echoed the voice of another UNDP governance advisor, who commented on the problem of demanding accountability from officials "who really have very limited powers" in the first place. Accountability, this person said, "is the weak part of the program right now,"[30] yet vitally important to the concept of a rights-based approach. So, what is the solution to this resistance? One solution is to work more closely with elected bodies, but "elected officials don't always see eye to eye" with the bureaucrats.[31] Another official stressed that further devolution of power—they mentioned the Panchayat (Extension to Scheduled Areas) Act of 1996 (see Mathew, 2003), which is legislation aimed at devolving local control over natural resources, as a further empowering move supported by UNDP.[32]

Still, what, ultimately, are the C&P rights implications of decentralization? As it is practiced by UNDP and other agencies, there is clearly an emphasis on accountability, although as we have seen, staff tend to shy away from the "hard" accountability of actually creating mechanisms to remove elected and appointed officials who fail to provide needed services; instead, the emphasis is on a "soft" one of training and sensitization, on creating feedback mechanisms so people can have their voices heard as programs are modified, and on empowering local groups to be more persistent in demanding results. Decentralization enables free speech in that it allows voices to be heard and civil liberties to the extent that local bodies are easier to rein in when they start to become destructive of those liberties. Decentralization is also closely tied to participation, which is itself an important C&P right, as discussed in Chapter 2. Perhaps more importantly, it is imperative to see how C&P rights are built into decentralization programs: through training on nondiscrimination and women's rights, through legal reform, and anticorruption strategies. When they do it right, UN agencies and the Government of India incorporate speech, nondiscrimination, and legal empowerment norms into decentralization programs and use them as a tool for citizen empowerment.

Conclusion

This chapter looks only at how some UNDP programs are integrating human rights issues into development. There are many other UNDP programs in India, and even within those covered there are any number of projects going on; this was meant to provide a representative sample of what is being done and how staff think about it rather than a comprehensive study.

It is certainly true that other UNDP programs have also considered how RBA fit into their operational agenda. For example, an expert on disaster relief and mitigation was very clear about the need to integrate a rights-based approach into their work. They shared an anecdote about discrimination in the distribution of housing aid after floods in northern India; not just discrimination based on caste but also on age and gender. UNDP disaster mitigation planning, they insisted, had to include training to eliminate such discrimination. Projects to help build rural livelihoods also take into consideration gender and caste issues, much as those projects noted above, although not always as explicitly. Disaggregation of data, in particular, is an important element of this strategy, as was targeting women and other vulnerable groups in particular. Staff members working on HIV/AIDS, not surprisingly, were also well-informed on the rights implications of their work. HIV/AIDS is another vital program area where RBA has important ramifications. It is left out here both in the interest of space and because it is one area where C&P rights are most explicitly mentioned, in terms of the rights of those with HIV/AIDS or who might have it. There is substantial resistance, but the policy is clear. Section 377 of the Indian Penal Code, outlawing homosexual sex, has been noted. In interviews with staff working on HIV/AIDS, there was substantial interest in working more generally with the LGBT community in India to support gay rights, both as a strategy to combat HIV/AIDS and as a worthwhile, rights-oriented goal in itself; although, this interest still seems in its infancy. However, there were discussions between LGBT activists and NGOs in India and UNDP staff working on HIV/AIDS issues that seem likely to lead to more focus on this area of rights in the future.

Overall, an interest in C&P rights—in the integration of real and measureable political change as part of the overall development paradigm—remains fairly compartmentalized in UNDP. Some see it as "their business." Others do not. Similarly, their interlocutors in the government have varied responses to questions about this: while some (for example, involved in legal training) say they are grateful to UNDP for bringing up these issues, others seem genuinely indifferent or unaware of RBA and its implications. Still, there is clear effort by some inside and outside the UNDP to consider what RBA means, and the level of resistance that some staff members meet is a reasonable testament to the effort being put into it. As explained in Chapter 2, the extent of integration of C&P rights has a lot to do with the bureaucratic nature of the UNDP. The staff is well aware of the general idea of RBA and realize that they are expected to consider how it should affect their work. As part of an "open system," UNDP staff takes cues from various places regarding how this should look: from UNDP directives, from academic work, from their own sense of what is important, and of course from their superiors in the organization. They then put their own stamp on it, both in terms of how to interpret RBA and how to implement it. The strategies of implementation—the way they push back against resistance and overcome pressure—is ad hoc, largely personal in nature, and only sometimes effective.

Still, there are strong areas of C&P rights implementation to go along with those where implementation is less effective. And among some staff, at least, a strong appreciation for the importance of developing new ways to push for an agenda they believe in. There is, in other words, adaptation to outside pressure, as well as a strong inner core of ideas to drive this adaptation and innovation.

Overall, it might be a good idea to focus on those areas where the promotion of C&P rights—rights to equal opportunity, the rights of people to receive and demand information from the government, democratic rights, and women's rights—are presented by UNDP interlocutors as *good in and of themselves*. The commitment to rights is not rhetorical—in the "we create conditions for increased employment, which allows people to afford food, thus implementing a right to food" mode—but a key element of how development is defined. This represents a real shift in what UNDP does, as evidenced by those within the organizations who will readily admit there has been a change in how the mission is defined. In the next chapter, there will be a greater emphasis on these changes and how they require a rethinking of more traditional development approaches and goals.

References

Ashraf, T. (2008). Empowering People Through Information: A Case Study of India's Right to Information Act. *International Information and Library Review, 40*(3), 148–152.

Banerjee, A. V., Rukmini, B., Duflo, E., Glennerster, R., & Khemani, S. (2010). *Pitfalls of Participatory Programs: Evidence From a Randomized Evaluation in Education in India*. Cambridge, MA: National Bureau of Economic Research.

Booth, D. (2012). Aid Effectiveness: Bringing Country Ownership (and Politics) Back In. *Conflict, Security & Development, 12*(5), 537–558.

Browne, S. (2012). *The United Nations Development Programme and System (UNDP)*. New York: Routledge.

Chatterjee, P., & Chowdhury, S. (2012). A Capabilities Approach to Access to Justice. *Journal of Indian Law and Society, 20*(1), 107–129.

DAC OECD. (2005). *Paris Declaration on Aid Effectiveness: Ownership, Harmonisation, Alignment, Results and Mutual Accountability*. Paris.

De Langen, M. S., & Barendrecht, M. (2009). Legal Empowerment of the Poor: Innovating Access to Justice. In G. Rizvi & J. de Jong (Eds.), *The State of Access: Success and Failure of Democracies to Create Equal Opportunities* (pp. 250–271). Washington, DC: Brookings Institution Press.

Government of India-UNDP. (2007). *India: United Nations Development Assistance Framework 2008–2012*. New Delhi: UNDP.

Government of India-UNDP. (2008). *Country Programme Action Plan Between the Government of India and the United Nations Development Programme 2008–2012*. New Delhi: UNDP.
Government of India-UNDP. (2013). *Country Programme Action Plan*. New Delhi: UNDP.
Human Development Resource Center. (2001). *Decentralisation in India: Challenges and Opportunities*. New Delhi: UNDP.
Hyden, G. (2008). After the Paris Declaration: Taking on the Issue of Power. *Development Policy Review, 26*(3), 259–274.
Masih, P., Singh, G., & Mishra, R. (2012). *UMMEED Live 2012: Third Gender Leadership Development Projecxt, Raipur, Chhattisgarh*. Raipur, India: United Nations Development Programme. Retrieved from https://issuu.com/undp/docs/ummeed-live-2012--third-gender-leadership-developm.
Mathew, G. (2003). Panchayati Raj Institutions and Human Rights in India. *Economic and Political Weekly, 38*(2), 155–162.
Mawani, R. (2015). Law and Colonialism: Legacies and Lineages. In A. Serat & P. Ewick (Eds.), *The Handbook of Law and Society* (pp. 417–433). Malden, MA: John Wiley and Sons.
Meene, I. v. d., & Rooij, B. v. (2008). *Access to Justice and Legal Empowerment: Making the Poor Central in Legal Development Co-operation*. Leiden, Netherlands: Leiden University Press.
Mukherjee, S., Chakraborty, D., & Sikdar, S. (2014). *Three Decades of Human Development Across Indian States: Inclusive Growth or Perpetual Disparity?* New Delhi: National Institute of Public Finance and Policy.
Murphy, C. (2006). *The United Nations Development Programme: A Better Way?* New York: Cambridge University Press.
Nanda, S. (2007). The Hijras of India: Cultural and Individual Dimensions of an Institutionalized Third Gender Role. In P. Aggleton & R. Parker (Eds.), *Culture, Society and Sexuality: A Reader* (pp. 247–249). New York: Routledge.
Oestreich, J. (2011). International Organizations in International Relations Theory. In B. Reinalda (Ed.), *The Ashgate Research Companion to Non-State Actors* (pp. 173–184). Burlington, VT: Ashgate Press.
Patel, T. (2010). Confronting Discrimination Through Affirmative Action in India: Playing the Right Music With the Wrong Instrument? In J. Syed & M. F. Ozbilgin (Eds.), *Managing Cultural Diversity in Asia: A Research Companion* (pp. 278–306). Cheltenham, UK: Edward Elgar.
Pellisery, S., & Jalan, S. K. (2011). Towards Transformative Social Protection: A Gendered Analysis of the Employment Guarantee Act of India (MGNREGA). *Gender and Development, 19*(2), 283–294.
Roberts, A. S. (2010). *A Great and Revolutionary Law? The First Four Years of India's Right to Information Act*. Suffolk: Suffolk University Law School Research Paper 10-02.

Roy, A., & Dey, N. (2002). Fight for the Right to Know in India. *Development Dialogue, 1*, 77–90.

Shrivasta, K. (2009). *The Right to Information: A Global Perspective*. Olympia Fields, IL: Lancer.

Singh, S. (2010). *The Genesis and Evolution of the Right to Information Regime in India*. Paper presented at the Regional Workshop: Towards More Open and Transparent Governance in South Asia, New Delhi.

UNDP. *Capacity Building for Access to Information (CBAI) Project*. New Delhi: UNDP. Retrieved from http://projects.cgg.gov.in/KPNRC/Documents/Publications/CBAI%20a%20case%20study.pdf.

UNDP. (2003). *Access to Information: Practice Note*. New York: UNDP.

UNDP. (2007). *UNDP Country Programme for India (2008–2012)*. New Delhi: UNDP.

UNDP. (2008). *Capacity Development for Local Governance: Factsheet*. New Delhi: UNDP.

UNDP. (2010a). *Hijras/Transgender Women in India: HIV, Human Rights and Social Exclusion*. New Delhi: UNDP.

UNDP. (2010b). *Rights-based Legal Guarantees as Development Policy: The Mahatma Gandhi National Rural Employment Guarantee Act*. New Delhi: UNDP.

UNDP. (2011). *National Implementation by the Government of UNDP Supported Projects: Guidelines and Procedures*. New Delhi: UNDP.

UNDP. (2011–2012). *Pathways for an Inclusive Indian Administration (PIIA)*. New York: UNDP.

UNDP. (N.d.-a). *UNDP and Access to Information*. New York: UNDP.

UNDP. (N.d.-b). *United Nations Development Programme Factsheet: Access to Justice for Marginalized People 2008–2012*. New Delhi: UNDP.

Vij, N. (2011). *Collaborative Governance: Analysing Social Audits in MGNREGA in India*. IDS 42. Oxford: Institute for Development Studies.

4

The United Nations Children's Fund

CHAPTER 3, ON THE United Nations Development Programme (UNDP), focused in particular on what sorts of civil and political rights were being promoted and implemented under the idea of a rights-based approach to development and what resistance was faced. The focus of this chapter will be a deeper consideration of how the notion of a rights-based approach informs and changes how the United Nations Children's Fund (UNICEF) plans and implements its existing operations. It is one thing, after all, to assert that you are promoting rights; but if this is to be more reality than rhetorical, there should be visible and significant changes in how development programs are conceived and executed. RBA has to be about more than just redefining service provision as "implementing rights": it should be about redefining what services are needed and creating the social and political conditions where citizens can claim those rights for themselves.

Unlike UNDP, UNICEF has an existing commitment to specific human rights that predates the development of RBA. That commitment comes from its earlier embrace of the Convention of the Rights of the Child (CRC) as a central programming document. Implementation of the CRC has been its stated, overarching goal, even though at times this commitment has been called into question (Oestreich, 2010). So in one sense, UNICEF is well ahead of UNDP and other agencies in its implementation of RBA: it has been thinking for quite some time about the connection between development, child rights, and programming. On the other hand, UNICEF (like other agencies) can at times seem to fall into the trap of thinking that *everything* is rights implementation; for example, that immunizing children is implementing a "right to health," that providing nutrition supplements is implementing a "right to nutrition," and so forth. The CRC can provide a convenient cover for "business as usual," or, more accurately, it can be a rhetorical tool that helps promote child welfare without really changing how it is provided. Interpretation of the CRC is not always easy. Thus, it is important to see to what extent development is truly reconceptualized from a rights-based perspective.

After a review of the overall programming goals of UNICEF in India, there will be detailed case studies of two programming areas where RBA has led to considerable reconceptualization of programming: in Education, and Child Protection (CP). A third case study will look at UNICEF's work in conflict zones: technically an area that comes under Child Protection, but in reality a special example of injecting UNICEF into a highly political situation where it would likely have preferred a lower profile in the past. In this case, RBA leads to a new sense of what its responsibilities are to children affected by armed conflict. For the sake of space, other programming areas will be dealt with a bit more briefly in the final section as with UNDP. It is simply not possible to go in detail through every programming area, and certainly not to then consider the various cross-cutting priorities, such as UNICEF's own work in decentralization or on equity. The case studies are chosen to give some sense of the types of changes RBA has brought to UNICEF, as well as some of the challenges, and the areas where change has not been pronounced.

UNICEF Programs in India

"The overall goal of the 2013–2017 Country Programme," according to UNICEF's documentation, "is to advance the rights of children, adolescents, and women to survival, growth, development, participation and protection by reducing inequities based on caste, ethnicity, gender, poverty, region or religion" (UNICEF-India, 2013a, p. 8). (This was almost the exact same wording used in the previous plan.) To a large extent, this "fulfillment of rights" is structured around the provision of services and accomplishing of fairly typical development goals: much of the country program is devoted to achievement of the Millennium Development Goals, whose benchmarks are put in terms of specific measureable outcomes rather than achievement of women's and children's rights. The document does, however, also give considerable attention to equity and nondiscrimination: "With adequate financial resources, a policy framework and large-scale national flagship programmes in place, the need is to enhance their effective implementation in a way that ends the inter generational cycle of deprivation among the poorest and most marginalised.

It is here that UNICEF aims to play a catalytic role in its support to government, by adopting a strong rights-based approach and using a combination of cross-cutting strategies, namely capacity development, decentralisation and improved governance, partnerships, social inclusion for equity, and knowledge management" (UNICEF-India, 2013a, p. 8).

The UNICEF action plan, and UNICEF-India itself, is divided into various program areas. These are:

- AIDS/HIV
- Child Protection
- Development and Nutrition
- Education
- Emergency Preparedness and Response
- Environment
- Reproductive and Child Health
- Social Policy, Advocacy, and Behavior Change (UNICEF-India, 2013b, p. 7)

Of course, all these programming areas are at least nominally expected to integrate a "rights-based approach." Staff in all units reported, in interviews, that they were, at least, familiar with RBA and its ideas, although, as will be discussed, the level of reported integration varied widely from unit to unit and even from person to person. As with UNDP, even the unit charged with responses to emergencies and disasters is clear about using RBA: a UNICEF Emergencies officer paid particular attention to the issues of equity and participation when discussing his unit's approach to disaster recovery. He listed children under five years of age, senior citizens, pregnant and lactating mothers, and others as "the most vulnerable" and stated that reaching and protecting them was a key priority. On the other hand, more than one staff person in the Child Protection unit, which deals with such complex and charged welfare issues as child labor, disabled and homeless children, sex trafficking, and child marriage, complained that other units felt they could safely ignore rights issues since they saw CP as the "guardians of the [Convention on the Rights of the Child]" and thus were "off the hook" for their implementation.[1] To be clear, this was just one person's anecdotal impressions, but it still speaks to the complexity of levels of interest and commitment to RBA within UNICEF.

Keep in mind that achievement of the Millennium Development Goals (MDGs) is a key goal of all UN agencies (See Langford, Sumner, & Yamin, 2013; United Nations Development Programme [UNDP], 2009). In some cases, achievement of the MDGs is seen as working counter to implementation of a meaningful right-based approach. There is a perception—widespread in UNICEF and those who watch it, not just in India—that pursuing technical goals like those of the MDGs draws attention away from the rights agenda. A widespread complaint is that the MDGs and other "results-based management" (RBM) systems (see Hulme, 2010) entails too much of a focus on numbers and the achievement of specific statistical benchmarks—a particular reduction in malnutrition rates, a specific increase in immunizations—that leave little room for the "fuzzier" notion of rights (Alston, 2005; Kaufmann, 2004). Indeed, many staff reported frustration with the move to RBM systems at all levels of the UN's work. While an emphasis on producing quantifiable results and showing specific outputs from money spent might seem an admirable goal, it necessarily privileges service delivery models over RBA. It is easy to show how many schools have been built or teachers trained; it is less easy to measure whether school management committees are truly empowered to speak up and make their voices heard. Staff in every agency studied here mentioned the ways that RBM made their work more difficult.

Further, achievement of the MDGs can hinder and even conflict with the pursuit of equity and reaching the most vulnerable: while some interview subjects felt that focusing on the poorest and most vulnerable would *help* in the pursuit of numerical goals like MDGs (by allowing a focus on children and women who would benefit the most from interventions), others feared that it would *hinder* that pursuit (by directing resources to small, expensive-to-help groups). The debate here shows how difficult it is to understand how the MDGs and RBA interact and work either to reinforce each other or work against each other.

At the most extreme, one division chief in a technical field stated that their division had essentially *no* rights policy. There was, this staffer said, some effort to reach out to underserved groups and to introduce "equity" in the program but said there was "not much beyond that."[2] Similarly, several staff in the CP unit complained that since they were perceived as the division with a specific rights focus, other units of UNICEF felt free to ignore rights in their own programming. On the other hand, as will be shown below, plenty of UNICEF staff had the opposite perception: their work was deeply informed by the Convention on the Rights of the Child; their emphasis on issues like equity, inclusion, and empowerment was pervasive and effective; and the organization as a whole had embraced a rights-based approach to programming in meaningful ways. Naturally, it is normal for different people in a large bureaucracy to have different perceptions of what their bureaucracy is doing. As an example, the same staff person who denied that there was a rights-based model in their field also admitted that their highly technical training made them less open to the benefits of RBA than others might be. They accepted that others might have a better sense of what RBA meant. Still, they were not alone in their feeling that RBA was not central to UNICEF's work. There remains a level of disagreement among officials as to how much rights are a rhetorical or practical exercise. This seems to derive from confusion about exactly what a rights-based approach means. For every thoughtful answer about rights as empowerment and political change, there were others who seemed to think it was sufficient to say, we provide services that people have a right to. The transition to RBA, in other words, is incomplete.

Education

Millennium Development Goal number three is the achievement of universal primary education. The stated goal of UNICEF's education department in the 2008–2012 plan was to contribute to achieving that goal, as well as the goals of gender equality and empowerment of women. (These goals, of course, are continued in the 2013–2017 programming period.) Education is a core component of all UNICEF programming, and an important priority in India. In 2009, the Indian government passed the Right of Children to Free and Compulsory Education Act (RTE) (Sripati & Thiruvengadam, 2004), which declared an education to be a fundamental right of all Indian children. Yet education remains a fundamental challenge in India, where there are vast numbers of poor children; where schools are often of terrible quality; and where corruption and lack of capacity undermines efforts at school reform (Govinda & Diwan, 2003; Kumar, 2006).

The 2008–2012 Country Programme Action Plan (CPAP) (in similar, but usefully more detailed language to the later plan) divides the education program into the following sectors:

- *Systems strengthening and capacity building* to contribute to strengthening norms and standards to contribute to a quality education, namely system performance, teacher performance and social inclusion. Key areas of focus will include child-centered teaching/learning practices; management of multi-level, multi-grade situation; physical environment and infrastructure; community participation; and teacher performance and support.
- *Knowledge management and policy influencing* to review and disseminate the best international practices in the areas of multi-level, multi-grade education, multilingual education; and English language teaching …

the programme will also provide technical assistance to the [government Education For All bureaucracy] in knowledge development in areas such as school management practices, quality education and English language teaching.
- *Advocacy and partnerships* to advance the education sector agenda on social inclusion and quality ... the programme will also bring together a broad-based national coalition to advance Girls' Education with a special emphasis on [Scheduled Castes/Scheduled Tribes] and minority girls.
- *Equity and quality promotion* to strengthen the capacities of major duty bearers to better meet their obligations in providing quality, inclusive education....The programme will contribute to ensuring that there is broad consensus on the major elements of quality and that these are progressively extended to the whole system.
- *Advocacy and social monitoring*, in particular strengthening the ability of communities to do social monitoring and audits. (UNICEF, 2008, pp. 37–38)

There is some right-oriented language here—from the reference to social inclusion and equity to an emphasis on duty-bearers, but it is fairly vague and open to interpretation. And, in general, providing children with a "right to education" is not the same as a "rights-based approach to education." The difference provides a useful lens through which to view RBA in India. It usefully illustrates how UNICEF programs in seemingly "ordinary" or nonpolitical areas still try to adapt to a rights-based paradigm. Education in India also has to adapt to a wide variety of situations, from ethnic minorities to conflict areas.

Just as UNDP could use legislation regarding RTI or MGNREGA to advocate for its preferred policies, UNICEF's education program is able to point to the Right of Children to Free and Compulsory Education Act in its efforts to advance Education through RBA. RTE was not yet law when the previous country program was developed, but it is central to the 2013–2017 UNICEF plan, which notes, "the Education programme will help to strengthen government efforts to provide quality education by reducing gender and other social disparities. While retaining a focus on elementary education under the Right to Education Act, the programme will look at a wider gamut" (UNICEF–India, 2013, p. 10). It was also incorporated into the period under study.

While UNICEF isn't usually cited as having played a strong role in passage of the RTE legislation (indeed, it is hard to find UNICEF mentioned in any histories of the act's passage), staff at the New Delhi office insisted they were active behind the scenes. Regional UNICEF offices also said they were active in pushing for state-level ratification of RTE. It would be odd if UNICEF did not express an opinion about legislation on this topic, but it became clear in interviews that they preferred to be quiet about their work in the Indian legal process, for fear of appearing to be injecting themselves in domestic politics. The term nearly every interview respondent used was "convening power": UNICEF's strategy was primarily to use its offices to support and bring together the civil society groups who were working on behalf of this legislation. As an example, the UNICEF Country Director specifically used her office to organize state governments and get them "on board" with RTE. As well, UNICEF was important in having the "child friendly schools" concept (see UNICEF, 2009a) incorporated into the final legislation, according to well-placed interview subjects.[3]

This is in no way intended to overstate the importance of UNICEF; the RTE movement was an indigenous one and no one at UNICEF took any real credit for its success, any more than UNDP claimed to be responsible for passage of RTI (Alston & Bhuta, 2005). Still, it is noteworthy that RTE legislation was passed and that UNICEF was willing to involve itself at all in the political process to help get it passed. Rather than shying away from becoming involved in domestic politics, UNICEF personnel understood the importance of the process to advance the organization's goals, and they acted positively on its preferences.

RTE commits the government to provide a free and compulsory education for all children ages 6 to 14. It commits the government to build schools where they are not available and to fund them appropriately from both federal and state sources. There are specific provisions in the act to guarantee an education to minority children, children from Scheduled Castes, child laborers, migrant children, and other disadvantaged groups; and also provisions regarding educational quality and child-friendly schools, that is, schools designed to actually promote education and participation (e.g., by providing sanitation facilities for both genders, by ensuring teacher quality, and addressing other factors that might deter children from attending school or be unable to actually learn while there).

Implementing a right to education might seem a simple question of building enough schools, providing enough teachers, and then finding children who might not otherwise be in school (Kington, 2007, p. 190; Mehrotra, 2012). To operationalize it as a rights-based approach, however, requires more than this. One important issue—central to nearly every conversation with UNICEF staff—was improving quality of schools (see also Kalyanpur, 2008), a term used repeatedly above in the set of UNICEF goals. Quality might seem like a desirable goal, although not one with a specific rights connection, but UNICEF staff was insistent that the connection was vital One top education official put it this way: "Is it a right to education or a right to learning?"[4] The low quality of many government schools in India is a well-known problem, perhaps inevitable in such a vast country: teachers are poorly paid and poorly trained; resources are stretched thin to the breaking point; corruption siphons off both materials and educator's time; and a host of other problems (L. N. Dash, 2010). Another interview respondent said: "It is easy to get Delhi bureaucrats to pass laws; harder to make a difference in 1.3 million schools." The goal in the quality sector was to "unpack" and "simplify" what quality means.[5] The "right" was to an education, and simple metrics like "how many schools have been built?" and "how many teachers hired?" or even "what is the literacy rate among girls?" failed to capture the question of whether real learning was going on. They look too much at the old service-delivery metrics rather than true human development. At least one UNICEF official was convinced that some states that have lagged in ratification of RTE legislation have done so because of the quality issue: fearful that they can't afford to meet the quality requirements of a right to education, this person said, they prefer to hold off on making any commitments at all.[6]

More tangible in terms of separating a rights-based from a service-based approach is the focus on creating school management committees (SMCs) (Verger & VanderKaaij, 2012). The Indian RTE legislation provides for the creation of these committees, made up of local people in each school district, to oversee education and hold officials accountable for its provision. Strengthening SMCs is a top priority of the UNICEF education staff in India, despite the fact that it is not specifically mentioned in the 2013–2017 Action Plan (although it is in many other planning documents). UNICEF works closely with Shiksha Ka Haq Abhiyan (Right to Education Campaign), an initiative to strengthen and build on existing community structures and empower local citizens. "Today, a parent can walk into school and ask 'where is my child's education?' " said one respondent: there is, this UNICEF staff person said, more "accountability" than, say, ten years ago, and attributed that to the creation of SMCs. Another pointed to "creating demand" for education as a key component of the SMC movement and said UNICEFs role was "in the background" to "create awareness" among parents and children of what their rights are and how they can claim them.[7] Said the same respondent, "it is the people's perception" of whether they are "asking for this because it is an entitlement," rather than simply requesting a service from the government (or being afraid to ask and simply hoping a service will be delivered), that is the key rights element in the SMCs. SMCs, Panchayats, and other local bodies become key for "demanding rights," and UNICEF, through its partners, conduct demonstration projects to show how this demand can be channeled and used effectively.

Examples from district offices of UNICEF illustrate how many of these ideas are put into practice. One state office official noted that with RTE legislation, the government was committed (albeit sometimes more in theory than in practice) to providing resources for education, and therefore the field office of UNICEF was turning more to "building up the demand side." This included not just supporting SMCs but also creating "child collectives" to "make children aware of their rights." Their office had also engaged in supporting litigation in court to make sure that underserved or especially vulnerable populations—for example, children in institutions (e.g., disabled children or those in detention facilities)—were able to access and call for their rights. The respondent was clear that UNICEF could not bring such litigation itself, but it had supported civil society organizations in doing so. "We build the capacity of people to understand the needs" of children, and "work with Justices of the High Court to understand the rights of those children."[8] The same office listed a variety of other techniques to bring in a rights-based approach to education. These included training legal functionaries and "front line government workers" on education as a right; "mobilizing civil society organizations" and linking them with government on issues such as institutionalized children; and developing "reference materials" for "front line workers" on child rights.

Another UNICEF official in a different region used similar language. This respondent also was helping to train government officials and civil society organizations to use the legal system as a way of demanding their rights—to move, in the respondent's words, "from welfare to rights." The state official stressed in particular the interaction between RTE and the Indian National Commission for Protection of Child Rights (NCPCR)—a federal body created in 2007 to ensure that both the terms of the Indian Constitution and the CRC were being implemented in the realm of child rights. This official cited the "Education Is My Right" program with the Ministry of Human Resource Development; training "block volunteers" to inform people in specific areas about education rights; drafting, in cooperation with the government, a "national vision for girls' education in India—Roadmap to 2015" which "envisages a 12-month community mobilization campaign on right to education, and increased and improved investment for girls' education, strengthening of system for effective service delivery and child friendly schools" (Gohain, 2011).

Also, perhaps most controversially, these initiatives include a push toward language inclusion in Indian schools (Pattnaik, 2004, pp. 183–185; Sridhar, 1996). "Language," this respondent said, "is a political issue" when UNICEF pushes for multilingual education in schools with minority enrollment. There are, by some counts, over 1,500 languages spoken in India, and many more dialects; and language is an important marker of identity for Indian minorities (Mohanty, 2009, p. 263). Students speaking minority languages are often excluded from education because it is entirely in the dominant regional language, and this is particularly acute for indigenous groups. As an example of "navigating" the politics, the interview subject pointed to UNICEF cooperation with Jawaharlal Nehru University in New Delhi, where a center has been created to promote bilingual education. This is part of the larger push to promote equity and inclusiveness in education rather than merely a focus on increasing crude numbers like children in school or literacy rates; it promotes the rights of minority children to be educated.[9] The larger imperative, mentioned by respondents many times, is to disaggregate educational data to reach underserved populations (UNICEF, 2007, p. 10). The importance of disaggregating data, and the source of that data, cannot be overstated; separating data to help find those who face persistent discrimination, exclusion, and social hardship, is central to how UNICEF defines RBA.

The key elements, then, of a true rights-based approach include informing people of their rights under RTE and empowering them to demand these rights from government officials; focusing on inclusiveness and equity; decentralization of power and creation of vocal and confident school management committees; and efforts to be more inclusive through bilingual education, outreach to underserved groups, a focus on the most vulnerable, and other ways of seeking equity through disaggregation of data. There was in many cases a strong commitment to doing things in a rights-based model and talk of moving from a service-provision model to one where rights are demanded by mobilized citizens. That said, asking what a "rights-based model" was, exactly, provoked mixed reactions. The provision of adequate toilets, to use one example, was cited as key to RBA in education since it meant that girls in particular could go to school (and not have to leave in order to relieve themselves); but how that separated a rights-based approach from a merely practical one was left unclear other than to make statements about how such services were "rights" of girl children. Many clearly innovative ideas about community empowerment were often mixed up—sometimes with limited coherence—among more anodyne statements about "providing children with their rights," often by the same people. To some extent, this thinking was likely facilitated by the passage of RTE legislation, which allowed the term "rights" to be attached to *any* educational intervention, since "providing children with an education" and "helping children realize their rights" became easily conflated.

The politics of education advancement can be as complicated and fraught as that of freedom of information, political devolution, or other issues dealt with in the last chapter. Although the focus of this chapter is policy change, it is worth noting, as with UNDP, how much is revealed about the politics of RBA in education from the sort of opposition it faces. Opposition can be seen as an indication that the program has moved beyond the merely technical or rhetorical and is instead impinging on underlying societal issues. One education section respondent, asked about the politics of education, said "no one opposes the right to education" and contrasted it with the issue of child marriage, which remains somewhat controversial.[10] Yet even this person noted that "emergency education" programs (e.g., those in zones of civil conflict, discussed in more detail below) had to "be more careful." Similarly, the staff person quoted earlier on the importance of teaching in minority languages— a controversial issue in regions where people are trying to preserve use of their traditional language, against the pressure from New Delhi to have children learn Hindi. The staff said there was a need to employ "subtle ways" to navigate the controversial politics of language, such as using "evidence-based research" on the benefits of indigenous language education that the government could not deny (using their own figures), and that these problems were not uncommon in educational programs.[11] A high-ranking official noted that convincing local governments to devolve power to the SMCs could be difficult, although this person denied it was a "major problem." Instead, they described it as an "issue to notice."[12] Another staff person noted that that while the government said it was supporting RTE, "my concern is that the government is not passing along other things needed," such as greater financing or devolving the necessary powers to the local level. They said that the transformation to RBA was "a continuous journey where you work with [a] government conditioned to thinking in [terms of] service provision."[13] Perhaps the most revealing story had to do with the "Road Map to 2015" document on girls' education, where UNICEF ultimately took its name off the cover of the document because the damning statistics inside (from the government's own Annual Survey of Education report) were so upsetting to the government (although UNICEF's involvement *is* clearly mentioned elsewhere in the report).[14]

Some of the political issues noted by the Education department were similar to those noted by other staff throughout the UN: discomfort in the government over devolving power, resistance to helping groups such as Scheduled Castes and tribes, and dislike of UN meddling in general. Others, like the issue of multilingual education, were more specific to the education field. None rose to truly serious levels, but all seemed to be at the back of the minds of the education staff. The discussion about the education road map is maybe the most revealing since the respondent spoke of a considerable amount of hand-wringing within UNICEF over exactly how much of a stand to take on what they considered a vital report. In the end the policy was to "stick to principles, but explain and go ahead."[15] Much, but not all, of the political issues seem to stem from the larger question of how RBA has altered the approach to education programming. Pointing out to the government, for example, that its education outcomes fall badly behind what should be expected would be important in any education program.

Child Protection

As noted already, a number of staff in the CP unit in New Delhi have commented, in one way or another, that they feel other units consider them "the rights unit," and that this somehow weakens the commitment of other units to a rights-based approach. Mention this to staff in *other* units, and you get various reactions; clearly some staff are deeply committed to rights-based approaches, others feel they are largely window dressing, and still others seem to mostly agree that Child Protection is the natural home of rights language. The Child Protection unit UNICEF was born largely in tandem with the creation of the Convention on the Rights of the Child. UNICEF's interest in "children in especially difficult circumstances" (CEDC)—for example, street children, working children, and children with disabilities—had a lot to do with former UNICEF Executive Director (1980–1995) James Grant's interest in the CRC in its early years. It is no surprise, then, that a 2011 information document on Child Protection in India begins with the disclaimer, "Child Protection is NOT about protecting all the rights of the child (education, health, nutrition . . .), which is everyone's job at UNICEF" (UNICEF-India, 2011, p. 1).

The 2013–2017 action plan states, "The objective of the child protection programme is to ensure that boys and girls grow up free from violence, exploitation, abuse and unnecessary separation from their families," and it "emphasizes preventing practices such as gender-biased sex selection, child labour, child trafficking and violence against children in all settings: at home, in schools, in institutions and in areas affected by violence" (UNICEF-India, 2013a, p. 11). The list of projects supported by UNICEF in Child Protection, like that of projects in other fields, is too long to go through comprehensively here. Some typical examples include cooperation with Swedish furniture giant Ikea in the Indian states of Uttar Pradesh and Andhra Pradesh to fight child labor (for a discussion see Mellahi, Morrell, & Wood, 2010, pp. 208–211); efforts to combat child trafficking (see Ghosh, 2009) that range from working with government interlocutors on revising laws to supporting police training to help fight local traffickers; and a variety of programs being supported to help homeless girl children in particular learn the skills they need to survive and get an education.

Child Protection work existed before the establishment of RBA, under the rubric of CEDC, and UNICEF has had to think about how a rights-based approach changes their work (Beigbeder, 2001, pp. 163–170; UNICEF, 1986). We can again see how the CP unit has tried to change from a service-provision to an RBA model. One high-ranking CP official addressed the link between CEDC and CP by explaining that CEDC was about *problems*: for example, children in prison. But the "global child protection strategy," as this person put it, was about a "systemic approach" to "protection and creating a protective environment" rather than merely addressing technical issues like prisoners, working children, or the disabled. Or, putting it more bluntly, they stated that Child Protection "*comes from RBA*": it is about asking "what are the conditions that create vulnerabilities?" and then addressing those conditions, not just the vulnerabilities themselves. RBA, in this person's mind, means tackling the social and political problems that lead to putting children in situations of extreme vulnerability in the first place, not just treating the vulnerabilities after they endanger children's welfare.[16]

Creating this environment meant focusing on "laws, policies, capacities, and monitoring . . . the system" that would create a protective environment for children, "for example, a health care system" that addressed all aspects of the needs of children at risk. As a second point they also noted that "social norms, attitudes, and practices . . . are a big chunk of the CRC."[17] In this person's view, issues like child trafficking, child labor, sex-selective abortions, and child marriage were about the *beliefs* of a society, and a rights-based approach, along with looking at the political and social systems that create difficult situations, also has to tackle changing social norms. It is about getting to issues at their source. Of course this is a fairly broad way of defining rights, but it draws on a rights analysis in the sense that it assumes the best way to promote rights is to prevent their violation in the first place, not to simply identify abuses and try to fix them after they happen.

A different UNICEF social policy specialist, looking particularly at issues of social exclusion, had a similar approach to what RBA meant to programming. This respondent said their key job was to "train the powerful to look at exclusion and powerlessness." How, they asked, can UNICEF build a process to help those who are powerless? Their focus was also on the *social structures* that put children in vulnerable situations. Another respondent used child labor as an example: to combat the problem, they said, you need to focus on the conditions that force families to have their children work just to survive. "Change society," they suggested, "to create a protective environment."[18] "Inclusion" and "identity" also "permeate everything," the respondent said, which allows a focus on the most excluded groups and how social structures continue that exclusion. Another Child Protection officer stated that they felt RBA meant "you are trying to change the mindsets of power structures;"[19] RBA necessitated both a strong connection between programming and the CRC and an effort to strengthen government systems for Child Protection.

How do these attitudes toward programming play out in practice? One central legal element used by UNICEF is India's adoption, in 2010, of an "Integrated Child Protection Scheme" (ICPS) under the auspices of the Ministry of Women and Children of the India Government (Deb, 2013, pp. 195–197). According to the Ministry, ICPS "articulates the rights agenda for the development of children" (Ministry of Women and Child Development, n.d., p. 2). As with other legislation considered in this volume—such as Right to Information and Right to Education laws—UNICEF staff insisted they were active in supporting ICPS but did so quietly and "behind the scenes." ICPS was created by the government to address what were perceived as glaring problems in the legal protective environment, including limited focus on preventing abuse; a lack of coordination among various government bodies; inadequate services, infrastructure, and personnel; and weak accountability and monitoring (Ministry of Women and Child Development, n.d., pp. 6–7). UNICEF's Child Protection strategy worldwide emphasizes legal reform and the creation of a protective environment by government agencies. Helping create ICPS was a key priority to move UNICEF toward this goal.

Interviews with UNICEF staff show that they consider supporting the ICPS as a key priority, perhaps *the* key priority. Speaking of implementation of ICPS, a respondent noted two challenges. First was the actual implementation of the scheme, considering the limited capacity available, limited resources, and limited "will" on the part of the government. The second was the problem of social change, which, the staff person said, was still central to the implementation of legal changes. Legal protection is not enough; attitudes and social structures must be addressed as well. It is worth noting, however, that one UNICEF staff person working closely with ICPS described its very existence as a rights policy since "child rights is about ensuring that every child is protected," yet noted also that "the accountability element is lacking."[20] The distinction between a "true" rights approach and one that is mostly focused on simple legal regulations was not always made clear. Protection of children was a right: therefore ICPS, with its legal status, was a rights-based strategy.

Several respondents here stated that there was, still, some resistance to rights language—partly because it was perceived as a "Western" ideal that was inappropriate in the Indian context, and partly due to its general unquantifiability. "If I call it 'this,'" said one, referring to rights language, "there is going to be a raising of eyebrows." Instead, "you camouflage the language."[21] Noted another, "we would like to go in [to community-level organizing] with human rights discourse," but "sometimes the human rights discourse is not the one we should use to break in . . . but it's a progressive process to start making the rights clear."[22] ICPS was a good example of how a rights approach was adjusted to make it politically palatable. A highly placed official stated that their strategy was to "Indianize" the argument for how ICPS should operate to make it seem indigenous rather than imposed from outside. It needed to appear more in keeping with domestic norms and needs. Referring to their cooperation with ICPS, this person said the strategy was to advocate for a direction the country "has already decided to go in" rather than push for policies that the government was not prepared to follow.[23] This "Indianization" was a political strategy to overcome resistance to outside pressure for human rights—another good indication that UNICEF programs were challenging entrenched political interests.

Along with the political challenges, the CP unit also addressed the problem of advocating RBA in an organization increasingly driven by the MDGs and results-based management. One UNICEF observer repeated the desire to see greater resources and also monitoring, noting that the monitoring efforts in ICPS were too focused on "outputs": it was, they said, about numbers, not the "quality element" addressing "whether children's rights are really being affected by these inputs."[24] Another UNICEF employee, on the same topic, noted "right now we're ninety percent outcome, ten percent approach" and said their top goal was to "reverse" that proportion.[25] The general sense was that the government still perceived legal protection as a matter of addressing violations rather than creating a "system" that prevented them in first place.

A true rights-based approach required focus on creating a culture of rights protection; yet that was resisted both by some within the Indian government, who perceived political meddling, and also some elements of UNICEF itself, intent on achieving easily measured goals rather than sweeping social change.

In cooperation with the government and civil society partners, and in the framework of the ICPS, the CP unit also tackles a variety of specific issues in India, including child labor, trafficking, and others mentioned previously. A handful of examples can be mentioned here. In Karnataka state, UNICEF supports a program to train police regarding children's rights issues; the goal is to both make them more aware of various children's rights laws and instruments and enhance their sensitivity to a child's psychological and social needs. In response to high-profile rape cases (before those of 2012–2013 that garnered particular international attention), UNICEF has been supporting the "ENDviolence" campaign initiative to create a more protective social environment for girl children in particular. It has worked to build capacity and awareness to fight child labor among employers and has cooperated with Ikea and other businesses to fight the practice. Since 2008 in Rajasthan state, UNICEF has cooperated with the government and civil society partners to bring at-risk girls to school by employing various interventions, such as providing transportation, working with Panchayat leaders on the school environment, and providing "out of the box" tools to teachers to improve the school environment.

A few high-profile examples, however, illustrate the work that needs to be done in completing the move to a rights-based approach in CP. One respondent used the issue of child trafficking in India—particularly from Bangladesh—as an example of where UNICEF had tried to move itself and the Government of India past an intervention policy and toward one that takes rights seriously. Trafficking of women and girls into India from Bangladesh stems from a variety of causes, from prostitution to the shortage of women in India due to sex-selective abortion (discussed in Chapter 5) (Nair & Sen, 2005, pp. 17–18). The respondent pointed out that while the government had taken a policy largely based on *prevention* of child trafficking through law enforcement, "our focus is to put the procedure in place with a child-centered focus."[26] This meant a focus on training police regarding the legal rights of women and children and on international human rights norms in the area. The police, the UNICEF staff person said, "don't understand" rights standards and are interested only in the issues of the criminal laws against trafficking: "They need 'what do I do?' information," regarding how to take a rights-based approach. In specific terms, this meant respecting girls' "entitlement to access to justice" and "procedures that respect international principles." The respondent cited efforts by UNICEF, Save the Children, Catholic Relief Services, and local partners to create "community vigilance groups" to both fight the attitudes that allow trafficking and help in the repatriation of trafficked women and girls. Repatriation is a particularly important issue since this is a vital step missing from a purely "law enforcement" approach that simply arrests those responsible, leaving the women open to further exploitation.

Approaching child labor (see Das, 2011; Weiner, Burra, & Bajpai, 2007) offers other insights into both the approach taken and more political ramifications of a rights-based approach. Child labor in India, for example, is illegal only for children under the age of 14; but UNICEF's CP officers have challenged this as inadequate, wanting children under 18 to be protected. When UNICEF first started talking about child labor issues, reports another UNICEF CP official, "we were told to keep it to this building" since the issue of child labor raised both political and economic problems. The CP expert recounted working hard on bonded labor (or *Jeetham*), for example, in Andhra Pradesh state. Simply presenting the elimination of child labor as a "right to childhood" issue was met with skepticism and a lack of understanding. Instead, the rights issue, to be politically effective, had to be linked to other, more concrete and palatable priorities. So, for example, gathering data on the number of bonded laborers, or statistics linking it with caste or gender, helped solidify the issue and make the rights argument into something that seemed less foreign and imposed. One interviewee identified strategies for promoting protection of those 14 to 17 years old, including data collection and a *judicious* use of media: "We do not talk to the government through the media," they said, but data can be shared with the government and then discussed with media and NGO partners in a way that does not "surprise" government officials but does put pressure on them. The UNICEF staff person leading this effort told of a ten-year effort to gather data, build NGO coalitions, and sensitize government officials. They also told of being threatened by a textile factory owner and knowing of a government official whose car was bombed by people profiting from child labor! UNICEF and its partners were able to show that girls in particular were often employed in hazardous sectors in Andhra Pradesh and also the connection with caste and tribal status.[27] Here, too, the creation and mobilization of self-help groups was cited as a way of changing community attitudes while also reframing a problem—child and bonded labor—in rights terms rather than legal ones.

It is useful here to point out that for all these efforts, UNICEF's influence in India is quite limited. "Politically," said one CP specialist, "we aren't really a force the government is worried about . . . this is your sandbox [is the government's attitude], you can play there."²⁸ Another official put it more optimistically. "You have to be modest" when talking with the government: the government does "treat the UN with respect," but it also has a level of pride that makes overt cooperation in the rights area difficult. UNICEF recognizes, this person said, that "we can't transform" a government and country the size of India, but it remains a mission to both change attitudes about Child Protection issues and to sensitize officials.²⁹ A number of government respondents, while polite about their relationship with the UN, also admitted that they felt they were able to largely pursue their agenda without UN help or that the UN provided only technical assistance rather than new ideas.

Conflict Zones

To really get an impression both of what UNICEF is doing that is new and different and of the political implications of RBA at the extreme, it is worth looking in detail at UNICEF's work in conflict zones in India. Leaving aside the tension along the Indian-Pakistani border—a particularly sensitive area from which UN bodies are almost entirely excluded by the Indian government—India contains a number of areas where the government is battling relatively low-level civil conflicts. Often these conflicts are against Naxalite movements: a term used to cover a variety of political insurgencies, often with a Marxist or Maoist political agenda, but also often based on tribal or local political grievances, and even banditry (Mehrotra, 2012, 2014). Eastern India is particularly affected by Naxalite and other violence, which is usually in rural areas and those populated by Scheduled Tribes (S. P. Dash, 2006, p. 97).

UNICEF's work in conflict zones raises particularly sensitive political issues. The way it has handled those issues also says a great deal about how it perceives the role of rights in programming. The Indian government is very sensitive about these regions and prefers to be able to operate there with a free hand rather than under the gaze of international agencies. When speaking about rights to UNICEF staff in the Chhattisgarh state field office, an office directly working in the regions of Naxalite conflict in the Bastar District of South Chhattisgarh (Sundar, 2006), the first thing mentioned is usually the fact that UNICEF operates there *at all*. While staff will certainly point out that they consider it normal and natural that UNICEF should be functioning in conflict zones—its job, after all, is to protect and help children, wherever they may be—there is also an awareness that they operate in a very politically sensitive area. This in itself demonstrated, to them, UNICEF's commitment to rights, since it was the child rights mission ("all children, everywhere") that allowed UNICEF to argue that they needed to be working in these areas. Their justification for pushing the limits of what the government might tolerate is that children have *rights*, and UNICEF's job is to be sure those rights are respected. In this case, RBA is less about an *approach* to programing than a justification for a more muscular, or overtly political, approach to programming. But it clearly feeds a perception in UNICEF, and provides a rhetorical tool, that UNICEF should be operating wherever it is needed, not just where the government would like it to be helping.

No UNICEF staff said that the Government of India actually tried to stop them from functioning in conflict areas (again, other than in Jammu and Kashmir, which is a very particular situation), but a lot of care is needed. A visit to these regions reveals just how cautious the staff is, yet also how much pride is taken in their efforts to navigate the tricky political terrain. An excellent example of this terrain has, again, to do with the language used by UN agencies: in particular, referring to areas like Chhattisgarh as "conflict zones" at all. A staff member in New Delhi explained that UNICEF studiously avoided using the term "war" in any documents, instead using formulations like "children in areas affected by violence," to assuage government sensitivities. Another member of the field staff put it differently: "For the government, we say 'left-wing extremism'"; in official documents, "civil strife"; and internally, "civil unrest."[30] Another respondent pointed out that the Government of India has avoided any reference to the Convention on the Rights of the Child's optional protocol on children in armed conflict (Coomaraswamy, 2010), insisting that they are not involved in any conflicts and that it therefore does not apply.[31]

Another UNICEF official explained that India is annually listed by the UN Secretary-General's office as an "area of concern" for children involved in armed conflict: this respondent stated quite clearly that the Indian government considers UNICEF responsible for getting it named to that list, yet has not "blamed" it or otherwise taken action against UNICEF. The respondent went on to claim that UNICEF had not even cleared it with the Government of India before taking that action, which was itself, they thought, a fairly bold decision by UNICEF and indicative of the importance they put on the CRC and rights obligations in general.[32] Another local Chhattisgarh official seemed to make much the same point when describing the attitude of top UNICEF leadership early on: "Do your own thing, but don't make a song and dance of it" was how they described their instructions from country headquarters in

New Delhi.³³ The district office was told to do what they needed to do to help children in the conflict zone without publicity and without drawing attention to themselves.

So UNICEF has not been hesitant about operating in conflict zones despite the political landscape, and in Chhattisgarh, for example, the UNICEF Country Director has been directly involved in promoting children's rights. Chhattisgarh was only formed as a separate state in 2000 (before that, it was a region of Madhya Pradesh state), and UNICEF soon after created an office in Raipur, the capitol, to work more directly in the regions. In 2006 UNICEF was invited to work with internally displaced persons as a result of the Naxalite conflict; according to staff, this was used as an "entry point" to gradually move into a more direct political role. "We . . . have credibility," as one interview subject said; UNICEF has "the faith and trust" of the government through its years of work in the region, "so they respect us . . . today, we don't shy away from saying unpleasant things to them," although it was emphasized that these "unpleasant things" are said carefully. The staff relates stories about traveling—rather bravely, by their telling—to conflict areas, protected primarily by the goodwill of their UNICEF vehicles, and being perceived as honest brokers by all sides of the conflict. By 2009 UNICEF felt confident enough in its work to move to "more difficult areas" even within the primary conflict regions.³⁴

So, what is new here in RBA compared to service-provision models? Within the conflict areas, RBA focuses first on community engagement in the development process and a concern for the most vulnerable populations. There is not, however, a really explicit emphasis on civil and political rights, and conversations with field staff show even more reluctance to address C&P rights than in overall programming by UNICEF or other agencies. ICPS does guide UNICEF's work here, too. "Child rights protection committees" have been promoted, along with other forms of community engagement, to advance children's rights and give more community voice and power to the process. The Chhattisgarh office has also implemented a model of "child reporters" (also being tried in other regions) in which children are trained to act as journalists reporting on the rights situation in their regions—a way of empowering children as well as increasing transparency and accountability among duty-bearers. When asked specifically about civil and political rights, area staff mentioned a few issues that more clearly involve RBA: these include pressing for the right of children to learn in their native language, and pressuring the government to keep children under 18 out of "hazardous situations" as part of the larger right of children under 18 to be exempt from military service. Respondents repeatedly also cited their efforts to work through and with local civil society organizations; Chhattisgarh has a vibrant civil society sector, and UNICEF has worked to engage them in helping children in conflict zones and elsewhere.[35]

One interesting priority has been to create schools as "zones of peace" within the conflict area. An aspect of this is convincing the Indian military to move away from schools: school buildings are often the tallest and most solid buildings in a region, and they or their grounds get used as barracks or observation posts by the military; this, in turn, scares children away from schools, makes the schools targets of the Naxalites, and opens girls in particular to abuse by soldiers as they try to go to school. Simply moving the military away from these areas is perceived as creating a child-safe environment, one key part of the CRC.

Building on the "every child, everywhere" principle incorporated into UNICEF planning, UNICEF must not only operate in safe zones and in camps for the internally displaced—where much of its early work on children in conflict zones was one—but also in Naxal-controlled areas also. This, in turn, means pressuring the government for access to these areas, when the government would rather not grant it, and navigating the complex political terrain this entails.[36] New Delhi headquarters itself decided to expand out from the camps, for example, because of the every child, everywhere principle and because to work only in the camps would have been perceived as tacit support for the government over the Naxalites. It would have meant UNICEF was working only for those children in zones where government supporters lived. Here again, however, the strategy was to act with tacit government support but not be seen as working arm in arm with the government, and definitely not to talk to the police or security forces in any direct manner. It was, said one respondent, important not to appear to be a tool of the government; yet, it was equally important not to be viewed as directly negotiating with the Naxalites either.[37] It has helped that most UNICEF local staff are from the region and are able to understand its subtleties; still, the staff was "taking risks" (both politically and physically), and the New Delhi office understood and supported their risk-taking.

Speaking with UNICEF staff in Chhattisgarh and working in the conflict regions of the South, a few things become obvious. UNICEF has been cautious but determined in its efforts, starting around 2006, to move out of the camps and government-controlled zones and to cover children in all parts of the state. They have done so with a careful eye on the politics of the situation. And they have done so in a way that defies the Government of India's policy of denying that it faces a conflict in these areas—UNICEF's policies are quite specifically aimed at the problems of children in a conflict zone—but not openly challenging the government's policies (see also Human Rights Watch, 2008).

When asked about the "rights" component rather than service delivery, a few answers are repeated. First, as we have seen, the mere act of determinedly working across conflict lines is itself a rights policy. Second, addressing the particular needs of children in conflict areas—their need for psychological and physical support, their need to be protected from violence, and the problem of providing quality care in such hard-to-reach regions—are part of a rights-based approach. Third, it is true that many of these interventions are done cautiously and therefore are not as fully rights-based (defined casually) as they might be in areas that do not have as many challenges. That said, many of the specifics of working in the conflict zone are sometimes confused regarding the meaning of human rights and RBA. There are, as always, answers about how simply providing an education is a "right to education" policy, and that sort of thing. It was in relation to schools in Bastar that "sports days" for children was mentioned as a rights-based policy: promoting sports leads to better self-esteem and helps children recover from the trauma of the surrounding violence, and since this is a part of their right to a healthy (mental) environment, sports days become a component of RBA. However, other, much more thoughtful answers are also provided. The UNICEF staff remains concerned about sexual violence and abuse against children committed by soldiers, who, as mentioned, are often stationed in or near schools. Getting the military to withdraw from school grounds might not be a C&P rights issue per se, but it certainly involves UNICEF in areas much trickier and more political than the issue of child sports. All in all, the key issue remains protecting children's civil rights in the face of conflict and political repression, an area they cautiously but insistently enter.

Other Programming Areas

For the sake of space, it makes some sense to group some of the more "technical" issues in a single section here. Many of the same considerations that were central to the education issue repeat in other of these fields; but it is worth considering the extent to which RBA truly percolates into these areas and how.

What emerges from the examination of RBA in the fields of Nutrition, Health, HIV/AIDS, and Water and Sanitation, perhaps more than any other observation, is the continuing, even magnified, unevenness of how the idea of rights is perceived. So, for example, one department head—a very high-ranking official, whose department can't be identified or even hinted at for obvious reasons—began our interview by stating they didn't think UNICEF was doing much on rights in *any* operational category, much less their own.[38] Another department head stated that the idea of rights mattered to their department, but that their budget was too limited to afford to hire a rights specialist.[39] A third department head insisted that rights were important but defined them as encompassing everything from "holding duty-bearers accountable," to focusing on equity, to challenging entrenched power structures.[40] The clear impression given from interviews with various department heads and others—including Education!—was of an organization still working out the details of what RBA meant.

Another difficult issue that seemed common to the more technical areas in general (again including education) was the tension, already referred to, between results-based management and rights-based programming. Results-based management is defined by the UN as "a management strategy by which all actors on the ground, contributing directly or indirectly to achieving a set of development results, ensure that their processes, products and services contribute to the achievement of desired results (outputs, outcomes and goals)" (UNDP, 2011, p. 1). RBM aims to create, in the UN development family, nothing less than a "results culture" that emphasizes a project life-cycle built around real, measurable results and management accountability for achieving those results. This has become steadily more important in a UN environment that, in the past, had trouble demonstrating results and had been open to criticism about wasted money and failed projects. Several interview subjects worried that an emphasis on measurable inputs and results undermined the effort to promote human rights and to fully implement RBA (official documents deny this: see United Nations High Commission for Human Rights, 2006, p. 31). The two priorities were seen as working in opposition to each other: rights are difficult to quantify, are about long-term change, and have a moral component as well as an economic one. Yet pressure to show measurable inputs and quick, statistically significant outputs pushed programming back to traditional programs that had easy-to-measure inputs and outputs. A "blind devotion to process"[41] was the summation of one staff person regarding RBM. On the other hand, another department head was more optimistic. Good process, they argued, was essential, as it brought together all concerned parties to a program they can agree on. Yet even this person argued that where there was a crisis, it might not be possible to wait "until everyone is on board."

New Delhi and New York want *process* and *results*, but sometimes they are not compatible.[42]

Still, there were various strategies for implanting RBA, which often were similar among the various departments—although, at times, not as similar as one might expect, suggesting that each program was thinking independently about how to approach the issues. A staff member in HIV/AIDS worried that the "medical response" had "hijacked" the HIV/AIDS response throughout the UN family, leaving little room for rights issues—although they did also state that the Joint United Nations Programme on HIV/AIDS (UNAIDS) had a more rights-based set of principles that had not "percolated down" yet to other agencies.[43] Staff complained the government "does not think in terms of a rights-based approach."[44] Both government and UNICEF efforts, they felt, were still dominated by the standard medical approach to HIV/AIDS of preventing mother-to-child transmission, pediatric care and treatment, protection of children affected by AIDS, and prevention of infection among adolescents and young people (the "Four P Approach"; UNICEF, 2011). Still, the goal was to do more work correlating deprivation and discrimination with HIV/AIDS transmission, making a case on nondiscrimination rights for more work with these groups. Staff also pointed to work done by the National Aids Control Organization—a key partner in India—to defend the rights of those who have been kicked out of school or refused hospital admission on the basis of HIV status. And there is an effort to address stigmas in society regarding HIV/AIDS as part of an overall strategy. The dominant approach, staff thought, was a "charity approach": "Oh, look at these poor people with disease, lets help them" was how it was described.[45]

Similarly, a Nutrition staff person described asking, "Who are the most vulnerable?" as a starting point for approaching RBA: the "equity agenda," this person said, brings together the various issues involved in a rights-based approach. To "progressively operationalize rights," you start with the hardest to reach and most vulnerable.[46] Tribal children, in particular, identified as among the very worst off, were to be the focus of the 2013–2017 program. Staff in a field office had the same approach: RBA to them meant, first and foremost, disaggregating data, finding the most vulnerable, and making sure they were being served. One field office staff, like nearly every other nutrition official, spent a lot of time talking about the political implications of India's appalling malnutrition rates (for competing views on this see Panagariya, 2012; Vishita, Keyur, & Harshil, 2013). In a country where nearly half of all Indian children suffer from at least some level of malnutrition, they said, one "does not think in terms of a rights based approach," but instead the focus was on equity.[47] Their point was that such intense problems required first a focus on basic service provision. It became clear, however, that many other nutrition sector staff see these figures as *necessarily* political: "I do talk about rights," another field staff person said. "This is a fundamental right of children." They continued, "I've never had anyone complain when I say eight million severely malnourished children is a rights violation." Nutrition, this well-placed staff person said, must become a political issue. Rather than appearing to be worried about the political implications of a rights-based approach, they said the key challenge was to create a political debate around nutrition issues.

Health sector staff also spoke a great deal about changing paradigms: they mentioned, for example, moving from a "build a clinic and we're done" model to one where "people demand their rights"[48] (again this phrase of demanding rights!) but lacked specific notions of what this meant in terms of practical changes. Although officials in the Disasters section freely admitted that they were "still figuring out" what RBA meant to them, "equity" and reaching "the most vulnerable" (those under five years old, senior citizens, pregnant and lactating mothers) were important, along with caste: "We have to deal with these issues of services . . . to reach those who are normally bypassed by normal development practices."[49] The Emergencies sector staff take on the government's approach was that they "paid lip service" to these ideals, that "it's easier" to "say, provide rice to everyone!" than to say "help women or the physically challenged first." A UNICEF official working on Water and Sanitation at the state level also mentioned using data to uncover discrepancies in coverage. Conversations with C4D staff turned up a similar focus on equity and helping the most vulnerable.

Decentralization of decision-making and giving "voice" and "participation" to those affected by projects is also a constant theme of what makes a rights-based approach rather than a more traditional one in programming. Not much has been said in this section about UNICEF's work in promoting decentralized planning and implementation, which parallels the work being done by UNDP (as described in some Chapter 3), but this informs much of how traditional programming is converted into RBA. So, for example, conversations with several state staff personnel brought up a comprehensive set of ideas for decentralizing decision-making and involving community members, NGOs, and Panchayats, among other actors. In Water and Sanitation, the UNICEF office is mobilizing women's groups to demand better sanitation services, on the premise that women's dignity demands more attention to provision of latrines; in the Health sector, as well as Sanitation, there is a focus on working with village Health and Sanitation Committees to demand better health care as an entitlement (UNICEF, 2009b, pp. 20–21). Female PRI members are also being recruited into grassroots efforts at empowerment; staff focused on their efforts, for example, to involve women PRI members in the creation of district planning in the health sector. Similar efforts to involve local voices with the National Rural Health Mission—a 2005 government initiative to aid the health sector in target regions of the country—are also a priority: "No District Collector can say no" to these local initiatives, according to a key UNICEF state organizer.[50] Speaking on nutrition, cooperation with local civil society organizations was brought up, and in particular those active in the "right to food" movement (see Srivastava & Tiwary, 2009). Staff stressed the need to connect nutrition interventions with other rights issues—particularly the right to life. "At all levels," a local staff member said, "sensitization to rights are taking place ... we build and continue to build [local government's] capacity to talk about ... rights."[51] The HIV/AIDS department also cited participation as a key issue for them, used to "overcome social norms" not "head on" but by finding "acceptable solutions" from civil society and grassroots partners.[52]

Another staff member working on HIV/AIDS discussed the need to address difficult, societal causes of the spread of the infection. "There's a complex reason why they are where they are," a "society issue that requires huge social change."[53] They expressed their opinion—very much not for attribution, as they made clear in the interview, since it was so highly critical of the government—about the politics of HIV/AIDS in India. This staff person expressed frustration at the pace with which the Indian government had been implementing programs to encourage treatment, during pregnancy and into the breastfeeding stage, to prevent mother-child transmission of HIV. They cited bureaucratic disorganization, foot-dragging, and lack of resources. The solution, as they saw it, was efforts by UNICEF to mobilize communities through UNICEF's cooperation with civil society organizations to build demand for these services. "Are we going to wait another decade until literacy levels are high enough for people to understand their rights and make demands?" this person asked; "we must accelerate the process."[54] Pilot programs being created were intended to bring government and CSOs together to better create demand for social services.

An anecdote from the Nutrition sector illustrates a similar point. Malnutrition, recall, has also been a substantial cause of embarrassment for the Indian government, and, according to the UNICEF staff person in one interview, the government responded by simply refusing to conduct more comprehensive nutrition surveys. The nutrition sector, however, wanted more data, and in particular sought a study that "listened to mother's voices" as a way of combining advocacy and empowerment. The solution was to support an indigenous NGO, the Naandi Foundation ("Naandi" is Sanskrit for "new beginning"), in conducting its own study, which was released in 2011 as the HUNGaMA Survey Report (Naandi Foundation, 2011). As the interviewee tells it, UNICEF was politically not in a position to do a report on malnutrition, given the political sensitivity, and couldn't even commission another agency to do it; in fact, UNICEF's name is hardly mentioned in the report. There was, according to the staff member, no memorandum of understanding and no financial transaction; "We didn't ask them to do it, but we made sure it was done well."[55] The ultimate goal was political mobilization and a demand for rights—in this case, the right to food and proper nutrition—to move from a service-based to rights-based approach.

Conclusions

The UNICEF office in India is large: it involves a number of programming areas and also several "cross-cutting" priorities such as decentralization and child rights. This complexity makes any single, simple analysis of its work very complicated. However, few general trends can be derived from how UNICEF thinks about the meaning of a rights-based approach.

First of all, it would be naïve not to focus on the fact that much of what is mentioned as part of a "rights-based approach" in UNICEF remains as much rhetorical as practical. Much of what UNICEF does remains very technical and practical: distributing nutrition supplements, immunizing children, and providing training on proper sanitation techniques. Discussions with UNICEF staff—particularly outside the CP unit—uncovers a lot of discussion about "rights" that doesn't move much beyond a reformulation of what UNICEF is already doing. Thus many staff reply to questions about RBA by talking about "making food a right," or "holding duty-bearers accountable for providing education," without a great deal of discussion about how to move this past a more typical service-provision model. The interventions are the same, but the rhetoric is shifted. In some ways, staff members are quite serious in seeing this as an important shift: in their mind, this means that people have a rhetorical tool they can use to help make a recalcitrant government more responsive; however, in other ways it changes very little. The programming is the same, only how it is sold to officials is different.

Beyond that, clearly the most common programmatic change is the deliberate, determined effort to disaggregate data to show gaps in equity. This, too, places the primary responsibility on UNICEF: it often retains a service-provision model but does so in a way that recognizes the problem of marginalized groups. The "right" most commonly mentioned by staff in interviews was the "right to have a certain service": it remains the "right to nutrition," for example, but with the added question of what specific groups are being discriminated against. That includes, of course, the issue of whether people's right to equal treatment and nondiscrimination is being violated, but typically this is considered less than the question of whether duty-bearers are being fair in their treatment of underserved groups.

It is also important to keep in mind UNICEF's cross-cutting priorities, particularly promoting decentralization and citizen participation. Decentralization was dealt with extensively in Chapter 3; UNICEF's policies of promoting this are similar, as are its efforts to develop the capacity of local governance. UNICEF staff reports the same mixture of acceptance and resistance among local officials that UNDP staff does. One governance expert in particular noted the problem of "elite capture" of local governing bodies as something to be overcome and that decentralization should also involve promoting "child participation" in the decisions that affect their lives, as stipulated by the CRC. Participation is "a vehicle for children to be aware of their rights and entitlements," he said. He also stated that *resistance* to child participation varied: "Our strategy is to identify people who support it and work with them."[56] The resistance, several UNICEF staff noted, was at the local level, not national; this response was similar to what UNDP staff reported.

Overall, the UNICEF experience once again shows that the level of rights promotion and integration varies depending on programmatic area, but, that in certain areas, there is a good-faith effort to think through the rights implications of UNICEF's work. This comports with the overall thesis of this work: that international bureaucracies like UNICEF are large and flexible, and they have the ability to change in accordance with new priorities, albeit unevenly. UNICEF's priorities have remained largely stable: promoting education, child health and nutrition, a healthy environment, reform of systems to protect vulnerable children, and other traditional program areas. The way they are interpreted in light of RBA, however, varies in both type and effectiveness. Still, there are enough good efforts to really change how UNICEF's work is being done, and what is being pursued, to show how seriously the idea of rights and programming is being taken.

References

Alston, P. (2005). Ships Passing in the Night: The Current State of the Human Rights and Development Debate Seen Through the Lens of the Millennium Development Goals. *Human Rights Quarterly, 27*(3), 755–829.

Alston, P., & Bhuta, N. (2005). Human Rights and Public Goods: Education as a Fundamental Right in India. In P. Alston & M. Robinson (Eds.), *Human Rights and Development: Towards Mutual Reinforcement* (pp. 242–268). New York: Oxford University Press.

Beigbeder, Y. (2001). *New Challenges for UNICEF: Children, Women and Human Rights*. New York: Palgrave.

Coomaraswamy, R. (2010). The Optional Protocol to the Convention on the Rights of the Child on the Involvement of Children in Armed Conflict—Towards Universal Ratification. *International Journal of Children's Rights, 18*(4), 535–549.

Das, D. (2011). *Child Labor in India: Rights, Wefare and Protection*. New Delhi: Deep and Deep.

Dash, L. N. (Ed.) (2010). *Education and Inclusive Development in India*. New Delhi: Regal.

Dash, S. P. (2006). *Naxal Movement and State Power*. New Delhi: Sarup & Sons.

Deb, S. (2013). Socio-legal Measures for Protection of Child Rights in India: A Review. In R. N. Srivastava, R. Seth, & J. van Niekerk (Eds.), *Child Abuse and Neglect: Challenges and Opportunities* (pp. 193–205). New Delhi: Jaypee Brothers.

Ghosh, B. (2009). Trafficking in Women and Children in India: Nature, Dimensions, and Strategies for Prevention. *International Journal of Human Rights, 13*(5), 716–738.

Gohain, M. P. (2011, 9 December). Gov-Unicef Drafts National Vision for Girls' Education. *Times of India*.

Govinda, R., & Diwan, R. (Eds.). (2003). *Community Participation and Empowerment in Primary Education*. London: Sage.

Hulme, D. (2010). *Lessons from the Making of the MDGs: Human Development Meets Results-based Management in an Unfair World*. Sussex, UK: Institute for Development Studies.

Human Rights Watch. (2008). *Dangerous Duty: Children and the Chhattisgarh Conflicxt*. New York: Human Rights Watch.

Kalyanpur, M. (2008). Equality, Quality and Quantity: Challenges in Inclusive Education Policy and Service Provision in India. *International Journal of Inclusive Education, 12*(3), 243–262.

Kaufmann, D. (2004). *Human Rights and Governance: The Empirical Challenge*. New York: New York University School of Law.

Kington, G. G. (2007). The Progress of School Education in India. *Oxford Review of Economic Policy, 23*(2), 168–195.

Kumar, R. (Ed.) (2006). *The Crisis of Elementary Education in India*. London: Sage.

Langford, M., Sumner, A., & Yamin, A. E. (2013). Introduction. In M. Langford, A. Sumner, & A. E. Yamin (Eds.), *The Millennium Development Goals and Human Rights: Past, Present, and Future* (pp. 1–34). New York: Cambridge University Press.

Mehrotra, S. (2012). The Cost and Financing of the Right to Education in India: Can We Fill the Financing Gap? *International Journal of Educational Development*, 32(1), 65–71.

Mehrotra, S. (Ed.) (2014). *Countering Naxalism with Development: Challenges of Social Justice and State Security*. Thousand Oaks, CA: Sage.

Mellahi, K., Morrell, K., & Wood, G. (2010). *The Ethical Business: Challenges and Controversies*: Palgrave MacMillan.

Ministry of Women and Child Development. (N.d.). *The Integrated Child Protection Scheme (ICPS)–A Centrally Sponsored Scheme of Government–Civil Society Partnership*. Retrieved from http://www.crin.org/docs/1._the_integrated_child_protection_scheme_icps.pdf.

Mohanty, A. K. (2009). Multilingualism of the Unequals and Predicaments of Education in India: Mother Tongue or Other Tongue? In O. Garia, T. Skutnabb-Kangas, & M. E. Torres-Guzman (Eds.), *Imagining Multilingual Schools: Languages in Education and Globalization* (pp. 262–283). Tonawanda, NY: Multilingual Matters.

Naandi Foundation. (2011). *The HUNGaMA Survey Report–2011*. Retrieved from http://naandi.org/HungamaBKDec11LR.pdf.

Nair, P. M., & Sen, S. (2005). *Trafficking in Women and Children in India*. New Delhi: Orient Longman.

Oestreich, J. (2010). UNICEF: A Human Rights Agency? In D. P. Forsythe (Ed.), *Encyclopedia of Human Rights*. New York: Oxford University Press.

Panagariya, A. (2012). *The Myth of Child Malnutrition in India*. Retrieved from http://academiccommons.columbia.edu/catalog/ac:156283.

Pattnaik, J. (2004). A Critical Examination of India's National Language Policy in Primary Education. In O. N. Saracho & B. Spodek (Eds.), *Contemporary Perspectives on Languaeg Policy and Literacy Instruction in Early Childhood Education* (pp. 181–215). Charlotte: Information Age.

Sridhar, K. K. (1996). Language in Education: Minorities and Multilingualism in India. *International Review of Education*, 42(4), 327–347.

Sripati, V., & Thiruvengadam, A. K. (2004). India: Constitutional Amendment Making the Right to Education a Fundamental Right. *International Journal of Constitutional Law*, 2(1), 148–158.

Srivastava, A. K., & Tiwary, M. (Eds.). (2009). *The Right to Food*. New Delhi: Human Rights Law Network.

Sundar, N. (2006). Bastar, Maoism and Salwa Judum. *Economic and Political Weekly*, 41(29), 3187–3192.

UNICEF. (1986). *Children in Especially Difficult Circumstances* (E/ICEF/1986/L.3). New York: UNICEF.

UNICEF. (2007). *A Human Rights Based Approach to Education*. New York: UNICEF.
UNICEF (2008). *Country Programme Action Plan 2008–2012*. New York: UNICEF.
UNICEF. (2009a). *Child Friendly Schools*. New York: UNICEF.
UNICEF. (2009b). *Community Approaches to Total Sanitation*. New York: UNICEF.
UNICEF. (2011). *Thematic Discussion on Results and Lessons Learned in the Medium-Term Strategic Plan Focus Area 3: Children and AIDS*. New York: UNICEF.
UNICEF-India. (2011). *India. Child Protection Basics*. New Delhi: UNICEF.
UNICEF-India. (2013a). *India Country Programme Document 2013–2017*. New Delhi: UNICEF.
UNICEF-India. (2013b). *Country Programme Action Plan 2013–2017*. New Delhi: UNICEF.
UNDP. (2009). *Human Rights and the Millennium Development Goals: Making the Link*. Oslo: UNDP Oslo Governance Center.
UNDP. (2011). *Results-based Management Handbook*. New York: UNDP.
UN High Commission for Human Rights. (2006). *Frequently Asked Questions on a Human Rights-based Approach to Development Cooperation*. New York: UNHCR.
Verger, A., & VanderKaaij, S. (2012). Global Policies: Public-Private Partnerships in Indian Education. In A. Verger, M. Novelli, & H. K. Altinyelken (Eds.), *Global Education Policy and International Development: New Agendas, Issues* (pp. 245–266). New York: Bloomsbury Academic.
Vishita, K., Keyur, U., & Harshil, G. (2013). Child Malnutriton in India: A Brief Review. *Asian Journal of Research in Social Sciences and Humanities*, *3*(9), 213–217.
Weiner, M., Burra, N., & Bajpai, A. (2007). *Born Unfree: Child Labour, Education, and the State in India*. New York: Oxford University Press.

5

Other UN Agencies Involved in Rights-based Approaches

THIS CHAPTER WILL look briefly at some of the other United Nations–affiliated agencies operating in India. In particular, it will focus on the World Bank (which, again, is not an agency of the UN but is in a formal legal relationship with the UN, and it is expected to uphold its principles and to participate in the UN Development Assistance Framework discussed earlier); UN Women; and the United Nations Population Fund (UNFPA). These agencies are chosen because they all are working on projects with a high degree of salience with rights-based approaches (RBA) and have extensive on-the-ground operations in India. Rather than going through all the work of these agencies—which in many instances parallels that of UNDP and UNICEF—each section will be content to focus on some specific elements of their work and to bring out relevant points about the politics of RBA in India. These largely build on what has been said before, but each agency is also different from UNDP and UNICEF, and thus interprets RBA differently. The World Bank is substantially larger, and, of course, a financial institution first and foremost; UN Women and UNFPA are much smaller, and their mandates are more malleable. Thus they show different, important aspects of how interpretation of RBA can depend on organizational type. It is not the case that all UN agencies see things the same way, and that is important.

The World Bank and Equity

This section will look at the World Bank Group's work in India. In particular, it will discuss the "equity agenda" that has guided much of the Bank's work and remains its central social priority. "Equity" was discussed briefly in Chapter 2, and many other UN agencies have taken note of its importance within a rights-based agenda. "The Bank's equity agenda" is a common phrase heard among staff in various agencies and also from Indian government officials and academics; the issue of equity consumes a great deal of time and attention in India as the country becomes wealthier. As for what equity actually means and how it is best attained, the World Bank is the thought leader, and others defer to its definition. It is important to see how equity—as opposed to equality—is conceived of as part of development and as a "right" to be promoted.

Despite being relegated to Chapter 5 of this work, the World Bank Group is the largest of the UN specialized or affiliated agencies operating in India and the most important by most metrics. The World Bank's country strategy for the 2013 to 2017 period expects annual commitments to India averaging about US$3billion. In 2014, India "graduated" from the World Bank's concessional International Development Agency (IDA) window, although it still qualifies for temporary, transitional lending from IDA (Kirk & Yadav, 2015). This marked the Bank's recognition of the enormous gains India has made in growing its economy and alleviating poverty (Kanbur, 2015, pp. 73–74). However, India currently risks hitting the overall US$17.5 billion limit for exposure of a single borrower, which could restrict its ability to borrow in the future. Yet even these sums are not terribly significant in a country the size of India, and the Bank's strategy recognizes that "World Bank Group finances will always be modest compared to India's Challenges," while noting that "support can be a catalyst for change at this crucial time" (World Bank, 2013a, p. 9).

The Bank's 2013–2017 plan of action makes only two mentions to a "rights-based approach to development," both times referencing India's own development strategy rather than any strategy adopted by the Bank itself. And there are no references at all to human rights per se. Even this, however, is an improvement over the 2009–2012 plan, which makes no mention of rights *at all* (other than property rights). In no way does this mean that the World Bank Group has no policy on human rights or on RBA; rather, it becomes clear when talking with Bank staff that there is an interest in rights, but that it is once again almost always spoken about in camouflaged terms—references to empowerment, decentralization, access to information, participation, and so forth. One Bank staff member, who was deeply interested in RBA, nevertheless insisted on speaking with me while strolling through New Delhi's beautiful Lodhi Gardens, which are located behind the World Bank's India headquarters; a decision clearly intended to prevent me from recording our conversation or taking notes. Not all Bank staff was equally cagey, but there was clearly more reluctance among Bank staff than that of UNDP, UNICEF, or UNFPA.

What accounts for this heightened reluctance? The Bank's plan of action notes approvingly of India's adoption of a "rights-based approach to development" and pledges its support for that approach, although it does not say that the Bank itself is using such an approach in its lending; and, if one looks at the Bank's vast portfolio of loans to India, work in areas related to RBA and social programs in general is a very small part of the overall portfolio. As will be discussed in below, some of the Bank's work—its support for decentralization and for the right to information, its desire to reach Scheduled Castes and Scheduled Tribes, and its focus on gender—certainly has a rights focus, which few in the Bank would deny. On the other hand, the World Bank has traditionally been nervous about taking on human rights issues. This nervousness stems from its basic mandate, which is to promote development and to steer clear of anything that would seem overtly "political." A human rights agenda is seen by many within the staff as violating that mandate (Cahn, 1993; Clark, 2002; Darrow, 2003; Lawyers Committee for Human Rights, 1995). On the other hand, the Bank is expected to respect the principles of the UN Charter and decisions of the Security Council, among other bodies, and thus should be supporting human rights as well as development (Shihata, 1988). These competing priorities have led to some confusion about exactly what the World Bank is expected to do in this area. Adding to this confusion is that the World Bank has been accused, often and vociferously, of actively *undermining* human rights in developing countries in a variety of ways—funding infrastructure projects that displace people, ignoring the needs of indigenous populations, propping up corrupt and repressive regimes, and many other activities (Bello, 1994; Easterly, 2015; Hancock, 1994).

The World Bank's current strategic partnership with the Indian government is fairly vague and general about the work to be done; any effort to reduce such a large portfolio into a single strategy will require a lot of condensing. The Country Partnership Strategy 2013–2017 identifies three priority areas:

- *Integration*, with a focus on knitting the country and various industries together through infrastructure improvement, and also improving the business climate through legal reform and better human infrastructure.
- *Transformation* of outdated industries, better service delivery, and a change in urban areas in particular to cope with the rural-urban migration that is accelerating in India.

- *Inclusion,* by promoting human development and social programs so that the most underserved, particularly Scheduled Castes, Scheduled Tribes, women, and other groups benefit from education, health care, sanitation, and other improvements.

It is important to see what these fairly broad ideas mean in practice. No other UN affiliated agency working in India is more focused on the traditional metrics of development—GNP growth, income generation, poverty alleviation, and Human Development indicators—than the World Bank, and "equitable" or "inclusive" growth is at the heart of all its work. Speaking with World Bank staff, it is clear that they do understand the rights implications of their work and, more importantly, that they care about incorporating RBA, even while disguising the language. And in many ways, the World Bank is working on rights issues covered in earlier chapters: it is, for example, active in support of Right to Information laws, governance reform, decentralization, and appropriate implementation of MGNREGA. Still, the stroll around Lodhi Gardens, with the expert on governance issues, demonstrated the sensitivity of these issues, as discussed already.

Equity, as mentioned, is a term used particularly by the World Bank, although one that has wide traction in all conversations about development in India (as well as beyond). It can seem almost impossible to talk in India about the future of economic development without discussing how the fruits of this development can be shared more equitable. (The other unavoidable topic is how India compares with China.) "Equity" means something different than "equality." There is no "right" to equality in terms of having equal resources or equal wealth, and no UN agency posits that there is. In international law (Franck, 1998, pp. 47–50), as in the Indian Constitution, equality refers to equal treatment, socially and before the law. Equity is different. The emphasis on equity is traced to the World Bank's 2006 *World Development Report*. That document defined equity this way: "By equity we mean that individuals should have equal opportunities to pursue a life of their choosing and be spared from extreme deprivation in outcomes" (World Bank, 2006, p. 2). According to the World Bank, equity does have an important political aspect, and one that specifically takes on existing power structures: "First, the best policies for poverty reduction could involve redistributions of influence, advantage, or subsidies away from dominant groups. Highly unequally distributed wealth associated with unduly concentrated political power can prevent institutions from enforcing broad-based personal and property rights, and lead to skewed pro-visioning of services and functioning of markets"

(World Bank, 2006, pp. 9–10). Similarly, Amartya Sen draws a crucial difference between "income inequality" and other things—"unemployment, ill health, lack of education, and social exclusion"—that hold people back from a fair shake in life (Sen, 1999, p. 108).

As the UN Assistance Framework puts it, however, "While Gross Domestic Product growth rates have been high, India also exhibits the paradox of high growth rates and high levels of poverty. Approximately 32% of the population lives below the poverty line and poverty is expected to rise in eight states" (UN-Government of India, 2013, p. 11). (The Reserve Bank of India [2015, p. 253] puts the number lower, at about 22%, and there is substantial debate about how poverty is to be measured; see Deaton & Kozel, 2005). The government has been accused of intentionally undercounting the poor by using its own, more restrictive definition of poverty (J. Ghosh, 2011).) As we have seen, malnutrition among children, according to UNICEF, approaches 50%, and roughly a quarter of the population remains illiterate. The World Bank 2013 planning document, while describing the remarkable economic growth in India over the past decade and praising the government for its policies, notes dryly that "India's rapid growth in the last decade has not benefitted everyone uniformly," and that the Gini coefficient—a measurement of consumption inequality—"is on the rise" (World Bank, 2013b, p. 11), although, at .34 it is not especially high by global standards. Helping to ensure that the benefits of India's economic growth were shared more equitably among the population was the issue that consumed more thought and space in the planning report than any other.

In international law, as in the Indian Constitution, equality refers to equal treatment, socially and before the law. This right to equality is well defined and well established in human rights law and has been central to what a RBA to development is about, as we have seen. Equity, however, is different. In interviews, many UN staff in India—in and outside the World Bank—stated that equity was a vital priority and referred specifically to what they called the "World Bank's equity agenda."

As Sofia Gruskin notes (in relation to health in particular, but intended to be generalizable), "equity ... is the absence of systematic disparities ... between groups with different levels of underlying social advantage/disadvantage—that is, wealth, power, or prestige. Inequities ... systematically put groups of people who are already socially disadvantaged (for example, by virtue of being poor, female, and/or members of a disenfranchised racial, ethnic, or religious group) at further disadvantage" (Gruskin & Braveman, 2003, p. 254). So equity—both as a philosophical matter and one for the Bank—is potentially as much political as economic where poverty reduction is concerned. "Empowering the poor," a Bank poverty expert said, with reference to Amartya Sen in particular, "is not uncontroversial."[1]

The argument here should be familiar after the preceding chapters: for the Bank, equity parallels RBA, even if it isn't called by that name, as it requires a look at the systemic forces that create and maintain unequal access to economic and social opportunity. A different Bank employee, also discussing Bihar, noted the importance of RTI implementation from the Bank's perspective;[2] not just to ensure government accountability, but also to use RTI requests as a way of gauging the effectiveness of policies aimed at promoting political empowerment.

How does "equity" fit in with "equality?" The Universal Declaration of Human Rights, of course, guarantees equality before the law, and equal rights to social services, to marriage and starting a family, to access to education, and other basic rights. Other UN documents promote equal rights in similar ways—the right not to be discriminated against, to be treated as a full citizen, to enjoy government services, and so forth. The World Bank often argues that severe inequality of income hinders economic growth; thus, inequality (and not just inequity) can be a "technical" issue, divorced from a question of rights or ethics: addressing equality can be seen as merely good development policy. Still, the link between inequality (an ostensibly economic issue) and inequity (a more obviously political and moral one) is made quite clear in a RBA, and they cannot be separated. Working for equality of rights should lead to greater equity; the equity agenda and RBA combines to recognize that much of the inequity in India is caused by discrimination and historical factors that will not go away on their own. Unequal distribution of wealth is not itself a rights violation; but severely lopsided distribution does not just cause slower growth, it also leads to violations of many other rights since it leaves so many powerless and without voice. Similarly, unequal wealth distribution becomes a rights matter when it is *caused by* discrimination and political powerlessness—it is to be fought against because it is a cause and an effect of systemic violations of human rights. The two issues are, of course, intimately linked, and thus must be attacked together. Thus the "equity agenda" is unmistakably a rights agenda, even if it is not always framed that way.

Dealing with equity issues and inclusion, Bank staff reports many of the same frustrations and challenges that staff in other organizations face. "As staff we must be apolitical," one told me. This staff person complained that a new government had been recently elected in Uttar Pradesh state, complicating their work. "When I pushed this issue [before a recent state election] I could just talk about excluded groups. Now I have to be more cautious."³ This person went on to say, "In India, the Bank does not use rights language at all"; World Bank headquarters in Washington, DC, spoke of rights, they said, but "gender justice, justice for the poor, are terms that we use now."⁴

Approaches to "equity" run across the various programs within the World Bank. The list of Bank-sponsored projects, again, is vast, and it is impossible to go through them all here. Those Bank programs specifically targeted at the very poor have a large equity component, as expected. Conversations with Bank staff brought forward a fairly nuanced idea of what equity would mean in an antipoverty program. Raising incomes, of course, and doing so in a way that targets "the poorest of the poor" is part of it. So, for example, the "Bihar Rural Livelihoods Project" in India's second-poorest state, a US$70 million project to (according to the project's website) "help poor farmers climb out of debt, become entrepreneurs, claim electricity and roads, and access government food and employment programs." A social exclusion study sponsored by the Bank and done in conjunction with the Asian Development Institute found:

> Rural landless and those belonging to the Scheduled Caste community form [an] integral part of poverty stricken and marginalized groups. Access to education and other capacity building inputs, sources of production, technology and institutions define and determine level of poverty as they are important tools to ensure access and control over opportunity and productive assets. . . .
>
> The poor have restricted access to social and economic opportunities as the elite and dominant, within the society, do not allow their easy entry and they do not have the articulation nor means and wherewithal to conform and compete at their level of operations. . . .
>
> As an extension of the societal milieus, norms and aspirations secondary institutions like cooperatives, SHGs, farmers' associations maintain hard walls and are restrictive to the entry of the poor. The externally designed and crafted institutions do not represent the needs and aspirations of the poor and therefore do not offer an institutional frame to grow with. SHGs and cooperatives have been found to have been co-opted by the elite and the dominant and the state opportunities for the poor to be delivered through such institutions are usurped in and misappropriated. They promote dependency and inaction rather than action, innovation and initiatives.

> PRIs, as instruments of decentralized governance, have too been found not quite favorable to the poor although the constitutional mandates of the PRIs with certain affirmative provisions have helped the poor assert their constitutional rights and privileges. There is a need for further reflection and fresh thought about how the PRIs could emerge as representing and safeguarding the interest of the poor,
>
> There is a definite nexus between the state agencies, the elite and the dominant and local level governance institutions who out maneuver the poor and marginalized. They (the poor) have feeble voice and instrumentality to counter their maneuvers,
>
> The tribal communities and poorest of the poor among the Dalits ... are still at the fringe of development who find themselves helpless and outmaneuvered at the hands of the dominant and the rich. (Mishra, 2007, pp. 9–10)

Poverty reduction, here, takes on a political side; the political implications of the various forms of discrimination mentioned here are clear and closely related to what has been discussed in earlier chapters. Drawing on Amartya Sen's work on "capabilities," it recognizes equity as not just a matter of distribution but also a matter of access to things like education and health care that enable people to fully develop in their lives. The reference to the failures of the PRIs to help the poorest people is particularly notable: both a reference to the political empowerment side of decentralization of governance and a recognition of the failure of standard modes to do what is really needed empower the weakest members of society. Even greater efforts are needed to address the politics of equity.

The significant point, then, is not equity defined in terms of poverty reduction or even changing Gini coefficients, but, rather, a more complex notion of political empowerment. In the Bank's case the transformation is closely tied to the goal of economic growth. Growth remains the principle goal of the Bank, although, again, how that growth is distributed takes on an additional, more political importance. Another example of this dynamic of empowerment, pointed to several times by staff, was the Bank's large National Rural Livelihoods Project, supporting the National Rural Livelihoods Mission, a large, ambitious antipoverty program intended to "shift away from a population and entitlement-based approach for resource allocation to a demand-driven approach" to poverty reduction (World Bank, 2010, p. 3). It includes a provision for "social inclusion [to] systematically mobilize the rural poor—focusing particularly on marginalized groups—into participatory institutions that they manage and lead" (World Bank, 2010, p. 4). Equity is promoted through social inclusion, participatory development, the creation of self-help groups, and better financial systems. As the Bank's website puts it, "mobilization will ... empower the poor, vulnerable and differently-abled to improve their access to public programs to which they are entitled such as old age and widows' pensions, livelihoods programs such as those under the National Rural Employment Guarantee Act (NREGA), and food security programs."

Still, promoting equity is often not particularly straightforward or even uncontroversial. Equity and equality are both complex topics, not easy to reduce to any one definition; and both are only two of many priorities Bank staff needs to keep in mind. One staff member pointed out that while equity was an important goal—one that she, as a poverty expert, entirely supported— it was also necessary to keep in mind that *growth* was essential as well, and sometimes the two might not go together entirely. As with UNICEF and UNDP, Bank staff debates whether there is greater benefit in helping the poorest of the poor—a strategy with high rewards but also great expense and a targeted approach—or helping people who might be less poor, but are a larger group and easier to reach. In this case, promoting economic growth might have the bigger overall benefit on welfare, even if it leaves the most powerless behind. This particular staff person suggested that there were debates within the Bank about which should be prioritized: the issue wasn't whether equity was important, but whether it was the top priority.[5] Similarly, an agriculture expert noted that although helping the poor was vital, this could sometimes conflict with increasing agricultural productivity, which was also extremely important. Besides, they pointed out, most farmers, even those who are not among the very poorest and marginalized, helping them is helping the poor, even if not the poorest of the poor.[6]

Another World Bank employee brought up the issue of working with schools when discussing equity. As with the UNICEF education staff, this Bank staff person said that the condition of schools in India was deplorable overall and that "equality of opportunity" required improving education. However, she said, Bank staff were divided over whether this meant improving public schools or working with private ones. On the one hand, the public schools were there for the poorest people, and thus helping those schools meant reaching the neediest and most powerless population; on the other hand, public schools might be of such low quality that an acceptable standard would be incredibly difficult to achieve, while some private schools of adequate quality might be made available to those of very limited means.[7] Yet another staff member mentioned "institutional platforms" set up to parallel—but also to circumvent—the PRIs, while supporting the rural livelihoods programming. PRIs are supported by Bank programming in governance reform, yet, at the same time, are still often captured by elites and not representative of the poorest and most marginalized.[8] Thus, the Bank might want to work outside the PRI structure rather than shoring it up and making it more important in development policy.

Targeting underserved groups was also difficult for Bank staff, even when the goal was clearly a priority. Different ways of targeting excluded groups are incorporated into different projects. Going outside the PRI system, to avoid its elite capture problems, can mean working with self-help groups directly, as the Bank "establish[es] institutional platforms for the poor"—often comprised only of women.[9] Targeting Schedule Tribes, one expert argued, was easier than Scheduled Castes, since the groups tended to be more homogenous and geographically limited.[10] "Geographical targeting" was mentioned by another staff member, with a recognition that this was an imperfect way of dealing with equity issues.[11] At the national level, there was a debate (mirroring the above-mentioned one on growth versus equity) between whether to focus on lagging states, where the need is greatest, or the more advanced ones, where more can be done more quickly. Country Assistance Strategies, in fact, have been progressively shifting to a "focus state" strategy to promote equity in the poorest areas (see Kirk, 2011), showing the gradual victory of this way of thinking. However, the process was neither easy nor entirely uncontroversial, since it meant moving attention from places where a great many people could be quickly helped.[12] Numerous staff mentioned that while higher level bureaucrats supported the equity agenda, at the local level there was less acceptance, and sometimes outright resistance; this has been a theme among all the agencies covered in this book and requires no further explication here. As Jason Kirk has noted, the Bank's strategy of working with both the national government and state governments often meant separate strategies depending on the level of operation and a complex strategy of keeping all sides of the relationship happy.

As with the other agencies, Bank staff repeatedly expressed frustration with the implementation of a rights agenda (however it was actually called) at the local level—the "last mile," as more than one staff person referred to it. Again, this sort of resistance has been covered in previous chapters and does not require reiteration here. The local level of resistance is often the most tenacious, and thus the World Bank—far larger than UNDP or UNICEF (or, for that matter, UNFPA or UN Women) faces the same challenges and expresses them in much the same language, when speaking of equity. "At the local level there's a backlash," as one put it. "In Uttar Pradesh Dalits get excluded from everything because of politics."[13] This from the same staff, quoted above, who argued for the importance of appearing apolitical. But, they added, the scale of the Indian projects was enormous. It was, they said, incredibly difficult to take the equity agenda, operationalize it, and apply it appropriately. For example, the Rural Livelihoods Mission alone included 400 million people within its scope!

Equity is hardly the only issue the Bank is concerned with, and much of the Bank's work, even around RBA, parallels that being done by other agencies. Governance reform, particularly decentralization and support for PRIs (even as other projects might seem to be undermining them in some ways), has repercussions discussed in other chapters. The same is true of support for Right to Information legislation and implementation. The Bank has supported RTI implementation with funding and technical assistance, and, as with UNDP, it argues that RTI is central to a RBA and better development outcomes.

Another noteworthy area is the World Bank's system of safeguard policies. These are a set of policies related to civil society actors, indigenous peoples, environmental impact of Bank projects, and forced resettlement, among other issues (Umaña, 1998; World Bank, 2002b). They set standards and lay out oversight and enforcement mechanisms to make sure that policies are not violated by the Bank or by Bank-funded projects. The rights of indigenous peoples, for example, and those affected by forced resettlement (for example, due to dam construction), as well as forest rights and other issues, must be built into policies of the World Bank. In some cases these policies have very clear human rights implications, for example, making sure that indigenous peoples have their lands protected and that they are fully informed about and allowed to participate in decisions that will affect their lives (a change from many earlier practices).

The Bank's safeguard policies have certainly been subject to considerable criticism (Buntaine & Parks, 2013; Rich, 2013; Weaver, 2008). It has been argued that they are mere window-dressing on existing policies or they are too little, too late. There is also the question about just how much the safeguard policies are being followed within the Bank—whether the staff really pays attention to these new policies, or whether institutional culture is simply too strong (Wade, 1997). There is also continual discussion of revising, and weakening, these policies, to the consternation of international civil society organizations (Human Rights Watch, 2015). For what it's worth (and these claims are never easy to verify), Bank staff in India insist that, if anything, there has been *too much* caution involved when imposing rules protecting these rights areas, to the extent that some worthwhile projects have been bypassed due to some concerns that were unlikely to pan out. It seems true, for example, that the Bank has taken a very cautious policy toward forest rights and indigenous peoples in India, particularly since some early disasters received international attention (Karlsson & Subba, 2006, p. 6).

A final issue to be mentioned, surely, is women's rights; gender mainstreaming has been World Bank policy since the 1980s (World Bank, 2001, 2002a), and this is one of the relatively few areas where the term "rights," in this case women's rights, is used fairly freely among Bank staff. It is striking that Bank staff will speak so openly about women's rights while being often so cagey about other rights issues. Rather than dealing with this very important topic here, however (which, befitting its importance, could take up considerable space), women's empowerment will be the focus of the next section, on UN Women. But it remains vitally important to all UN agencies.

UN Women

UN Women is by far the newest of the organizations studied here. Also known as the United Nations Entity for Gender Equality and the Empowerment of Women, UN Women was proposed in 2006 as a way of bringing together various work being done across the UN Development Group on behalf of women under a single umbrella (Charlesworth & Chinkin, 2013, p. 36). Its specific goal is to work for gender equality and women's empowerment across the globe, with the Convention on the Elimination of All Forms of Discrimination Against Women (CEDAW) as a foundational document, along with other UN documents such as the Beijing Declaration, adopted at the Fourth World Conference on Women in 1995. The mandate of UN Women is to consolidate and coordinate the work of the UN on women's empowerment and advancement, creating some coordination among the various UN arms working on women's rights and development. Women's rights and empowerment are central to almost all the work done by UN agencies and are an accepted and vital part of the rights agenda. This section on UN Women will focus in particular on expanding the concept of empowerment with reference to women.

As an organization, UN Women identified five "priority areas of intervention" in its 2014 Annual Report. These are:

- Leading political transformation
- Claiming economic rights

- Ending violence against women and girls
- Making equality central to peace
- Planning and budgeting for empowerment (UN Women, 2014, pp. 11–15)

Four of these five priority areas are also considered central to the work of the UN Women office in New Delhi (which also covers Bhutan, the Maldives, and Sri Lanka). "Making equality central to peace" is not listed as a priority, although work in conflict zones is certainly one of the priorities of the New Delhi office and listed on their website. The sensitivity of the Indian government over the issue of conflict, however, makes it useful to downplay that particular priority.

Still, empowerment of women is the single central strategic priority of UN Women; all the other advances, UN Women strongly believes, will come only through women's empowerment in India as elsewhere. The programs mentioned above are part of the empowerment process and are expected to fit into this larger strategic category. Empowerment is to come from economic advances, from removal of the fear of violence, from greater political participation, and other changes. Although empowerment as a concept has been raised often in other contexts in this project, it is important here to keep in mind that as a concept, it initially entered the development lexicon in relation to women's empowerment. A study of women in India from the 1970s—the beginning of the global women's movement—listed a number of ways in which women were disempowered in India and the challenges they faced. These included pervasive child marriage, low literacy rates (estimated at the time as 18.4%, compared to the also-dismal rate for males of 39.5%), low participation in the labor force, discriminatory property laws, and highly restrictive religious norms, among many other issues (National Committee on the Status of Women, 1975). More recent studies point out that the situation has not substantially improved in many areas—the issue of sex ratios (the effect of strong cultural preferences for boy children over girl children, discussed later in relation to UNFPA), being only one indication of that (Kumar & Varghese, 2005).

The concept remains tightly connected to gender and takes on additional meaning when used that way. More than just allowing people to participate in the decisions that affect their lives, or to hold government accountable, "empowering women . . . means strengthening them to confront family, community, caste, religion and traditional forces and biases working within government departments" (Arya, 2000, p. 147). True empowerment of women "acknowledges inequalities between men and women in relation to resources and family, the community, the market, and the state, and emphasizes race, class, colonial history and their country's position in the international order" (Kumar & Varghese, 2005, p. 57). Empowerment, in other words, requires looking at all the forces—social, economic, cultural, and so forth—that hold women from full enjoyment of their rights. At the same time, helping women claim their rights is the key to empowerment. Legal change—passing, or even enforcing, laws designed to protect or empower women—is not enough (Coomaraswamy, 2011); only social change can bring about real respect for rights and real empowerment.

UN Women, for the most part, does not do much programming by itself, nor does it have the capacity to do so; it primarily works though UN and NGO partners, building on other successful programs from UNDP, UNICEF, and other agencies. It also provides support directly for government programs. Interestingly, staff admitted that they do some direct implementation on "sensitive issues." Working in conflict zones was cited as one area. (This for the same reasons as mentioned in earlier chapters, primarily that the Indian government denies that many of these zones have conflicts in them, preferring to call it unrest.) UN Women mostly sees itself as bringing its particular "comparative advantage" on women's issues to the operations of other agencies. UN Women also recognizes the importance of building capacity among local actors, including government officials: "Sustainability will happen if government structures take ownership of programs," one official states, as "only they have the capacity to push for real change." The same UN Women official also states, bluntly, "[we're] challenging taboos, social customs, and patriarchy, so we *need* partners" to take on such enormous challenges.[14]

Many of the specific programs, then, undertaken by UN Women will sound familiar to those who have read the preceding chapters. UN Women has been particularly active in promoting women's political participation and leadership, from the PRIs up to the national level. At the level of the Panchayats, UN Women has sponsored, through partners, training for women about modes of participation in public life, similar to (and in conjunction with) UNDP programming. As of 2015, the program worked with 65,000 elected women in 16 districts of India. In Bihar, for example, UN Women has supported "Strengthening Women's Empowerment through Electoral Process," using contacts from radio programming to one-on-one meetings to promote women's leadership (*Promoting Women's Political Leadership and Governance in India and South Asia*, 2011, p. 5). UN Women also has projects on "gender responsive budgeting," providing advocacy, technical support, and knowledge at the national and state levels. UN Women estimates at least 400 people have been trained in gender responsive budgeting at the national level and other trainings for officials in the banking sector.

Other issues have also been extremely important. Violence against women has been a problem in India as it is in many countries. Working with UNICEF and other agencies, UN Women has supported legal change, anti-trafficking programs, and other antiviolence campaigns, such as one to deter sexual harassment of women in public in New Delhi and elsewhere. In human trafficking, for example, a UN Women–supported project has taken steps to teach women and girls about human trafficking laws, to mobilize communities against trafficking and create vigilance committees, and to offer livelihoods to those rescued from traffickers. It has also provided support to build capacity in the legal system for enforcement of laws and punishment of traffickers (UN Women, 2013b, pp. 15–18). UN Women has also aided programs to empower widows—in India, widows have often faced terrible difficulties, sometimes unable to remarry, inherit land, or overcome stigma (UN Women, 2013a, pp. 3–5)—and other women in particularly vulnerable situations. Along with UNDP there are programs to support rural livelihoods and to ensure women's access to MGNREGA, the rural employment guarantee scheme discussed earlier. These programs also work from pilot projects at the local level to training of national bureaucrats.

As we have seen in other chapters, there are various legal prescriptions in Indian law to address the status of women (see also Poonia & Poonia, 2011, pp. 141–168). Success has been limited; for example, there is mixed evidence whether reserved seats for women in the PRI system has led to women's empowerment or greater political participation (Ambedkar & Nagendra, 2006, pp. 260–265; Mathur, 2011, pp. 250–251). Violence against women and girls continues to present tremendous obstacles to women's empowerment and economic progress (Solotaroff & Pande, 2014), and other severe rights violations, from trafficking to caste and tribal discrimination, also hold women back from full participation in the economy and from equal status.

In this context, the work of UN Women in India has the most radical agenda to press for social change, and speaking with UN Women staff shows, again, a willingness to press for radical revisions in India politics and culture that might surprise those accustomed to more traditional modes of UN operations. "The climate," one highly placed UN Women official told me, "has changed"; while it "used to be you couldn't talk about [rights and social customs]," there is now "at least a semblance, if not a real commitment, to rights" and particularly to CEDAW.[15] The press for real social change is particularly visible in UN Women's programming, where there is a pronounced emphasis on community-level work and public information campaigns aimed at changing attitudes of ordinary people as well as policymakers. Promoting CEDAW has the same central place to UN Women as the CRC for UNICEF, naturally, and provides the same sort of foundation of rights language and programming on which to build.

The importance of changing cultural norms—of involving themselves in the most basic level of Indian society—was central to how UN Women's staff saw their work. Rights were described to me as "nonnegotiable" by UN Women; but when the "conflict with custom" and cultural norms arose, it was necessary to tread carefully, particularly if religious-based norms were at issue. "Who dare question religion or a thousand years of tradition?" I was asked rhetorically.[16] One example from a UN Women official was their cooperation with UNFPA on the issue of sex-selective abortion—a very serious and tragic problem, discussed in depth in the next section on the UN Population Fund. UN Women has been working with Panchayat leaders on the issue: "It's all about cultural norms," they said, and "you begin to open up their minds." Passage in 2005 of the Protection of Women from Domestic Violence Act was cited as another important milestone (B. Ghosh & Choudhuri, 2015); not just because of the legal rights it placed in Indian law, but also because of the effect it has had on transforming attitudes. Staff made it clear that while passing laws protecting rights was important, social change was the only way to effectively translate those rights into real improvement and empowerment. Laws without social change are mere window-dressing. Government officials attend trainings by UN Women and other agencies; people see posters and hear social workers explain the importance of gender equality. But persuading them to truly internalize these issues is another story, and the only way to make real progress.

UN Women, like other agencies, recognizes that this type of rights-based social engineering is a strong departure from what is normally expected of UN agencies. UN Women recognizes the challenges that this represents. Women's empowerment is not only a matter of legal change—nor is a RBA to development properly understood (Pillai, 1995). A UN Women staff person contrasted UN Women's approach to rights with that of UNDP; "we *use* the word rights," she said, unlike her perception of UNDP, which was that it avoided rights language. "But we don't rub their [officials'] faces in it."[17] Empowerment is understood then as a recognition of *all* rights; and the role of UN Women, to the extent that their extremely small budget allows, is to promote all women's rights, including (perhaps particularly) civil and political rights. UN Women is to act as an agent of social change. This elevates the programming from rhetorical posturing to real transformation. There is also recognition that the process of promoting real social change around rights is not an easy task, nor an uncontroversial one: but without social change, legal rights would be all but meaningless. Empowerment is not simply providing economic opportunity, legal protection, or political voice; but also transforming the social structures that prevent women from actually living the rights they are promised. More openly than the other agencies here, and despite the talk of not "rubbing their faces" in rights language, the revolutionary nature of this project is not lost on UN Women staff, nor the need to effect real social change.

The revolutionary nature of this work should not be understated. As Coomeraswamy (2002, p. 484) put it, "In a world where western imperialism has historically been the champion of third world females in Asia or Africa, the struggle for women's rights acquires another dimension. How does one fight for women's rights without being complicit in the racism and prejudice that characterizes Northern attitudes toward Southern countries?" The UN has not been immune from the critique that it represents a sort of cultural and ideological imperialism, and, as noted in the first chapter, the process of working so actively for such basic social change is not without controversy. More so than with other agencies, however, UN Women staff seems unconcerned about the implications of imposing a "Western" notion of women's rights. Rights, again, "are what we do," in the language of staff mentioned earlier. They too are aware that this is an enormous change in what is expected of UN agencies and tread carefully because of that, but also do so unapologetically.

This is not meant to sound overly laudatory in terms of UN Women's work on human rights. UN Women has the advantage of being a small organization, with a small footprint in India and a budget that constrains it to provide support for other, larger agencies. As discussed in Chapter 7, and shown below with the UN Population Fund, it is easier to take controversial or politically sensitive positions when you are largely flying "under the radar" of government officials. UN Women does also, like UNICEF, benefit from having a specific human rights document, widely accepted around the world, to furnish its social work an extra level of international legitimacy, and they use that opportunity to good effect. CEDAW provides a very convenient and sometimes powerful instrument of persuasion. So they are freer than some others to talk about significant social change and able to be entirely open about their rights policies. On the other hand, their small size and relatively marginal role (as mentioned, mostly supporting other, bigger agencies and government bureaucracies) means that (as

Chapter 6 will discuss) solid accomplishments are hard to point to. UN Women has the freedom, to some extent, that comes with being a relatively small player on a very, very large stage.

United Nations Population Fund

The UNFPA (formerly the United Nations Fund for Population Activities) is the UN agency promoting population planning, maternal and reproductive health, and safe childhood and adolescence. It is also charged with promoting gender equality and equity and cooperates substantially with UN Women in particular. In India as elsewhere, UNFPA has a small physical presence, both in Delhi and in UN field offices in targeted states and regions. As with UN Women, much of its work is in cooperation with other agencies. Part of the United Nations Development Group (UNDG), UNFPA works in close collaboration with UNDP and UNICEF as well as other UN agencies such as the World Health Organization. It is able to leverage its limited resources partly through these close collaborations.

In the 2013–2017 programming period, UNFPA has about US$14 million per year to spend on its operations in India (United Nations, 2012). As with UNDP, it operates entirely through "national implementation," working with government partners and other agencies. Given its limited resources, it primarily seeks to create successful pilot projects that will later be scaled up by national and other government bodies. UNFPA has a long history in India, which since gaining independence has struggled with the implications of a vast and fast-growing population. Staff members of UNFPA are well aware of this and consider themselves to have a particularly close and long-term relationship with the government. Government officials seem to feel the same way, speaking with considerable familiarity about their work with UNFPA and the importance of population issues in India's development. Population control, safe motherhood, and related issues have long been highly visible issues in India.

The UNFPA strategic plan for 2014–2017 focuses on achieving three primary outcomes:

- Increased availability and use of integrate sexual and reproductive health services (including family planning, maternal health and HIV) that are gender-responsive and meet human rights standards for quality of care and equity in access;
- Increased priority on adolescents, especially on very young adolescent girls, in national development policies and programmes, particularly increased

availability of comprehensive sexuality education and sexual and reproductive health services; and
- Advanced gender equality, women's and girls' empowerment, and reproductive rights, including for the most vulnerable and marginalized women, adolescents, and youth. (UNFPA, 2014, pp. 6–8)

The 2014 Strategic Plan reflects a 2011 rethinking of the direction of UNFPA, which itself was an increased focus on sexual and reproductive health (SRH) and reproductive rights as the key goals—the "bulls-eye," in their terminology—of UNFPA action. Achievement of human rights, gender equality, and sustainable population dynamics were identified as the three key inputs, or strategies, that would lead to achievement of the primary target. The UNFPA strategic plan, in contrast to some others, is full of the language of rights, encompassing both C&P rights and ES&C rights, in a manner that suggests a fairly good consideration of the interrelation between the two categories. Statements like "all couples and individuals have the right to decide freely and responsibly the number, spacing and timing of their children" might reflect a fairly broad or vague use of rights language; but "reproductive rights are comprised of a constellation of civil, political, economic, social and cultural rights protecting the freedom of individuals and couples to make autonomous, informed decisions . . . free from discrimination, coercion and violence" suggests a deeper consideration (UNFPA, 2014, pp. 7–8). Further on, specifics like gender-based violence, female genital mutilation, gender equality, poverty, and food and water security are mentioned as factors in reproductive health and rights.

The research period covers the transition between an earlier (2008–2012) and later (2013–2017) Country Program Action Plan. The latter plan, on which this section will focus, notes a number of priority issues to be addressed in India, including:

- Significant levels of "inequality and social exclusion," particularly for Scheduled Castes and Scheduled Tribes;
- Fertility rates that have dropped significantly in most parts of the country but remain high in some states, and a likely population of 3.5 billion (overtaking China) by 2030;
- Deeply-rooted practices of child marriage and early fertility, also particularly pronounced among Scheduled Castes and Scheduled Tribes;
- Rapid urbanization and increasing numbers of children and adolescents living in peri-urban slums;

- Low literacy rates, which prevent access to reproductive health information;
- Low contraceptive use rates, and an emphasis on female sterilization;
- Declining, but still high, maternal mortality rates.
- A demographic transition to an older population in the future.
- Natural disasters, particularly floods and earthquakes. (UNFPA, 2013, pp. 4–8)

Once again, the list of total programs being supported by UNFPA is too long to consider in toto. And as with other programs, the list seems entirely too long to believably be carried out by the small staff available! Indeed, there always seems to be a shockingly small number of staff tasked with carrying out way too many projects at the same time.

The current country strategic plan calls for pursuing five "outputs":

1. Young people, especially the marginalized (Scheduled Castes, Scheduled Tribes and minorities) have acquired gender-sensitive knowledge on sexual and reproductive health and services;
2. Adolescents have access to gender-sensitive, life skills-based sexual and reproductive health education in schools;
3. Health systems are strengthened to provide high-quality sexual and reproductive health services, including family planning services, with a focus on vulnerable and marginalized populations;
4. Strengthened capacity of state and non-state entities to reverse son preference.
5. Strengthened national capacity to incorporate population dynamics in relevant national and sub-national plans and programmes, with a focus on gender and social inclusion. (UNFPA, 2013, pp. 9–10)

Naturally, some of the rights implications of these five priorities are more tenuous than others. The Country Programme Action Plan says about priority 1, for example, "A safe and successful passage from adolescence to adulthood is the right of every child. This right can only be fulfilled if families and societies make focused investments and provide opportunities to ensure that adolescents and youth progressively develop" (UNFPA, 2013, p. 10). Here again, the RBA language is fairly vague, defining the health and welfare of children as a "right" without a great deal of explanation. On the other hand, a key strategy in pursuit of that goal—"leverage national programmes to reach vulnerable adolescents and young people with information on reproductive health"—at least puts the emphasis on education and choice among the young, and, as with most other programs studied here, focuses on vulnerable and poor groups rather than the populations as a whole. The targeting of "underserved" and vulnerable populations is continued throughout the program of action. Key issues like reversing "son preference" and sex-selective abortion have obvious relevance to women's rights. Fighting the ingrained preference for male children obviously includes a great deal of social pressure and public relations—nothing less than changing a basic societal norm in India—and has broad implications for what a UN agency can involve itself in, much as UNDP and UNICEF have also set for themselves the goal of changing basic social dynamics.

Interviews with UNFPA staff suggest many really do understand the rights implication of their work, and also how complex those implications make their jobs. That said, staff reported at all levels that they do consider the Indian government generally open to human rights talk about key UNFPA issues. India, at least one well-placed staff person believed, wants to be seen as a "global player" and feels that openness to rights promotion was an important part of global image-building. There was the usual feeling that there was more receptivity to rights talk at the upper levels of government; while highly placed officials in New Delhi were well informed about the implications of RBA and concerned with its implementation, working with local governments was more difficult, if only because of less awareness of what rights meant.

It has been argued elsewhere in this book that a focus on the "demand side" of development and rights is vital for a clear understanding of what RBA is—empowering citizens to hold governments accountable is different than a traditional service-provision model of development. Interviews with UNFPA officials quickly turned to a discussion of how to "actualize" (a word used more than once) a policy of empowering citizens to demand the elements of a healthy reproductive life. "The intent is rights," said one official, "but we don't want to say this is a policy to promote rights."[18] The official gave as an example the fight against "gender-based violence" (GBV). Simply raising the issue, one official noted, was not a problem, even when it was put in explicitly rights-based terms. To go further into the "demand side" of women's rights, UNFPA has sponsored public forums to develop awareness about the problem of GBV. UNFPA has also piloted a program in Rajasthan to train PRI candidates about GBV and other issues (such as sex selection and forced sterilization, mentioned below). Still, "the government gets jittery," they said, when the work could lead to "confrontation with the public."[19] The official in this interview was quick to mention that, despite this jitteriness, the government was "receptive" to the work and generally supportive, but the political nature of it was obvious. And they suggested that the government's concern over its international image was a problem UNFPA was able to exploit: "India needs its MDG indicators and other numbers to get better" and knows that UNFPA's demand-side work is a way of accomplishing this.

Asked what they consider their key priorities, top staff will list a few issues. "Information and knowledge" is a top priority of UNFPA, as we have seen, and was listed as the most important rights priority. "Access and quality" of services was second; "everyone deserves access and quality . . . they are rights" was the justification for bringing up what might otherwise be seen as a service-provision priority. Third was community empowerment, the primary cause of the jitteriness and possible confrontation mentioned above.[20] Within these general priorities were included other, more solid concerns, for example, effective supply-chain management to make sure that reproductive-health needs are met with quality medicine and other goods.

As an example of progressive programming, staff in Odisha (formerly Orissa) state pointed to their work with "ASHA" ("hope" in Hindi and several other languages of the subcontinent), a program of the National Rural Health Mission to "create village level social activists . . . to provide primary medical care, advise the villagers on sanitation, hygiene, antenatal and postnatal care, escorting expectant mothers to hospital for safe delivery, etc." (Nandan, 2008, p. 1). ASHA councilors are community-based volunteers, largely intended to help with things like distributing contraceptives, teaching about optimal timing between births, providing information regarding proper sanitation and safe motherhood, among other issues. These are not rights issues per se, except, of course, in the sense that citizens are thought to have a "right" to information on these issues, and to safe motherhood and childhood. But when asked what they consider to be the most important human rights issues in India, top UNFPA officials in New Delhi and elsewhere listed "information and knowledge" as their first priority: "Girls," one said, "must be educated to be empowered: they have more agency and make better choices" with information.[21] Again, education of girls and women about their reproductive choices and rights is not, in itself, necessarily a well-considered RBA. No one denies the importance of education in promoting healthy behaviors, whether you think of it as an issue of rights or good public health policy. But there was a strong awareness among staff that this education was about changing power dynamics, as well as teaching health habits. One staff person, for example, noted that there was an effort to "build the self-confidence of shy teachers," assuming this would make them more effective at teaching girls about their rights;

not, once again, exactly a rights approach in the way spelled out in the first part of this volume, but at least an awareness of the complex nature of empowering citizens.

However, two vital issues particularly dominated all discussions of human rights within UNFPA: sex selection and forced (or coerced) sterilization. The issue of sex-based selection among parents has been well documented and is an ongoing problem in India and elsewhere, aided by the development of new technologies that are able to tell parents the sex of their fetus well before delivery (Arnold, Kishor, & Roy, 2002; Madan & Breuning, 2014). According to some recent figures, the number of girls ages 1 to 6 per 1,000 boys dropped from 927 in 2001 to 914 in 2011 (Jain, 2013, p. 1). There are many reasons why there are "missing women" (to use Amartya Sen's phrase [Sen, 1992]) in South Asia and elsewhere. Primarily, a deeply ingrained preference for boys over girls leads to various behaviors, from sex-selective abortion to preferential treatment of boys over girls in terms of access to nutrition, health care, and education. These manifest throughout the lives of girls, and even into adulthood, and are combined with gender-based violence and other factors.

The problem of sex-selective abortion is both particularly acute and shocking in terms of the obvious issues it raises. UNFPA and other UN agencies fit sex selection within the larger context of gender discrimination: According to a key report, "Many pervasive social, cultural, political and economic injustices against girls and women ... constitute violations of the right of women to non-discrimination. This was clearly recognized at the International Conference on Population and Development (ICPD) in 1994 and in the associated Programme of Action which enjoined governments to 'eliminate all forms of discrimination against the girl child and the root causes of son preference, which result in harmful and unethical practices regarding female infanticide and prenatal sex selection'" (World Health Organization et al., 2011, p. 3). The same report goes on to insist, "Sex selection in favor of boys is a symptom of pervasive social, cultural, political and economic injustices against women, and a manifest violation of women's human rights. Such injustices must be addressed and resolved without exposing women and children to the risk of death or serious injury through denying them access to needed services—and thus further violating their rights" (World Health Organization et.al., 2011, p. 4). Imbalanced gender ratios also lead to a host of other rights violations against women, from trafficking of women to forced marriages, to marriages, in some parts of India, to multiple men. There are other pernicious implications as well, dangerous to the stability of society and dangerous to women in particular (Bose, Trent, & South, 2013; Kaur, 2013).

Sex-selective abortion is illegal in India; the 1994 Prenatal Diagnostic Techniques (Regulation and Prevention of Mis-use) Act limits the use of prenatal diagnosis to a list of selected congenital conditions and makes it illegal to use ultrasound and other techniques to determine the sex of a fetus. It is also illegal for doctors to tell parents the sex of their child, and mobile ultrasound devices (which can be used by unscrupulous people to offer sex tests to parents) are also outlawed. The Indian Supreme Court has issued detailed directives to the national and state governments to raise awareness on the law on sex determination and called for increased surveillance of all clinics providing ultrasounds. UNFPA, along with UNICEF and others, provides support to law enforcement, medical clinics, and other partners to help enforce these laws and has advocated for further legal change to make ultrasound and other similar testing more difficult to use for sex selection. Social change is also vitally important, and UNFPA supports public information campaigns to change opinions about male child preference. UNFPA staff complained to me that as recently as 2007 there was little enforcement of laws to prevent sex-selective abortion and no state-level system to deal with the problem. Currently, however, the government is taking the matter more seriously, and "show-cause" notices (a form of legal challenge to a suspected lawbreaker) are regularly issued to medical clinics suspected of complicity in sex selection.

UNFPA respondents also report that the Government of India is highly receptive to this work and to the use of rights language to describe the fight against sex selection. Yet even in such an uncontroversial area, there remain pitfalls. UNFPA staff reported that sometimes they felt that rights language "backfired" and led to unintended, and often counterproductive, consequences. (Similar concerns, it should be noted, were voiced by staff in many other agencies also and even by at least one government respondent.) There was worry that the language—or rhetoric—of rights might complicate an otherwise fairly simple public health campaign. One example given was in relation to sex-selective abortion. If agencies phrase the issue in terms of rights (the rights to equal treatment of girls), the danger is that "the men say, 'yes of course it is my right to decide if I want to have that child or not.'"[22] Thus the government has come to understand the complexity of rights language here and tries to avoid it when discussing this particular issue. Further complicating matters is that abortion is legal in India, and UNFPA has supported legalized abortion since it prevents dangerous "underground" abortions from threatening women's lives. So the rhetoric of rights is even more problematic because women have the right to abortion in India, yet the problem of sex-selective abortion constitutes its own rights issue. "We avoid using the term feticide," for example, "because then we get into a debate over abortion."[23] Rights can sometimes clash, while simpler public health campaigns are not so open to misinterpretation or misuse.

Another issue felt very strongly by UNFPA staff is the history of forced or coerced sterilization of women in India, something that has been too common as a way of controlling population in India for decades (Ledbetter, 1984, pp. 742, 747–748). Family planning services and policies have evolved since Indian independence, but by the 1980s there had developed a strong emphasis on using sterilization (focused particularly on women who already had three or more children) as a means of population control; and, concurrently, government offered cash incentives to both women and providers to have the procedure performed. Local officials tasked with overseeing populations efforts were also provided incentives to hit target numbers of women sterilized: while those targets were officially removed in the 1990s because of the abuses they caused, many officials still feel pressure to reach certain numbers (Dugger, 2001; Matthews, Padmadas, Hutter, McEachran, & Brown, 2009, pp. 699–703). This has led to the "hidden" problem of forced or coerced sterilization that UNFPA has been fighting as a violation of women's rights to choose their own best way to control family size. A meeting with high-level officials in Madhya Pradesh state was cited as a key element there in convincing the government apparatus to promote alternatives to sterilization;[24] state UNFPA officials also cited efforts to pursue "target-free" approaches and the promotion of condoms, birth spacing, and other means of family planning as alternatives.[25]

In addition to these priority areas, there are many other places where UNFPA uses the rhetoric and reality of RBA to promote their work. Staff in state offices noted, for example, putting up notices in health clinics to inform clients about their rights, for example, to free medical care during childbirth; to confidentiality; to a careful explanation of what was being done in simple local language; and to informed decisions about their own health care.[26] Other staff mentioned privacy in particular as a key right of women seeking maternal and child health care, contextualizing it as part of a right to "dignity."[27] On the other hand, asked about RBA, another interviewee brought up the issue of "reproductive health commodity security," that is, efforts to ensure a steady and reliable supply of reproductive health materials as a matter of providing a right to adequate health care; this included working with software systems to track supplies and improving distribution networks.[28] Another commented generally on "access and quality" as rights issues since "everyone deserves access and quality as a right!"[29] Again, a loose and rhetorical idea of rights mixed in with much more specific ones.

Reaching the underserved, particularly Scheduled Castes and Scheduled Tribes but also other groups that face discrimination, is also regularly mentioned as a rights priority by UNFPA, as it is with the other agencies examined in this volume. And, again, the "rights" issues involved in that effort range from the well-considered to the fairly vague and rhetorical. Promoting "Village Health and Sanitation Committees" (Venkatesh & Satpathy, 2006) is, for example, a key strategy of UNFPA (in conjunction with others) to promote healthy motherhood as well as demographic planning, and staff emphasized the desire to see Scheduled Caste members represented on the committees.[30] Others complained that while government's planning was supposed to be a "bottom-up" approach that empowered rural committees, the "reality is that it is still very top-down,"[31] and that UNFPA and its partners were trying to bring real change through efforts to further empower local committees. Without prompting, this official worried about the implications of this process: "We have to remain apolitical," they said, which required using "social" rather than "political" processes to make sure that the most vulnerable had their voices heard.[32] In this case, the "resistance" felt to these empowerment efforts was seen as coming primarily from local customs and traditions rather than from the government: fighting resistance "depends on how you align yourself" this official said in the same interview, noting that if the program was influenced by UNFPA "at the design level," then it would be seen as a government directive and therefore more likely to be accepted by those effected. Thus, empowerment in general, reaching the underserved, and promoting participatory development are seen as rights-based programs by UNFPA staff, although at times the idea of "rights," as with other agencies, seems more about equity and participation than real changes to existing power structures.

UNFPA remains a fairly small player in the Indian development space, leveraging its relatively limited budget and influence through partners—both NGOs and other UN agencies. Its limited ability to act on its own is further hampered by the wide range of issues it wants to tackle. As with UN Women, it sees its primary strategy as "nothing less than the empowerment of women," as it seeks to achieve the goals listed at the start of this section. That empowerment can mean a RBA, when it is well thought out, but, as we have seen, empowerment and rights fit together imperfectly. UNDP officials do talk about resistance at the social and, sometimes, government level, but it tends to be fairly subdued. The larger issue was appearing "overtly political," which is not quite the same thing as fighting political opposition. Still, the concern over this at least points to the wide-ranging and sometimes controversial issues being pursued by UNFPA. On the other hand, UNFPA is somewhat hindered by the more technical nature of its work, particularly concerning women's rights. While UN Women is unabashed in its promotion of certain rights issues, and its use of rights language, UNFPA is somewhat more cautious about what it says. Much of what UNFPA does, to be sure, is still quite technical in terms of family planning, child health, and safe motherhood. This gives it a bit more room to couch its work in technical terms, and a larger percentage of its work is, in fact, more about service delivery than rights promotion.

Conclusion

One other agency not mentioned here, but originally intended to be studied, is the World Health Organization. The WHO has a difficult relationship with RBA: while ostensibly supporting the concept, implementation has not been easy. Much of this stems from the highly technical nature of much of the WHO's work and from the technical training of their staff of doctors and public health professionals. Rights language and programming can seem a diversion from the technical work of promoting public health, and many WHO professionals are trained to distrust ideas that cannot be backed by scientific evidence. Of course, other agencies face these same issues, and they crop up over and over again. World Bank economists, UNFPA demographers, and even some UN Women staff face the same challenges. This is without saying very much about, for example, the World Food Programme or the Food and Agriculture Organization, which are still more technical in most of their work.

The World Bank dwarfs the other subjects of this chapter, and in that respect might be considered sui generis. As such a large organization, there is substantially more variation in the level to which various staff adhere to the principles of RBA or even perceive it as relevant to their work. There is a danger that some sections of the Bank—particularly those dedicated to governance reform—will be seen as the "RBA units," in the same way that the Child Protection unit in UNICEF is sometimes given the same moniker. Smaller agencies, not surprisingly, are more consistent in their application, with less bureaucratic spread and a more consistent mission. On the other hand, there is similarity across agencies in terms of some of the basic definitions of terms, if not in their use. Equity provides a good example: while it is the World Bank that defines "equity" for the entire system (and the term "the World Bank's equity agenda" is common parlance among all agencies), the concept is adopted fairly uniformly across the system. So, too, ideas about disaggregation of data, gender empowerment, and other basic development concepts. UN staff members talk frequently with one another and do receive direction from the Country Director's office.

As in other chapters, we see a mix of rhetoric and reality in the implementation of RBA. UNFPA and UN Women, for example, are firmly dedicated to what they consider a RBA, but they gather a great many different policies under the rubric of human rights—too many, perhaps, for a coherent notion of what it means. But still, much of what they do fits UN guidelines on what RBA means—empowerment, citizen mobilization, political equity, and a real commitment to helping the most powerless. But this commitment seems to overflow, sometimes, into more traditional (if still quite useful) programming areas, such as ensuring maternal health through better medical practices or promoting girls' education. On the other hand, the World Bank probably underestimates how expansive its rights-based programming is: while it shies away from the term "rights," a surprising number of staff worries about their impact on women, indigenous peoples, Dalits, and other groups. Most of what it does, to be sure, has little impact on rights, but it still tends to underplay its interest in real reform.

All the agencies described in this chapter have a higher level of commitment to RBA. And all of them are grappling with the political nature of this work and the resistance both outside and inside their agencies. Mostly their experiences reinforce what was described in the context of UNDP and UNICEF: the process of implementation is ongoing; it faces challenges; and it requires adaptation to political realities, which the UN is still learning to do. Even the boldest advocates admit to facing resistance and political challenges—as one would expect. Yet, the amount of thought being put into how to overcome this resistance is encouraging.

References

Ambedkar, S. N., & Nagendra, S. (2006). *Role of Women in Panchati Raj*. Jaipur, India: ABD.

Arnold, F., Kishor, S., & Roy, T. K. (2002). Sex Selective Abortions in India. *Population and Development Review, 28*(4), 759–785.

Arya, A. (2000). *Education and Empowerment*. New Delhi: Gyan.

Bello, W. (1994). *Dark Victory: The United States, Structural Adjustment, and Global Poverty*. London: Pluto Press.

Bose, S., Trent, K., & South, S. J. (2013). The Effect of a Male Surplus on Intimate Partner Violence in India. *Economic and Political Weekly*, *31*(35), author manuscript.

Buntaine, M. T., & Parks, B. C. (2013). When Do Environmentally Focused Assistance Projects Achieve Their Objective? Evidence from the World Bank Post-Project Evaluations. *Global Environmental Politics*, *13*(2), 65–88.

Cahn, J. (1993). Challenging the New Imperial Authority: The World Bank and the Democratization of Development. *Harvard Human Rights Law Journal*, *6*, 159–194.

Charlesworth, H., & Chinkin, C. (2013). *The Creation of UN Women*. London: London School of Economics. Retrieved from http://eprints.lse.ac.uk/53605/1/__libfile_repository_Content_Chinkin,%20C_Creation%20UN%20Women_Chinkin_Creation%20UN%20Women_2013.pdf

Clark, D. (2002). The World Bank and Human Rights: The Need for Greater Accountability. *Harvard Human Rights Law Journal*, *15*, 205–226.

Coomaraswamy, R. (2002). Identity Within: Cultural Relativism, Minority Rights and the Empowerment of Women. *George Washington International Law Review*, *34*, 483–490.

Coomaraswamy, R. (2011). To Bellow Like a Cow: Women, Ethnicity, and the Discourse of Rights. In R. J. Cook (Ed.), *Human Rights of Women: National and International Perspectives* (pp. 39–57). Philadelphia: University of Pennsylvania Press.

Darrow, M. (2003). *Between Light and Shadow: The World Bank, the International Monetary Fund and International Human Rights Law*. Portland, OR: Hart.

Deaton, A., & Kozel, V. (2005). The Great Indian Poverty Debate. *World Bank Research Observer*, *20*(2), 177–196.

Dugger, C. (2001, 22 June). Relying on Hard and Soft Sells, India Pushes Sterilization. *New York Times*.

Easterly, W. (2015). *The Tyranny of Experts: Economists, Dictators, and the Forgotten Rights of the Poor*. New York: Basic Books.

Franck, T. M. (1998). *Fairness in International Law*. New York: Oxford University Press.

Ghosh, B., & Choudhuri, T. (2015). New Protection Against Domestic Violence in India. *Indian Journal of Development Research and Social Action*, *11*(1), 111–128.

Ghosh, J. (2011, 4 October). India's Official Poverty Line Doesn't Measure Up. *The Guardian*. Retrieved from http://www.theguardian.com/global-development/poverty-matters/2011/oct/04/india-measuring-poverty-line.

Gruskin, S., & Braveman, P. (2003). Defining Equity in Health. *Journal of Epidemiology and Community Health*, *57*(4), 254–258.

Hancock, G. (1994). *The Lords of Poverty: The Power, Prestige, and Corruption of the International Aid Business*. New York: Atlantic Monthly Press.

Human Rights Watch. (2015). World Bank: Dangerous Rollback in Environmental, Social Protections. Retrieved from https://www.hrw.org/news/2015/08/04/world-bank-dangerous-rollback-environmental-social-protections.

Jain, A. (2013). Sex Selection and Abortion in India. *British Medical Journal*, March 25, 2013. Online resource. Retrieved from http://www.bmj.com/content/bmj/346/bmj.f1957.full.pdf.

Kanbur, R. (2015). Can a Country Be a Donor and a Recipient of Aid? In S. M. Dev & P. G. Babu (Eds.), *Development in India* (pp. 71–81). New Delhi: Springer India.

Karlsson, B. T., & Subba, T. B. (2006). *Indigeneity in India*. New York: Kegan Paul.

Kaur, R. (2013). Mapping the Adverse Consequences of Sex Selection and Gender Imbalance in India and China. *Economic and Political Weekly*, *48*(35), author manuscript.

Kirk, J. A. (2011). *India and the World Bank: The Politics of Aid and Influence*. New York: Anthem Press.

Kirk, J. A., & Yadav, V. (2015). From Swagger to Self-Advocacy: India's Postgraduate "Transition" in the World Bank. *India Review*, *14*(4), 377–398.

Kumar, H., & Varghese, J. (2005). *Women's Empowerment: Issues, Challenges, and Strategies*. New Delhi: Regency.

Lawyers Committee for Human Rights. (1995). *The World Bank: Governance and Human Rights*. New York: Lawyers Committee for Human Rights.

Ledbetter, R. (1984). Thirty Years of Family Planning in India. *Asian Survey*, *24*(7), 736–758.

Madan, K., & Breuning, M. H. (2014). Impact of Prenatal Technologies on the Sex Ratio in India: An Overview. *Genetics in Medicine*, *16*(6), 425–432.

Mathur, D. (2011). *Women Empowerment and Panchayati Raj*. Jaipur, India: Prism Books.

Matthews, Z., Padmadas, S. S., Hutter, I., McEachran, J., & Brown, J. J. (2009). Does Early Childbearing and a Sterilization-focused Family Planning Programme in India Fuel Population Growth? *Demographic Research*, *20*, 693–720.

Mishra, R. (2007). *Social Assessment Including Social Inclusion: A Study in the Selected Districts of Bihar*. Patna, India: Asian Development Research Institute. Retrieved from http://documents.worldbank.org/curated/en/566141468258313355/text/IPP2170IPP03941ialoAssessmentoFinal.txt.

Nandan, D. (2008). *A Rapid Appraisal of Functioning of ASHA Under NRHM in Cuttack, Orissa*. New Delhi: United Nations Population Fund. Retrieved from http://documents.worldbank.org/curated/en/566141468258313355/text/IPP2170IPP03941ialoAssessmentoFinal.txt.

National Committee on the Status of Women. (1975). *Status of Women in India*. New Delhi: Indian Council of Social Science Research.

Pillai, J. (1995). *Women and Empowerment*. New Delhi: Gyan.

Poonia, M., & Poonia, V. S. (2011). *Women and Human Rights in India*. New Delhi: Sonali.

Promoting Women's Political Leadership and Governance in India and South Asia. (2011). New Delhi: The Hunger Project. Retrieved from http://clientdisplay.com/unwomen/assets/Promoting%20Women's%20Political%20Leadership%20 and%20Governance%20in%20india%20and%20South%20Asia%20-%20Report.pdf.

Reserve Bank of India. (2015). *Handbook of Statistics on the Indian Economy.* New Delhi: Reserve Bank of India.

Rich, B. (2013). *Foreclosing the Future: The World Bank and the Politics of Environmental Destruction.* Washington, DC: Island Press.

Sen, A. (1992). Missing Women. *British Medical Journal, 304*(6827), 587–588.

Sen, A. (1999). *Development as Freedom.* New York: Random House.

Shihata, I. F. I. (1988). The World Bank and Human Rights: An Analysis of the Legal Issues and the Record of Achievements. *Denver Journal of International Law and Policy, 17*(1), 39–66.

Solotaroff, J. L., & Pande, R. P. (2014). *Violence Against Women and Girls: Lessons from South Asia.* New York: World Bank.

Umaña, A. (Ed.) (1998). *The World Bank Inspection Panel: The First Four Years (1994–1998).* Washington, DC: World Bank.

UN. (2012). *United Nations Population Fund: Final Country Programme Document for India* (DP/FPA/CPD/IND/8). New York: UN.

UN-Government of India. (2013). *India UNDAF: United Nations Development Action Framework 2013–2017.* New Delhi: UN-Government of India.

UN Women. (2013a). *Ending Violence Against Women.* New Delhi: UN Women.

UN Women. (2013b). *Mid-term Evaluation of UN Women's Anti-human Trafficking Programme.* New Delhi: UN Women.

UN Women. (2014). *UN Women Annual Report 2014.* New York: UN Women.

UNFPA. (2013). *Country Programme Action Plan 2013–2017.* New York: UNFPA.

UNFPA. (2014). *United Nations Population Fund: The UNFPA Strategic Plan, 2014–2017.* New York: UNFPA.

Venkatesh, S., & Satpathy, S. K. (2006). Human Resources for Health in India's National Rural Health Mission: Dimension and Challenges. *World Health Organization; Regional Health Forum, 10*(1), 29–37.

Wade, R. (1997). Greening the Bank: The Struggle Over the Environment 1970–1995. In D. Kapur, J. P. Lewis, & R. Webb (Eds.), *The World Bank: Its First Half-Century* (Vol. 2, pp. 611–734). Washington, DC: Brookings Institutions Press.

Weaver, C. (2008). *Hypocrisy Trap: The World Bank and the Poverty of Reform.* Princeton, NJ: Princeton University Press.

World Bank. (2001). *Integrating Gender in World Bank Assistance* (Operations Evaluation Department #23035). New York: World Bank.

World Bank. (2002a). *Integrating Gender Into the World Bank's Work: A Strategy For Action.* Washington, DC: World Bank.

World Bank. (2002b). *Safeguard Policies: Framework for Improving Development Effectiveness: A Discussion Note.* New York: World Bank.

World Bank. (2006). *World Development Report 2006: Equity and Development.* Washington, DC: World Bank.

World Bank. (2010). *National Rural Livelihoods Program: Project Information Document* (AB5993). New Delhi: World Bank.

World Bank. (2013a). *Country Partnership Strategy for India for the Period FY2013–2017*. New York: World Bank.

World Bank. (2013b). *Country Partnership Strategy for India For the Period FY2013–2017*. New York: World Bank.

World Health Organization et.al. (2011). *Preventing Gender-based Sex Selection: An Interagency Statement OHCHR, UNFPA, UNICEF, UN Women, and WHO*. Geneva: World Health Organization.

6
Strategies and Outcomes of Rights-based Approaches

Strategies of a Rights-based Approach

Development is *always* a political process. Even development projects that claim to look solely at economic growth, infrastructure improvement, and the like have clear political implications. They come from a set of economic principles grounded in a political ideology; they seek to "improve" society in a way that follows that ideology; they are implemented, ultimately, by governments, that know who will be the winners and losers. To paraphrase Robert Cox (1981, p. 127), there is no development theory for itself; development is always for someone and serves a particular purpose. It is never neutral, and it never fails to either reinforce or challenge existing political structures.

That said, this book began with the premise that rights-based approaches to development, if they are to be more than mere rhetorical exercises, must more explicitly embrace the political implications and challenges of development programming than previous UN efforts have done. The very definition of RBA includes a critique of existing political structures in almost any society. UN agencies cannot just redefine development as a "right" and then insist that governments have a duty to provide it, without engaging in empty rhetoric. Rights-based approaches, to have meaning, must question and challenge existing structures of society and identify the reasons people are unable to provide for themselves. It has been a basic premise of this book that a strong sign that this is happening will be resistance from privileged groups and the need to overcome that resistance through careful diplomacy by UN agencies (and, presumably, anyone else truly dedicated to RBA).

As shown in Chapter 1, many of the implications of RBA—or, at any rate, RBA done correctly—require a rethinking of how UN development agencies push for their preferred agenda. It was surely a myth all along that older development approaches were apolitical or, at any rate, uncontroversial. Still, it was a myth that had a great deal of importance to UN bodies. Recall that avoiding "politics" was a central concern for many UN agencies, which fear losing influence or being asked to leave a host country if their work is seen as overtly challenging to the political order. Moreover, the nature of the UN itself is supposed to be neutral—however that is defined.

"If you do this head-on," one key informant at UNICEF told me about pressing a rights-based approach, "you can undo all the progress you've made." "If you call nutrition a national shame," for example, "the Prime Minister's office will call you the next day."[1] "The resistance is never overt," said a UNDP staff member in a regional office; "we just won't let you into our town," is the reply of local officials challenged by empowerment efforts.[2] A telling anecdote came from a UNICEF communication specialist, describing efforts to organize communities in support of education. The staffer told of going through policy documents and replacing the word "mobilization" with "participation" since mobilization implied having people challenge their government rather than simply cooperate with it.[3] While clearly stating that the Indian government does have a commitment to decentralization and citizen participation that is both legal and practical, the staff member also noted that it is a delicate process when one is trying to directly change power structures and a traditional social order.[4]

Other UN personnel also mentioned the difficulty of pushing for human rights, when these can challenge entrenched power at various levels. "Our mandate," one UNDP staff said, "is to work with the most marginalized, but they are so because of the existing power structure."[5] One interviewee specifically mentioned resistance by upper caste officials to programs that aim to empower "untouchable" Dalits, and NGO workers who were "roughed up" by local people who resented these efforts.[6] A government official who worked with the UN called their Access to Justice programs "a joke," and he stated that the sophisticated government bureaucracy "can easily obfuscate any rights issues" or push back if outside agencies "cross a certain rubicon."[7] The Government of India, he said, was experienced at giving donors like the UN the "runaround," keeping the money and goodwill flowing while not really paying much attention to anything but their own priorities.

How, then, can rights through development be pursued while remaining aware of the political sensitivities this can engender? When asked if he faced government resistance to rights language, one staff person in a state field office responded, "If I wasn't in this chair, I could answer that."[8] And the notion of promoting rights under the radar might seem less than optimal to those, like Urban Jonsson, cited in Chapter 2, who see the essence of RBA in building the capacity of government to fulfill the rights claims of their citizens. Yet the reality of promoting C&P rights, in particular, requires more tact from UN agencies than used to be needed.

Several strategies that helped avoid state sensitivity and the restrictions of Article 2(7) of the UN Charter were mentioned repeatedly in interviews. Many of them are clear from the preceding chapters, but they are worth spelling out here.

First, and most common, is the careful and determined use of data—rather than anecdotes or vague moral arguments—to demonstrate to government officials how rights are being violated. We have seen the importance given to data about malnutrition rates, for example, and how that has been used to pressure the government. But, "you never go with UN-collected data," was the refrain, because government counterparts will simply say that your information is biased. This was a common point: the data had to be from the government itself or at least from third-party organizations (such as universities) that had a reputation for impartial reporting. Interview subjects often stated that they use government data in a way that their interlocutors cannot ignore or dismiss.

Interviewees also referred to the *Human Development Report* as a useful tool; in particular, India now publishes state-level Human Development Reports, which can be used to compare state progress. Pointing out to state officials that they lag behind other states turns out to be an extremely effective tool for spurring action. Various states would compete with others to do the best in on the Human Development Index, and this could in turn be used to press state and federal government officials for change. Perhaps not surprisingly, UNDP staff in particular seemed especially pleased with how the Index was becoming a vital advocacy tool.

Rights issues themselves are generally translated into matters of data by UN agencies or arise from data-driven techniques. Thus, for example, advocacy for the status of women is transformed into data about women's income versus men, or the poor nutritional status of girls versus boys, or the economic marginalization of Scheduled Castes or Tribal peoples. The importance of disaggregated data has been covered extensively already. Indeed, it can seem sometimes to be a synonym for RBA: as if this were all that was needed to identify the structures of deprivation. Talking to some

UN staff, it can seem as if simply pointing to discrepancies among various groups is their definition of RBA rather than what actually needs to be done to address those discrepancies.

A second strategy often mentioned was the judicious use of the media. UN staff agreed that the media is a vital ally in promoting rights standards and overcoming resistance from government. Using the media is important for making people aware of their rights and changing attitudes detrimental to rights, such as attitudes toward girl children. But it can also be used to pressure the government. Experienced personnel know the importance of building relationships with sympathetic reporters and others who can get the word out about serious problems and preferred solutions. The media can also be used to ensure transparency in government, and reporters can be convinced to ask questions about social issues. Most UN agencies conduct campaigns through media outlets on key human rights issues such as women's rights and child labor.

As a general rule, wise development agencies never go to the media first about serious issues; as a UNICEF official stated with respect to an area where the government is battling a Marxist insurgency, the "faith and trust" that the government feels toward UNICEF would be undermined if issues were discussed with the press before the government itself.[9] All interviewees agreed that good relations with government partners are vital and to blindside them by going to the media first would be disastrous. But once government is informed—often using government data to make the point—then media outlets can be used to hold the government's feet to the fire.

In the course of this book we've seen a third strategy, which is promoting rights issues without actually using the term *rights*; instead, policies are presented using less provocative language. UNFPA staff, for example, explained that while they speak of rights when talking with their national government counterparts, they avoid the term when interacting with lower levels of government and grassroots representatives. "Once you've gotten down to the grassroots level, you've already won the battle," said a highly placed UNFPA official; "talking of rights just confuses the issue, and might turn people off."[10] Recall the UNICEF official who noted, "If I call it 'this,' there's going to be a raising of eyebrows," so you "camouflage the language."[11] Interview subjects agreed that the comfort level of officials with rights language varied; some were open to the idea while others were not. "Once you've ratified [CEDAW] . . . at least you have to pay lip service to it," was the take of one UN Women interviewee.[12] But even with these documents in place, the language of rights sometimes had to be used judiciously.

One example of this was mentioned at the start of this chapter. Another was brought up earlier: avoiding the term "conflict zone" when discussing areas with Naxalite insurgencies or other ongoing violence. The government does not like to admit that such zones exist and are uncomfortable with the international legal implications of the term. And as noted above, potentially inflammatory language is sometimes avoided in direct discussions with government agents as well. In general, staff thought, at the higher levels of government there is more acceptance of rights language; greater difficulties were found lower down. This was not entirely in accord with some government and NGO staff, who thought that at the high level there was more lip service to rights but no greater true receptivity. Still, language matters, and good diplomats learn to use the correct language.

A fourth strategy commonly brought up was the "convening power" of UN agencies. UN staff in India repeatedly mentioned that their greatest power stems from their ability to bring parties together—notably elected officials, members of the civil service, civil society agents, local members of Panchayats, self-help groups, and other grassroots organizations. The term often used was *goodwill:* the UN has substantial reserves of goodwill, is perceived to be an "honest broker," and is able to leverage that status as it pursues goals like community empowerment. This must be done carefully: a UN Women interviewee, for example, noted that it was important to be "very careful" to bring together a balance of officials from both the ruling party and the opposition parties.[13] Similarly, a UNICEF state official described how it was important not to praise government efforts too much, or be seen working with them too closely around election time, for fear of appearing to favor one party over another.[14] Yet with care, this can be an effective way of bringing issues forward and putting pressure on the right parties.

The upshot of all this is that bureaucracies like those of UN agencies are strategic actors, with their own goals and desires (or multiple goals and desires) that they pursue despite resistance from outside. One question, which has not really been addressed here for the sake of time, is whether these goals have more to do with bureaucratic politics (that is, furthering the size and influence of the organization), the personal interests of staff, or a principled desire to further development and human rights. I tend to come down largely on a combination of two and three; but that is for Chapter 7 to discuss at greater length. But the ability of these agencies to push their agenda despite resistance—and the strategies they produce—is central to the argument that these are agents with great potential for rights promotion, whatever their motives. However, how much that potential is realized depends on the effectiveness of RBA, which is discussed below.

Evaluation of a Rights-based Approach

In 2013, the World Bank's Independent Evaluation Group, the semi-independent body that carries out assessments of a program's success or failure, had this to say about a reproductive and child health empowerment project the World Bank is financing:

> *Impact: Unevaluable*
> Maternal, infant and child mortality and total fertility are affected by a broad range of socio-economic factors, improved reproductive and child services being only one among many others. Given the timeframe of program implementation and the unavailability of health services and impact data after 2010, it is difficult to assess with confidence the extent of the program's contribution to documented trends in these outcomes, as well as the trends in these outcomes themselves for the project's latter years. Nevertheless, because of the good design of the program, it is *plausible to assume* that the program *might* be contributing to these outcomes, especially in the later years when implementation was more accelerated, and in the post-project years. (World Bank, 2013, p. 6; emphasis added)

A program evaluation report had something similar to say about work being done by UNDP: "In discussing the impact of any projects and programs, there are always concerns and disputes with respect to attribution and the extent to which any outcomes can be represented as the result of particular activities. . . . In India, this issue is further complicated by the size and diversity of the country and the budgets of central and state governments. . . . *Since the data collected are largely qualitative*, the problems of subjectivity and bias, on the part of both respondents and interviewers, cannot be entirely eliminated" (UNDP, 2012, p. 6; emphasis added).

It seems fairly obvious that an analysis of rights-based approaches to development in India—or anywhere else—needs to discuss the central issue of whether they *work*. Naturally, this depends on what it means to work; what the goals are, what time frame they ought to be achieved in, and the extent to which they are achieved. Development, as a concept, is always problematic—and political, as noted above. Any conversation about development projects ought to include what they are trying to accomplish (Jolly, 2004). One of the great journeys in development thinking has been the regular re-evaluation of what development projects ought to accomplish; and thus, any evaluation of development projects and agencies needs to take that into account. As goals change, so will the metrics used to assess progress toward them.

One striking element of UN efforts in RBA across various countries is the lack of consistent, project-level evaluation efforts. Some of the organizations under study have an independent evaluation office, for example the Independent Evaluation Group of the World Bank. Others do their own evaluations or commission independent consultants to prepare reports. Reports almost always differ in their terms of reference, the methodology used, and the metrics measured, as well as the time frame: sometimes individual projects are evaluated as they happen, other times an entire five-year programming cycle is reviewed at once. This makes it extremely difficult to get an overall picture of how programs are doing and make comparisons; there is no single system of evaluation and documentation that allows comparisons or the aggregation of data for a meta-study. Most of the evaluations of UN programs in India—particularly those aimed at social programs and human development—note that the data is largely qualitative, based on interviews with various "stakeholders" in the UN, in the government, among civil society partners, and occasionally those people who are intended to be helped. This will be shown in more detail below.

Of course, the rights-based approach has not really replaced other strategies; development doesn't work that way. Different approaches coexist, meld together, and sometimes even work against each other. Indeed, even within the UN, which has made RBA its central development paradigm, it works along with other strategies. It might be most accurate to say that RBA is less a fully developed paradigm of development than a set of principles. For example, it does not replace or invalidate notions like basic needs approaches, which focus on the provision of basic social welfare rather than economic growth (Stewart, 1989), or concern over gender or environmental sustainability as the keys to sustainable development (Elliott, 2012; Tinker, 1990). Instead, it is intended to sharpen and supplement them with new emphasis on the political nature of development. The interaction of human rights, politics (and particularly the powerlessness of the poor and other vulnerable populations), and economic development has garnered increasing attention in the past decade, and RBA seeks to uncover and address the political and power relations that hold back development for millions of people.

If we are to assess the effectiveness and success of a rights-based approach to development, it is important to be clear what we are trying to accomplish; it must, after all, be measured against what it is trying to achieve. There are a number of different ways that an RBA can be conceptualized: each will imply a different set of metrics.

- RBA can be seen as a more effective way of *producing development*, defined as economic progress either at the national scale (GDP growth) or at a more personal scale, such as the provision of basic human needs or human development. It is a new strategy that provides better outcomes—defined as poverty alleviation and rising standards of living (broadly defined)—than other development strategies. This builds on the notion that rights have an instrumental value—that they empower people and thus allow them to be more economically productive, as well as more able to demand services, hold government accountable, and participate positively in the development process. In this case, the success of RBA will be whether it is more effective at developing national or local economies than other approaches.
- RBA might be a *normative framework* into which other development efforts can be fit. In this view, development still aims to alleviate poverty, provide a social safety net, promote access to safe drinking water, etc. What's added, however, is a set of more values-based obligations that improve development by paying attention to the way it's approached and the sorts of outcomes it promotes. These values include equity, political empowerment, and respect for individuals. Development projects are then examined through the lens of this moral framework. It asks, in essence, whether development is being done in a way that has certain moral touchstones. The success of RBA will thus be whether these normative goals are met: whether development increases equity, empowerment, and other similar goals. As Urban Jonsson has put it, "A human rights approach to programming suggests an ethical dimension both to *what* should be done (desired outcome) and *how* it should be done (process). (2003, p. 20; emphasis in original)
- RBA can also be justified by saying that the policy is a moral imperative in itself. Although this justification is not much discussed in the UN development literature, it comes up frequently in interviews with UN staff, many of whom (although by no means all) feel that integrating rights and development is the "right thing to do." In this view, the success of

RBA will largely be measured by whether RBA policies are actually being implemented.
- RBA can also be justified by reference to the legal obligations of states to respect human rights as spelled out in various treaties. States, this argument goes, are legally obligated to respect rights, and the UN is obligated through its charter to assist this effort. The success of RBA will thus be measured through the achievement of human rights in states and the preparedness of states to live up to their obligations under human rights instruments.

Of course, these are not mutually exclusive; indeed, elements of most, if not all, of them coexist in many documents dealing with RBA, and practitioners also often refer to more than one at a time when discussing their efforts at RBA. Yet each of these implies a different set of metrics for assessing success. This greatly complicates how one ought to measure and justify RBA. A successful project might be one that helps deliver better services for the poor, or that is successful in having legislation passed to make some basic service a legal right, or one that leads to economic growth that benefits a wide range of people. There is no single way of saying a project is successful.

Assessing the Rights-Development Link

First and foremost, rights-based approach to development is seen by many as the most effective way of promoting development, as defined by UNDP and the rest of the international development community. "Fundamentally, a human rights approach to poverty is about the empowerment of the poor," according to one UN study; "human rights provide one way of weakening 'the web of powerlessness' and enhancing the capabilities of poor women and men so that they can take more control of their lives" (Hunt, Nowak, & Osman, 2002, p. 11). But is this the case? The link remains tenuous and hard to measure accurately. As one UN study puts it:

> The chain of causality, whether implicitly or explicitly spelled out, seems to be as follows: increasing citizens' voice will make public institutions more responsive to citizen needs and demands and thereby more accountable for their actions . . . this is particularly important in terms of supporting the empowerment, greater inclusion, and increased voice of traditionally marginalized groups . . . if they are to demand greater responsiveness and accountability from the state and have the opportunity to move out of poverty. . . . Rather than being spelt out, however,

the significance of voice and accountability is usually implied through their relationship to the institutional characteristics that define "good" governance. (Menocal and Sharma, 2008, p. 17)

Development assessment, done properly, should involve a "theory of change," or "chain of causality," defined as "a representation of how an organization or initiative is expected to achieve results and an identification of the underlying assumptions made" (Imas and Rist, 2009, p. 151). Good evaluations include a theory of change to establish a causal link between strategies and outcomes. Assessment should include a theory that connects inputs to outputs. UNICEF, for example, explains its theory of change by stating, "One of the most important assumptions in this context is that evidenced-based laws, policies and implementation plans combined with doable and cost-effective technical solutions can make a difference in the lives of disadvantaged children. This technical assumption is nurtured by the belief in the power of scientific arguments to act to improve the situation of children if they are provided with evidence and practical methods, tools and interventions" (UNICEF, 2014, p. 2). In evaluating the concept of RBA, particularly the argument that rights promote development, it is important to bring some clarity to why and how this is true. As a UNICEF India evaluation notes, "A primary purpose for this evaluation was to test the Theory of Change model. . . . The Theory of Change structures the individual strategies into a consistent overall model" (UNICEF, 2011, p. 30).

Ultimately, it would be useful to employ counterfactual analysis to development assessment: Would development progress have been greater had a different approach been applied? Would the achievement of rights-based social goals be different? In practice counterfactual analysis is quite difficult to employ because it is difficult to know what might have happened in such a hypothetical situation (Cracknell, 2000, pp. 128–130). The promise of RBA is greater effectiveness, and this ought to be measured in some way. UNDP, for example, conducts periodic "Assessments of Development Results" (ADR), which, while not actually employing counterfactual analysis, do analyze the overall development picture in a state and attempt to draw conclusions about where progress (or failure) came from.

Typically these assessments discuss RBA but don't focus on it in particular. Mostly these evaluations consider the overall success of projects; rights promotion is discussed only in a larger context. This is important: in reviewing the available documents on effectiveness, it isn't always possible to see precisely what the rights-based approach is. A lot gets lumped together. It's not always easy to discern what components are being considered part of RBA and what is a more traditional development approach.

Difficulties of Evaluation of RBA

Of all the agencies operating in India for the UN, UNDP has undertaken the most extensive set of evaluations. The latest UNDP overall evaluation report, covering the period 2004–2011, begins with an explanation of the difficulties of data collection and review of UNDP programming. It lists its data sources as:

- Three outcome evaluations commissioned by the country office for specific projects, that is, democratic governance; energy and environment, and poverty; and HIV/AIDS.
- "Stakeholder interviews" with government representatives, civil society organizations, private-sector representatives, UN agencies, multilateral organizations, bilateral donors, former UNDP staff, "and, importantly, the intended beneficiaries of the program in the states, districts, and localities where UNDP works."
- Site visits to target regions where the projects are being undertaken. (UNDP, 2012, p. 2)

The assessment team also notes the use of "desk reviews" of existing documents, the use of focus groups, and observation of projects underway.

Despite this data-gathering effort, the UNDP cautions, "since the data collected are largely qualitative, the problems of subjectivity and bias, on the part of both respondents and interviewers, cannot be entirely eliminated. Of course, these were sought to be reduced as far as possible" (UNDP, 2012, p. 6). Another UNDP study contains this very strong caveat, in a chapter devoted to the theory of change within UNDP programming: "The targets and indicators in the present results framework are skewed towards the quantitative and are not conducive to tracking or elucidating qualitative and process elements. The results framework needs to be revisited to remedy this gap" (Menon-Sen & Shiva Kumar, 2010, p. 51). It goes on to say about women's rights in particular that "At this point, the overall impact of UNDP's work on gender equality and women's rights in the country is not possible to assess...The need for technical support to undertake programme-specific gender analysis has been expressed by more than one programme division" (Menon-Sen & Shiva Kumar, 2010, p. 53). Other evaluation reports contain similar caveats. One particularly interesting one is contained in an assessment of UN Women's work on gender and the Indian budget process: "It is worth reiterating that this evaluation does not attempt to attribute gender equity achievements to UN Women's [gender responsive budgeting (GRB)] activities. The evaluation was not designed to infer causality; rather, the study seeks to understand the ways in which UN Women has contributed toward understanding and practice of GRB in the country" (UN Women, 2012, p. 7). A key UNICEF report contained a litany of problems involved with evaluation of the program in India: "little, if any, baseline data available to benchmark progress"; "UNICEF reporting indicators are mostly at the activity and intermediate result level, while the impact indicators are at the national level and often cannot be attributed directly to UNICEF. The lack of outcome level indicators (e.g., change in performance, change in quality of services, change in coverage of marginalized populations) ... made it difficult to attribute or demonstrate the contribution of the higher level outcomes to UNCIEF," and even "limited access to national and state government officials: in some cases it was difficult to access pertinent national and state level official for interviews" (UNICEF, 2011, pp. 20–21).

In other words, if "assessment" of programs by these agencies is defined as determining whether they have had a substantial outcome on the overall progress of development in India, then there is a sense that many of the most important metrics are simply unknowable. This becomes truer as agencies move away from traditional service-delivery models and really try to implement the social-empowerment ideals of RBA. For example, UNFPA can justly point to a successful effort (through consultants working with the government) to increase the number of "First Referral Units" (FRUs—clinics to provide basic health care) affiliated with 24-hour primary health care centers that meet the standards set by the Ministry of Health and Family Welfare. It considers this a successful intervention, raising the number of FRUs meeting the government standard from 30% to 52% of the total by the end of the assessment period (UNFPA, 2011, p. 15). UNICEF can point to a program to control anemia in the Tonk district of Rajasthan and assert that 80% of school-age girls were being reached in the target areas, although that report admits that the baseline study is inadequate, making it hard to know how much this is an improvement (UNICEF, 2011, p. 95). But it is much more difficult to say that a program aimed at, say, teaching the *hijra* community about their legal rights, has actually improved the situation of this group or truly made them more aware of their rights. UNDP, as will be discussed below, can point to the number of judges trained by its Access to Justice program, but proving that this has led to more respect for the rights of those caught up in the legal system is not easy to do. And even when progress is measured against an effective baseline, proving that a particular UN intervention was responsible is nearly impossible in a country as large and complicated as India.

If RBA is presented as a moral imperative in and of itself, then these connections are not so important. The proper metric for assessment would become simply whether the programs are being properly implemented or not; that in itself would be a success. And, as we have seen in the sections devoted to particular units of the UN, it is not always clear that RBA is even being implemented; recall, for example, the general feeling within UNICEF that the Child Rights section personnel are the "rights people," and therefore other officials can focus more on other issues—the measurable ones of delivering vaccines, building schools, and so forth. Thus, the evaluation section of UNDP, for example, regularly assesses country programs to determine their compliance with UNDP guidelines, including their use of RBA.

It is not unusual for the assessment to determine that there is spotty compliance. For example, a 2006 report on "gender mainstreaming" says, "There are commendable efforts to mainstream gender in most of UNDP's practice areas, but there is no clear strategy, and staff do not seem to know how to apply gender mainstreaming perspectives. . . . Overall, the evaluation concludes that UNDP lacks both the capacity and the institutional framework for a systematic and effective gender mainstreaming approach" (Evaluation Office 2006, pp. viii–ix) A substantial report prepared for UNICEF in 2005 by external evaluators (and provided to the author on the condition that it not be cited or quoted) looked exclusively at the extent to which UNICEF had been able to mainstream RBA and to implement a rights-based policy. It concluded that much progress had been made, but commitment to RBA remained uneven through the organization. (UNICEF has undertaken studies since then also to look at whether programs are being implemented in a rights-based way.) This example is particularly illustrative of the well-known difficulty of international organizations adapting to new priorities (Wade, 1997; Weaver and Leiteritz, 2005). Although UNICEF is just one of several leading development agencies, its long-standing efforts to use the Convention on the Rights of the Child as a programming tool has made it a thought leader on RBA, and many other agencies look to it for guidance and inspiration. Yet agencies continue to evaluate RBA from the perspective of "are we doing it?" rather than "does it work?" This is true not just in India but also around the world.

Agency-Specific Reports

How, then, are individual agencies doing in their implementation of RBA in India? Has it been a success measured against any of these metrics? Is there even an effort to see if there is? The five main agencies studied here—UNDP, UNICEF, UNFPA, UN Women, and the World Bank are discussed below.

United Nations Develoypwment Programme

Evaluation of the last programming cycle for UNDP consisted of an Assessment of Development Results report and three thematic reports mentioned above: Democratic Governance; Energy & Environment and Poverty; and HIV/AIDS. The ADR mentions several times that UNDP follows a rights-based approach to development in India and mentions in its executive summary, for example, the need for "greater economic justice" (UNDP, 2012, p. xi). The report notes that the largest problems continue to be the disproportionate number of women, Scheduled Castes, and Scheduled Tribes who remain in poverty (UNDP, 2012, p. 8). Despite the reference to a rights-based approach to development, however, the report overall focuses on achievement of greater human development outcomes rather than the achievement of rights, either ES&C rights or C&P rights. The report, interestingly, notes that a "lack of strategic focus" has been a hindering factor in the effectiveness of the UNDP's efforts (UNDP, 2012, p. xiii). RBA is certainly important to what UNDP is doing, but according to its own evaluation, RBA does not seem to provide a strategic touchstone that guides all work.

Overall the ADR is fairly critical of what UNDP has been doing in India. A central critique is that the work of UNDP is "skewed towards the 'supply side' of the development equation"; in other words, "the central strategy for addressing the issue of social exclusion—improving the targeting, outreach and management of government programmes—appears to be based on the assumption that equality of opportunity will automatically translate into equality of outcome for marginalized groups" (UNDP, 2012, p. 17). This finding mirrored an earlier medium-term report; it also found that helping marginalized groups required a much deeper and more nuanced understanding of the patterns of discrimination than can be captured in simple, "upstream" work such as training judges, changing legislation, or making Panchayats more inclusive. Both the medium term report and the ADR call for an articulation of a superior theory of change that can "place economic growth within the larger framework of human rights, demonstrating the integration of social and economic goals as equally critical to development" (Menon-Sen & Shiva Kumar, 2010, p. 49). Not surprisingly, it is easier for UNDP to be effective—that is, show measureable progress—working with government counterparts rather than though the more difficult work of social mobilization. The report notes, "The Government of India officially made 'inclusive growth' its slogan for the Eleventh Five-Year Plan" and that "there have been moves towards a more rights-based discourse in public policy, expressed in two important pieces of legislation that have already been passed—the Mahatma Gandhi National Rural Employment Guarantee Act . . . and the Right to Education Act" (UNDP, 2012, p. 9). Yet once again legal change is not enough, and that a focus on rhetorical changes is not the same as true empowerment.

A second, important critique contained in the ADR involves the number of projects being undertaken by UNDP, and a lack of "focus" that results from having so many different projects under way. This includes both the number of programming areas (from Energy and Environment to HIV/AIDS) and the number of projects being undertaken within any particular programming area. This was, in fact, *despite* a reduction in project areas starting in 2007. Related to this is an observation that many of the UNDP project staff seem lacking in expertise in their subject area, and that there is too much reliance on young, often expatriate staff who are supposed to be providing technical assistance and capacity for government counterparts. This seems crucial, considering the number of times in interviews (and in official reports) UNDP notes its ability to provide expertise. It also seems to correspond with a number of government informants, who, while noting the good intentions of UNDP, questioned its ability to make much headway against the extremely large, professional Indian bureaucracy, which is proud of its own capacity. We've seen how government officials claim to know how to appease UN agencies while working quietly to undermine them. These are not observations about RBA in particular; they speak only to the general work of the UNDP. However, the lack of expertise and the wide variety of programs being tackled is not unrelated to both the difficult and diffuse nature of the empowerment work being done by all UN agencies.

In terms of specific projects, the UNDP evaluation of Democratic Governance programs notes the same concerns. It details that the "technical cell" supporting MGNREGA "will need to comprise [*sic*] of more senior staff, with significant field experience and strong NGO networks at the grassroots" (Satyanand, 2012, p. 51). Similarly, it notes that UNDP relations with government counterparts are too irregular to be entirely effective: "One strategy is to keep influential officials apprised on major programme developments and achievements.... Equally useful would be to build relationships with other Ministries/Departments that might interface with a programme on the ground.... A final tip is to invest in relationships with junior officers, who generally keep their seniors abreast of pressing issues and commitment (Satyanand, 2012, p. 45)." It ends with the advice that "UNDP should also engage with politicians to drive reform politically, since the issues it works on are all extremely saleable politically. *UNDP needs to 'run a political campaign within the government'*" (Satyanand, 2012, p. 45; emphasis added). Similarly, the report on HIV/AIDS notes that UNDP can "gain greater leverage by taking much more proactive steps" in terms of bringing its social policy successes to the government (Rego, 2012, p. 21). Despite all the efforts—documented throughout this volume—to leverage the agency's political and diplomatic skills, evaluations still suggest that UNDP will have to do more to have an impact on government actions, to the extent of running its own "political campaigns."

Within the specifically RBA-oriented portfolio, the evaluation document also cites a number of important successes. State-level Human Development Reports, it notes, have been a very successful initiative. The report also notes the importance of the "Capacity Development for Local Governance" portfolio, saying "the training is generally seen to be useful, especially in some cases where particular trainers of trainers ... were very successful," although that success hinged on the quality of the trainers (UNDP, 2012, p. 26). Efforts to strengthen decentralized planning "have the potential to be extremely relevant," although implementation is often a struggle because district politicians too often ignore the input of the Panchayats (UNDP, 2012, p. 27). The specific study on governance does report that decentralization "has triggered a mindset shift in State and District planners and policy-makers.... Most importantly, communities have begun to become more assertive. Having contributed to the District Plan one year, they then demand results from block, district and state officials the next year, sometimes quite aggressively" (Satyanand, 2012, p. 19).

Here the overall ADR disagrees somewhat with the specific evaluation of the governance portfolio, with one much more optimistic than the other about the ability of newly empowered communities to change policy at the district level. This disagreement can be largely attributed to the qualitative and impressionistic nature of evaluations. The governance evaluation reports that "informants from among the '1000 potential leaders' identified and trained by the [UNDP and NGOs] said that the programme had 'inspired' them by giving them the opportunity to interact personally with senior politicians and by keeping them politically motivated" (Satyanand, 2012, p. 33), while the ADR notes the uncertain downstream results of this work. The difference seems to stem from one approach, which is satisfied that community organizers are "inspired" to press for their rights, compared with another, which evaluates the success of the program by looking at the concrete impact it has had on policy. It is easy to dismiss the first, but this report was not written by someone who takes for granted that all well-meaning efforts are important; it goes on to say that the Right to Information program has been successful at producing a wide variety of important training materials but "fell short on most of its other objectives." The report notes that "UNDP's investment in RTI training has not had the extensive national outcome that was intended ... many government offices around the country, particularly at the block level and below, still fail to report even the *most basic* information required by the act—that is, the name and contact details of the Public Information Officer!" (Satyanand, 2012, p. 35; emphasis in original). However, the vagueness of how outcomes are judged, and even of what is trying to be accomplished, leaves a great deal of room for interpretation as to what constitutes a successful program.

The conclusions note several times that it is very difficult to gauge exactly how effective UNDP efforts have been exactly because it is so difficult to assess the type of work UNDP does, and because there are insufficient monitoring and evaluation processes in place (UNDP, 2012, p. 56). The report notes, interestingly, "it may be necessary to reconsider the current use of the Results Based Management approach to move away from quantitative indicators that may provide only relatively simplistic and possibly misleading indicators and also not adequately capture impact ... requiring programme officers to submit quantitative indicators of success may trivialize the issue" (UNDP, 2012, pp. 56–57). Recall that UNICEF and UNDP staff had complained that results-based management practices had hindered their work in RBA by requiring quantitative indicators of success that did not adequately capture the social work intrinsic to their efforts.

Overall, the final evaluation of the last programming cycle for UNDP is a mixed bag, but more critical than praising of the results achieved. Along with noting the lack of strategic focus, the report states that even human development had lost some salience in the program but was "making a comeback," lack of capacity had to be addressed, and more work was needed with the government to align UNDP's and the Government of India's priorities. As for the measurement of effectiveness, the key issue was whether policies were being implemented effectively and efficiently, and in a sustainable manner (with the answer that it was also a mixed bag, but that great room for improvement existed). In other words, there was less concern with the effectiveness of the policy on development outcomes, than on whether the policy was being followed. Little was said in any of the evaluations about contributions to the national economic growth of India in the social development field (as opposed to work in, say, Energy & Environment). Success here, then, is largely (but not exclusively) defined as achieving the specific goals of RBA and human development programming. The policy is the goal, to a large extent, or, at least, there is an implicit acceptance that some results simply cannot be measured, so there must be faith that the policy, properly implemented, will have the desired results.

UNICEF

Like UNDP, UNICEF evaluations have determined that a shift to more "upstream" work is necessary to improve effectiveness. This has been referred to at UNICEF-India as "changing gears," a result of evaluations done in 2008. In language similar to that used for UNDP, UNICEF found "a 2010 study showed that capacity development has been adequately articulated for each of the programmes and their results. At the same time, the study found that these activities are not necessarily informed by an analysis of institutional and capacity constraints to help evolve capacity development plans, with the possible exception of HIV and Communication for Development programmes." It also noted, "A lack of systematic evaluation makes it difficult to ascertain the extent of the strategic shift of capacity development interventions and their impact on systems strengthening" (UNICEF India, 2011, p. 3). So, as with UNDP, the most recent analysis of development outcomes notes that "at the national level, the UNICEF overarching strategy is seen as less effective. Its ability to work in the upstream is not perceived to be a strength because of a perception of insufficient capacity in research and policy analysis, *and because it is not perceived as an organization that is always willing to push government on controversial issues*" (UNICEF, 2011, p. 11; emphasis added). The move toward upstream and policy-based work, it appears, is hampered exactly by the difficulty of pressing for rights-based development policies as they are understood in this volume; finding a way to advocate for them is both a key to their success and one of the biggest challenges facing UN agencies.

The terms of the UNICEF country evaluation were laid out clearly:

- Determine to what extent, and how, the key strategies employed by UNICEF have contributed to better positioning UNICEF in the national development agenda of India.
- Measure the extent to which the key strategies accelerated and strengthened the achievement of higher level results.
- Provide findings, conclusions, and recommendations to inform the 2013–2017 UNICEF country programme.
- Provide findings, conclusions, and recommendations that can be shared with other parts of UNICEF. (UNICEF, 2011, p. 18)

So, it looked both at how well RBA is being implemented (as a "key strategy") and to what extent it was actually leading to success in desired development outcomes (and thus could be shared with other parts of UNICEF as a way forward). The key parts of the evaluation were structured around the current theory of change; the relevance of UNICEF's work to India's development priorities and with overall UNICEF goals (e.g., inclusion and equity); the effectiveness of UNICEF interventions; the efficiency of its work given its resources; and program sustainability.

One important component of the UNICEF program review, again, was an analysis of whether RBA concepts are even fully understood by staff and effectively implemented in programming. The report found, for example, that gender issues and women's rights were "not clearly understood" by many staff members and "there is a gap between knowledge of gender concepts and their application to programmes/projects" (UNICEF, 2011, p. 28). On the other hand, "the evaluation found that social exclusion was considered in the majority of the case studies, particularly on the supply side (government as service provider)" (UNICEF, 2011, p. 35). The report, and the medium-term results report before it, also noted good understanding in other areas, such as "adopting strategies for the empowerment, representation, and inclusion of excluded communities" and "supporting responsive government services to ensure . . . inclusive services delivery" (UNICEF, 2011, p. 43). The UNICEF evaluation took whether RBA is understood and implemented as key metrics, before even considering the actual outcomes of those policies.

The overall sense of the report is a mixed bag of successes and failures. It notes, for example, that capacity-development programs (including those to help empower local-level committees and to train government officials to assist the socially excluded) are a strength of UNICEF, align well with the

Indian government's priorities, and have created many solid demonstration projects that can be replicated across the country. On the other hand, "despite the abundance of examples that the evaluation came across, the study did not find a lot of documented evidence of the actual outcomes of UNICEF's capacity development efforts" (UNICEF, 2011, p. 40). It also notes that "UNICEF's influence on the national agenda, with respect to social inclusion results mainly from its analytical studies, and advocacy in which it highlights underserved groups, problem areas in health and social indicators in socially excluded communities, [and] poor performance of government programs" (UNICEF, 2011, p. 41). This fits well with UNICEF's own perceptions, noted in Chapter 3 and repeated in the first section of this chapter, that its advocacy and use of data remains its greatest strategic asset. The report also singled out success in improving Panchayat-level performance and "the improved functioning of the government supported health, education, water and sanitation, and other facilities that are under the supervision of the Gram Panchayat . . . an indirect impact of the initiative is an improvement in panchayat-level governance . . . result[ing] in greater awareness of local issues" (UNICEF, 2011, p. 52). It also mentions that, for example, although it is difficult to get specific numbers, there are indications that decentralization efforts are, in fact, leading to better water and sanitation programs.

The report is skeptical about the push to codify new legal rights at the national and state level; it notes that while a great deal of rights-based legislation to help women and children has been passed by the government, there is little evidence that these laws are having an effect downstream. This criticism is remarkably similar to what was said about legal change in the UNDP report; passing legislation and making certain things "rights" is all well and good, but having the desired effect on citizen's lives is another thing. Laws are passed but enforcement is weak. Schemes, such as one intended to help women in conflict zones, have not "taken off." Plans that "moved towards the concept of a woman's agency and child rights . . . are clearly visible, albeit the progress has been slow." In language similar to the World Bank report cited earlier, the UNICEF report notes, "The fact is that many issues require much more socio-cultural research in order to determine the best strategy for addressing specific social problems. This is an area of potential support for UNICEF as addressing long term ingrained social attitudes and practices are sometimes *difficult for governments to address from a political perspective*" (UNICEF, 2011, p. 59; emphasis in original). Again, there is a need for more direct political participation from agencies that are still learning their way around.

UNFPA

UNFPA India assembled an evaluation team in 2011 to look over their country program (UNFPA's seventh official program since starting work in India) and issued a report in November 2011. The team spent three months collecting information, primarily qualitative, as the report states in its methodology section. The report covered all UNFPA actions in India during the 2008–2012 period (although not quite at the end of the period—this was in order to have suggestions ready in time for the next country program).

The various thematic sections of the UNFPA report open with sets of national-level achievement goals: for example, the section on reproductive health lists its desired results as:

- Reduction in maternal mortality ratio from 201 per 100,000 live births in 2001–03 to less than 100 in 2012
- Reduction in unmet need for contraception: 80% of unmet need to be met
- Reduction in adolescent fertility rate from 16.8% to 12% by 2012
- Reduction in adult HIV prevalence from the 2005 level of 0.36 (UNFPA, 2011, p. 23)

Other sections open with similar sets of goals. As with the other reports, the UNFPA assessment notes on several occasions that there is little it can directly do to achieve these goals given its small budget. It notes on the key issue of sex selection, for example, "UNFPA's own resources are not large enough to bring about rapid and extensive change. If UNFPA wishes to have national impact through its work on sex selection it may need to consider playing the role of a catalyst for advocacy" (UNFPA, 2011, p. 72). In other words, it is hard to know how to define success when there isn't really much you can accomplish under the circumstances!

On the other hand, the report does point to a number of positive signs. It observes, for example, "During the field visits and discussions of the evaluation team with government officials at the national and state level, it became abundantly clear that UNFPA state programme coordinators and programme officers are regularly called upon to participate in and provide inputs at various state level technical and core group meetings and consultations such as on maternal health and family planning. It is not an exaggeration to say that in many states, UNFPA and its officials are seen as an extension of the government" (UNFPA, 2011, p. 26). In other words, UNFPA has a close and effective relationship with government at the local level and is a trusted partner. Work against gender-based violence in health care settings is also cited as a very successful program, with greater cooperation with Panchayats suggested as way to build on this success, although no statistics are given to support the view of general success. The adolescent health program is credited with the "significant achievement" of developing a "sound conceptual framework" in target states. Even in the area of sex selection, where the report calls for greater work and acknowledges the difficultly of changing attitudes, it also has positive things to say, asserting that changes in sex ratios is the wrong metric to use: rather, if one looks at "intermediate measures of outputs and processes that will over the long term help to achieve impact," then there has been important work accomplished (UNFPA, 2011, p. 63).

The conclusion of the report includes successes and failures. In terms of the question of whether to work "upstream" or "downstream"—an issue that had also been raised for UNICEF and UNDP—the assessment has a decided answer: "UNFPA has not paid adequate attention to the demand side of health issues—improving health seeking behavior, demand generation, and increasing utilization of services" (UNFPA, 2011, p. 111). The study points to a number of ways UNFPA can increase its effectiveness, but these almost all concern strategic issues; the concern is whether UNFPA is pushing for the right things in the right way (that is, focusing on rights and empowerment) rather than on metrics of success such as changes in sex ratios, numbers of clinics staffed, and so forth. In this is a clear recognition that the key factor is whether the right things are being pursued in the right way, rather than on specific indicators of development "success." So once again the question is, How well does the agency examined align its activities with its strategic priorities? Whether these are having a discernible impact on India's overall development picture is unknowable, given the constraints in evaluating its programs.

UN Women

UN Women has the most explicitly rights-based sets of programs among all the UN agencies studied here. Advancing women's rights, of course, is its central mandate, and its assessment operations are designed to measure progress toward that goal. There is no single evaluation or assessment document for UN Women's work in India, but there are a variety of studies done since 2010 that illuminate their progress and show which metrics of success they consider vital. As with the other assessments, those from UN Women are conspicuous in noting that they rely on qualitative, not quantitative, data. However, since 2012 UN Women has been conducting a number of "baseline" studies of various women's issues in India—on human trafficking, the empowerment of widows, and safety of women and girls in cities—intended both to guide future interventions and to allow for better assessment of results. It is noteworthy that UN Women's assessments and evaluations have a decidedly more upbeat and positive tone than those of UNDP, UNICEF, or UNFPA.

A central 2012 report on UN Women's work on Gender Responsive Budgeting (GRB), for example, reviews the various efforts of UN Women to train, sensitize, and build the capacity of various government officials, and to empower local communities to hold those officials accountable. It concludes, "UN Women's work, alongside other organizations, has contributed to increasing stakeholders' awareness and understanding of GRB, and its relative significance, in India" (UN Women, 2012, p. 55). This conclusion is based primarily on the number of trainings held, the number of self-help groups reached, and the results of surveys of key stakeholders. In an echo of other programs, UN Women notes that "UN Women's early work made important contributions to GRB positioning in India despite limited staff, budget, and lack of a formal country strategy" (UN Women, 2012, p. 57). Still, the report asserts success at sensitizing government officials to GRB and suggests that GRB has been used at various levels, ranging from federal ministries to PRIs. It also admits that naturally much more work needs to be done before GRB truly becomes a national priority. The focus, to be sure, is squarely on whether the trainings are happening and if government officials are incorporating the ideas; not on the all-but-unknowable question of whether this translates into better outcomes for the women affected by government budgeting decisions.

On the other hand, a midterm assessment of efforts to combat human trafficking, while still largely a rundown of various statistics regarding what has been accomplished programmatically—how many households interacted with by peer educators, self-help groups received training, and vigilance committees established—concludes that "the programme appears to be on-track towards contributing to its overall objectives and goals to reduce the vulnerability of women and girls in source areas of trafficking." That conclusion is primarily based on the assumption that "collaboration between community and local law enforcement agencies and systems can build the capacities of both to reduce vulnerability of women and girls to trafficking" (UN Women, 2013, p. 57), rather than on hard statistical evidence.

The basic questions of an evaluation of a program to support women who are HIV-positive—the "Positive Women's Network" (PWN+)—were (1) Did UN Women supported PWN+ projects empower the lives of WLHA [women living with HIV/AIDS]? (2) Did UN Women support build sustainable organizational capacity of PWN+ and its members? (3) Was UN Women support strategic, and did it lead to engendering the work on HIV in India? (UN Women, 2013, p. 17). The report concludes, "UN Women support to PWN+ contributed to developing PWN+ into a powerful platform for social change where WLHA are informed about their rights and supported to make use of them; and with the support of UN Women and other organizations, PWN+ has been successful in creating a positive space for WLHA to meet and exchange experiences and achieve tangible improvements in living conditions of WLHA such as improved access to the health services" (UN Women, 2013, p. 20).

On a project for empowering Dalit women and increasing their ability to earn a living, UNDP notes that "*the participatory process used in the design, implementation and monitoring of the programme, guided by human rights and gender equality principles* has been very effective and an important contribution of UN Women ... [the initiative] has proven to be a cost effective investment made by UN Women Fund for Gender Equality because the economic gains made by Dalit women exceed the investment made by UN women ... even in a short time span" (Ojha, 2012, p. 41; emphasis in original). It also asserts the importance of changing "social attitudes towards women" and feels the program has been successful in that area, as well as bringing about legal change, and suggests that the program, while quite small, has the potential to be a model in other parts of India outside the targeted districts.

The World Bank

Determining how successful the rights-based portfolio of the World Bank has been—or even how they would define the success of that portfolio—is especially complicated, since, as we have seen, the Bank does not officially follow a rights-based approach to development. And, of course, its work is far broader (and better funded!) than that of other agencies. It does quite a lot of work that has little to do with RBA or with social development generally. Not surprisingly, the Bank's work on assessment is *substantially* more quantitatively based than that of the other organizations. In 2013 the Bank's Independent Evaluation Group undertook an overall assessment of the Bank's performance, looking (briefly) at all program sectors. The evaluation rated the performance of the country office as "moderately satisfactory" (Independent Evaluation Group, 2013a, p. 1). The report overall notes mixed results: effective in work on power, education, water and sanitation, and microfinance, among other sectors; "below expectation" in urban development, public-private partnerships, disaster management, and governance reform. Overall, the World Bank evaluation is the only one studied for this project that related its work to overall, national-level economic and social indicators, and it took economic growth seriously as a measure of development success (as opposed to simply asking if policies were being implemented correctly and in good faith).

Project-level reports take the same approach; for example, an assessment of work in the HIV/AIDS sector uses changes in overall HIV prevalence as a measure of success, rather than, say, looking at inputs such as condoms distributed, workshops held, and so on (Independent Evaluation Group, 2013c). On the other hand, that same report does not mention the word "rights" a single time, despite the importance of RBA in HIV/AIDS work. A report on child and maternal health—a sector, as we have seen, with important RBA components—has no mention of rights per se, but a considerable emphasis on inclusion and "reaching the poorest and most under-served," as well as the empowerment of local communities in terms of demanding improved services. In terms of reaching these underserved sectors, the report asserts that a "reduction of disparities in the use of skilled delivery services [for childbirth] also exceeded targets," but it adds that "maternal, infant and child mortality and total fertility are affected by a broad range of socio-economic factors, improved reproductive and child services being only one among many others. Given the time frame of program implementation and the unavailability of health services and impact data after 2010, it is difficult to assess with confidence the extent of the program's contribution to documented trends in these outcomes" (Independent Evaluation Group, 2013b, p. 5).

The overall assessment sees a mixed bag of outcomes. It states, "India made important strides towards greater inclusiveness. In addition to the acceleration of overall poverty reduction, the gaps in growth rates across states narrowed, real consumption and real wages in rural areas grew by 3.4% and 6.8%, respectively, between 2004/05 and 2011/12, and targeted assistance to vulnerable groups increased eightfold without a major increase in the total outlays" (Independent Evaluation Group, 2013a, p. 6). It also notes that data on poverty and exclusion is being more effectively used than in the past. The evaluation mentions efforts at inclusive growth several times; yet the word "rights" is used only once, in relation to indigenous land use and land rights. Overall, however, it suggests that inclusive growth, government reform, local participation, and reaching marginalized communities has been successfully implemented by the World Bank, if only as part of a much larger system of aid designed specifically to grow the Indian economy rather than pursue rights per se.

Conclusion

How do we judge the overall "success" (put in quotation marks on purpose) of RBA? It is worth reconsidering the four sets of criteria mentioned earlier in this chapter.

As we have seen, only the World Bank makes any real effort to tie its efforts in social development and governance—largely a stand-in for RBA—to the overall growth of the Indian economy or national-level indicators of welfare. None of the other agencies discussed here are much interested in national, or even regional, growth rates. The key issue is the changing nature of how "development" is defined. The evolution of development from a focus on simple GDP growth, to human development, and now rights promotion is well documented and needs no explication here. If development is defined *simply* as the promotion of a rights-based policy, then the question of whether RBA promotes development becomes easy, if dangerously tautological. Recall from Chapter 1, however, that justifications of RBA include the argument that people whose rights are promoted become more economically productive; this is central to the argument for the policy. Yes there is precious little evidence that this works in practice in India, or elsewhere for that matter, and much of the doubt over the ability to produce quantitative evaluations of the work of various agencies seems to implicitly accept that there ought to be *some* connection between the work of UN agencies and economic growth.

To some extent—perhaps to a large extent—the argument that RBA adds to national economic growth and traditional "development" goals is largely based on public relations. International organizations are not supposed to be involved in politics; RBA is, by nature, political. Claiming to promote growth through politics gives the UN some cover; it can say its work is apolitical and guided by the pure facts of economic rationality. Interviews with staff, including World Bank staff, suggest that few really concern themselves with measures of success at this level.

It must be noted that the successes and failures of RBA can be, and sometimes are, assessed in terms much better than those discussed in this chapter. As far as providing a "normative framework" for development work, several of the reports do discuss the ways in which RBA shapes the way the agencies think about what development means and how successfully those norms are translated into policy. These are successes themselves. Also, while many reports mention, as we have seen, the difficulty of finding good quantitative data on success, they also discuss how UN agencies disaggregate information based on need and social exclusion, and address those problems. There is no shortage of discussions of equity, empowerment, and similar concepts. These are central to defining how RBA is to be conducted, although they are not well integrated into assessment language in the various UN documents. The overall upshot here is mixed: while a number of government officials, for example, have been "sensitized" and "trained," it is also clear that the actual effect of all this is hard to measure, or where it is measured, the results are disheartening (if not altogether negative).

What's perhaps most striking about the collected reports, other than the fact that it is so difficult to measure success quantitatively, is the concern over whether RBA is being implemented in a way that is consistent and coherent. There is confidence that RBA is a part of programming, that it is morally important, and that it is supported by international legal obligations; but that it is being done in a way that truly represents a unified intellectual idea is lacking. Even if assessment is a measure not of specific outputs but of the degree to which RBA is truly being implemented, the results seem decidedly mixed. This does fit well with the evidence from interviews and site visits that there is an uneven understanding of what RBA is throughout the organizations being studied.

For RBA policies to be more effective, it is clear, there will need to be more clarity in their implementation and more resources provided, in terms of both expertise (the lack of which is noted by several reports) and simply general coverage by UN agencies. There also needs to be a greater appreciation of the types of policies that do and do not fit under that umbrella—which will itself take a strong commitment to determining what it means in an operational context. Finally, to really consider the effectiveness of RBA, there clearly needs to be a more consistent, methodologically sound, and widespread effort to assess development effectiveness in general among various UN agencies; at this time that process simply does not exist.

References

Cox, R. (1981). Social Forces, States and World Orders: Beyond International Relations theory. *Millennium, 10*(2), 126–155.

Cracknell, B. (2000). *Evaluating Development Aid: Issues, Problems, and Solutions.* Thousand Oaks, CA: Sage.

Elliott, J. (2012). *An Introduction to Sustainable Development* (4th ed.). New York: Routledge.

Evaluation Office. (2006). *Evaluation of Gender Mainstreaming in UNDP.* New York: UNDP.

Hunt, P., Nowak, M., & Osman, S. (2002). *Human Rights and Poverty Reduction Strategies: A Discussion Paper*. Geneva: UN Office of the High Commissioner for Human Rights.

Imas, L., & Rist, R. (2009). *The Road to Results: Designing and Conducting Effective Development Evaluations*. Washington, DC: The World Bank.

Independent Evaluation Group. (2013a). *CASCR Review: India*. New York: The World Bank.

Independent Evaluation Group. (2013b). *Implementation Completion Report (ICR) Review—India: Reproductive & Child Health Second Phase*. New York: The World Bank.

Independent Evaluation Group. (2013c). *Implementation Completion Report (ICR) Review—India: Third National HIV/AIDS Control Project*. New York: The World Bank.

Jolly, R. (2004). *UN Contributions to Development Thinking and Practice*. Bloomington: Indiana University Press.

Jonsson, U. (2003). *Human Rights Approach to Development Programming*. New York: UNICEF.

Menocal, A., & Sharma, B. (2008). *Joint Evaluation of Citizens' Voice and Accountability: Synthesis Report*. London: Department of International Development.

Menon-Sen, K., & Shiva Kumar, A. (2010). *UNDP India Mid Term Review of the Country Programme Action Plan 2008–2012*. New Delhi: UNDP.

Ojha, G. P. (2012). *Evaluation of UN Women Fund for Gender Equality Economic and Political Empowerment Catalytic Grant Programme: "Dalit Women's Livelihoods Accountability Initiative" India*. New Delhi: UN Women.

Rego, A. (2012). *Outcome Evaluation of UNDP India's HIV and Development Programme*. New Delhi: UNDP.

Satyanand, P. N. (2012). *Outcome Evaluation of UNDP India's Democratic Governance Programmes 2008–2011*. New Delhi: UNDP.

Stewart, F. (1989). Basic Needs Strategies, Human Rights, and the Right to Development. *Human Rights Quarterly, 11*(3), 347–374.

Tinker, I. (Ed.) (1990). *Persistent Inequalities: Women and World Development*. New York: Oxford University Press.

UN Women. (2012). *Evaluation of UN Women's Work on Gender Responsive Budgeting in India*. New Delhi: UN Women.

UN Women. (2013). *Mid-term Evaluation of UN Women's Anti-human Trafficking Programme*. New Delhi: UN Women.

UNDP. (2012). *Assessment of Development Results: India*. New York: UNDP.

UNFPA. (2011). *Evaluation Report of UNFPA India Country Programme–7*. New Delhi: UNFPA.

UNICEF. (2011). *Evaluation of UNICEF Strategic Positioning in India: Final Evaluation Report*. New Delhi: UNICEF.

UNICEF. (2014). *Supplementary Programme Note on the Theory of Change: UNICEF Strategic Plan, 2014–2017*. New York: UNICEF.
UNICEF India. (2011). *Country Office Annual Report*. New Delih: UNICEF.
Wade, R. (1997). Greening the Bank: The Struggle Over the Environment 1970–1995. In D. Kapur, J. P. Lewis, & R. Webb (Eds.), *The World Bank: Its First Half-Century* (Vol. 2, pp. 611–734). Washington, DC: Brookings Institutions Press.
Weaver, C., & Leiteritz, R. (2005). Our Poverty is a World Full of Dreams: Reforming the World Bank. *Global Governance, 11*(3), 369–388.
World Bank. (2013). *Implementation Completion Report (ICR) Review—India: Reproductive & Child Health Second Phase*. New York: The World Bank. Retrieved from http://lnweb90.worldbank.org/oed/oeddoclib.nsf/DocUNIDViewForJavaSearch/8525682E0068603785257A860058160D?OpenDocument

7

Conclusion

NEW WAYS OF PURSUING HUMAN RIGHTS PROMOTION

THIS PROJECT STARTED with a few basic questions about UN development programming. First, does a rights-based approach to development, as it is actually implemented, represent a new approach to development work, one that incorporates meaningful pursuit of human rights, especially civil and political rights? Second, how do these agencies navigate the tricky political terrain they find themselves on? Behind these two fundamental questions is a subsequent issue: To what extent does the move to RBA mean that UN development agencies are now active players in the promotion of human rights? How effectively can they make this transition, and how much is the old focus on "traditional" New York- and Geneva-based human rights bodies outmoded? This is important, as it could (and I think does) represent a real advance in the global human rights movement. In some ways, it is the most explicit move yet toward the concept of actually *implementing* human rights through international bodies (other than the last-line of defense represented by the Security Council) rather than merely *advocating* human rights.

Key Questions Revisited

Does RBA Represent More Than a Rhetorical Commitment to Human Rights?

Does RBA represent more than a rhetorical commitment to human rights? The quick answer to this is "yes, but not in every case." UN staff, as well as their national counterparts, continues to struggle with exactly what RBA means, and how it moves their work forward. As Chapter 6 showed, assessment is a particular problem: it is difficult to prove that RBA delivers measurable results and even difficult to know exactly what results one is looking for. RBA complicates the definition of development and thus avoids easy answers to the question of "does it work?" We have also seen how "results-based management" techniques—so important, in many ways, in a field where accountability has often been lacking (Khang & Moe, 2008; Kusek & Rist, 2004; Weiner, 2006)—make it still harder to pursue complex goals in development. The trend toward results-based management, while understandable, also means staff will prioritize straightforward and measurable goals over those harder to quantify.

Some of the problem has to do with the definition of RBA, which, as we have seen again and again, remains unclear and contested. For example, passing laws that codify rights in legal language is important but rarely adequate in itself. Helping India to pass Right to Education legislation is, certainly, an element of RBA: making education a legal right is of course a big step, but it is not enough. That right has to be justiciable, people need to have the economic and political resources to claim it, communities need to organize to provide for themselves when government fails to act, and so forth. In some areas these policies are progressing well, in others, progress has been slower. We have seen that "technical" areas tend to lag behind more "social" ones: the UNICEF Health staff is less sure what RBA means than, say, the Child Protection staff. But this is not true in every case; much of what UNFPA does is related to the technical aspects of health care, but their work is better informed by RBA than that of other agencies. Their small size and specific mandate seem to help: with less staff and a more direct focus, it is easier for the agency to change in response to new demands and strategies.

This book has focused in particular on civil and political rights. This is not an uncontroversial decision. The United Nations, we have noted, already officially considers rights to be indivisible: it does not prioritize one set of rights over another. And, as we have seen, RBA itself properly understood assumes an intimate and self-reinforcing relationship between civil and political rights on the one hand, and economic, social, and cultural rights on the other. They cannot be separated. Nevertheless, the distinction has important heuristic advantages. As Chapter 1 explained, UN agencies have always been charged with promoting economic development, and it has been easy in some cases to simply rebrand this development as "rights," for example, the right to education or the right to food. But they have traditionally shied away from an emphasis on civil and political rights, since an emphasis on this category of rights was much more likely to provoke an angry reaction from governments. So bringing this side of the rights equation to the fore would go a long way in showing a real change, rather than a rhetorical one, in how UN agencies think about their work. It is easy for states to pay lip service to ES&C rights without doing very much; they simply explain that such rights take time to implement. That argument becomes much harder when C&P rights are at stake. (Although it is true that these rights also can't be implemented overnight or without the appropriate economic supports.) So it is harder to hide behind rhetorical promises when dealing with free speech, the right to information, or democratic participation.

On the other side, it is also easy for UN agencies (and other development NGOs) to find themselves in the same trap. UN agencies have to often repackage their old, service-based programming as rights promotion, for example, calling food supplements a "right to nutrition" or building schools as a "right to education. A commitment to C&P rights is far harder to finesse in this way. To be sure, we have seen some efforts to do just that. Still, it was clear that some staff had thought very hard about what it meant to truly want to empower citizens to demand their rights and to move beyond mere rhetorical repackaging. Parts of the UNDP have thought seriously about transitioning from a service-delivery model to one where citizens demand their rights and have the freedom to hold government accountable. But this process is unfinished: members of UNICEF's health staff freely admit that they still grapple with what this means. To them, RBA is important in what it suggests but still a work in progress. Much of this is visible, also, in the effort to assess the value of RBA or its value added to the traditional work of these organizations. The truth is, the technical experts at some agencies are right: it is nearly impossible to say that these new approaches are really "empowering" citizens, really "changing the paradigm" of service delivery, or otherwise reaching more people or making them more capable of demanding what is rightfully theirs.

The Politics of Rights-based Approaches

As the previous chapters have shown, UN staff is well aware of the complexity of, and sensitivity surrounding, the relatively new paradigm of a rights-based approach to development. They tread carefully when they bring up rights and often face resistance or backlash from their government partners. Government officials, too, recognize what a sea-change it is to have UN agencies speaking of civil and political rights and express mixed feelings about it. Largely they are receptive but also skeptical that much can be accomplished by outsiders. UN agencies are often seen as well-meaning but ineffectual, too small and under-resourced to make much of a difference in such a vast country; or, at times, too ignorant of local culture to adapt their ideas properly (Easterly, 2015; Feeney, 1998; Ferguson, 1990; Hayter, 1971; Mihivc, 1995). It seems to be true that UN staff and Indian government officials see the difference between C&P rights on the one hand and ES&C rights on the other as far greater than many human rights theorists, who insist on their close connection. Talk about a right to food or shelter, and everyone agrees on the need for action; discuss legal rights and citizen empowerment, and there is far more wariness. A rhetorical commitment to their indivisibility does not necessarily translate into policies that see them as two sides of the same coin.

As summarized in Chapter 6, the more political nature of this work has required the development of new skills by UN staff to navigate the difficult terrain of rights talk. In many cases, the staff is directly and specifically aware of what they are doing in this area, and some of the longer serving staff in particular noted how things have changed since "the old days." This has been true of all organizations studied. The degree, though, has varied. Again, and not surprisingly, those engaged in the most technical work—health care delivery, nutrition programs, and so on—are the least adaptable, although there are exceptions. Some technical staff were very creative in terms of seeing how RBA could and should change their work.

Much of the change has been surprisingly ad hoc. There are no directives coming from headquarters about how to deal with political backlash; workshops on rights-based development touch on the topic, but provide few concrete guidelines for action. Developing such instructions may not be feasible. Every situation is different, and every country and topic brings its own challenges. Still, the process of learning the politics of RBA suffers from the lack of institutionalization. As discussed in Chapter 1, UN agencies and the financial institutions are bureaucracies, often very large ones; without specific guidelines and central direction, each unit is left to determine what is in its own best interest in terms of pursuing the trickier parts of RBA. So not only the definition of RBA tends to vary from unit to unit, even within a single agency, but also the way its pursued, the degree of politicization, and the extent to which staff is willing to take chances. World Bank staff members, for example, are fairly risk-averse when discussing their governance agenda. Their organization particularly shies away from the political implications of its work and is supervised more closely than others by member states. UN Women, on the other hand, is much more willing to take a confrontational stance. So, too, are *parts* of UNDP (e.g., those dealing with HIV/AIDS) but not others (e.g., those working on inclusion regarding the Rural Employment Guarantee Act).

Overall, however, the situation has changed dramatically since the days when the UNICEF Resident Representative in Dhaka reacted in horror to the suggestion that they involve themselves in domestic politics. Of course, what UNICEF and other agencies are doing today is not quite like actually expressing a preference among candidates in an election. But it is still far more political than anything such agencies would have considered 20 years ago. And we have seen some examples of agencies pushing the limits of what they can get away with politically, such as the case (mentioned in Chapter 6) of UNICEF staff being careful not to praise government officials too close to election time. Political involvement like this is not unprecedented, but the scale of these changes is picking up pace.

These new agenda items within UN agencies open a question about the role of the UN in international politics and development. Traditionally, the UN has been a "neutral" agency, ostensibly carrying out its mandate in a way that did not privilege any one political, economic, or cultural system over another. That has always been a fiction, of course, a sort of "organized hypocrisy" similar to some other traditions in international politics (Krasner, 1999). Human rights in general derives largely from Western political traditions (Cranston, 1962; Donnelly, 1985; Frost, 2002; Ghai, 2000; Zvobgo, 1979); the financial institutions have done a great deal to spread Western, capitalist economics around the world (Woods, 2006); international law has developed largely from Western legal systems and thought (Anghie, 2004, pp. 196–199); and so forth. Still, the political resistance prompted by some aspects of RBA shows that this process is continuing and perhaps accelerating. The focus on state push-back has been designed to show that a real, not just rhetorical, set of values are being incorporated and advocated, with real consequences. Staff is grappling with this but in an ad hoc way. It would make sense for there to be a more specific set of rules and directions for this process, but that might be itself politically sensitive, as it would be a clear recognition of an otherwise veiled process.

UN Specialized Agencies as Alternative Ways of Promoting and Protecting Rights

India, no one needs to be reminded, is hardly the world's worst human rights abuser. The country has a progressive constitution, a well-developed (if underfunded) legal system, and a commitment to democracy. That said, it is still a state that faces many challenges; regarding women, corruption, the treatment of Scheduled Castes and Tribes, and all the other issues discussed in this volume—not to mention the vast economic rights challenges.

India is a UN member and a signatory to a wide range of human rights documents and thus subject to their various monitoring and enforcement mechanisms. It files reports to the UN Human Rights Council as part of the Universal Periodic Review (UPR) process (see Charlesworth & Larking, 2015; Doninguez-Redondo, 2012) and submits reports to a number of treaty bodies—on civil and political rights, women's rights, children's rights, and so forth. Beyond that, however, the traditional human rights mechanisms are unable to do much to promote rights implementation and respect. That goes for both "positive" and "negative" rights, but as we have seen, there is more sensitivity around the latter. As is the case with any sovereign state, the standard mechanisms of human rights promotion, based in New York and Geneva, can do little beyond collecting information about rights abuses and issuing reports about those abuses, or otherwise bringing attention to them. The UN Human Rights Council has gained some ability through "special sessions" to address the most grievous human rights situations, and, of course, UPR has tried to learn and improve over time (Cowan & Billaud, 2015), albeit with uncertain results. The UPR process has been examined as a way to work more cooperatively on rights, an alternative to traditional naming and shaming. But the committee can do little beyond issuing reports or state opinions to pressure states. It is limited, among other things, by its lack of resources and only occasional scrutiny of state reports, as well as the politics inherent even in the improved system.

So, pursuing rights through development cooperation is an important alternative to a still-sclerotic human rights system and holds great promise to create a new way to promote rights. Yet this system has been almost entirely ignored by mainstream work on international human rights. Just to give a few examples, notable works like Jack Donnelly's *Universal Human Rights in Theory and Practice* (2003) or David Forsythe's *Human Rights in International Relations* (2000) make no reference to the role of UN specialized agencies in promoting and protecting human rights; Todd Landman's otherwise excellent *Protecting Human Rights* lists all the various treaty-monitoring bodies in a chapter on the "Human Rights Regime" but leaves out UN specialized agencies (Landman, 2005). This list can be extended almost indefinitely. Where works look at promotion of human rights or even enforcement outside the traditional bodies (including the Security Council, in the most extreme situations), they mostly focus on nongovernmental organizations, not the specialized agencies. Work on the effectiveness of existing agencies finds the results mixed, at best: while there are successes, these seem to be slow, and concentrated not among the worst abusers, but those states already somewhat open to rights progress (Flood, 1998; Hafner-Burton & Tsutsui, 2007; Hathaway, 2002). There is only so much that can be done through reporting, naming and shaming tactics, or even the dispatch of special rapporteurs and the like. A more cooperative model of rights promotion can add to the existing model and correct many of its weakest features.

There is no arguing that development agencies contribute to the promotion of economic, social, and cultural rights. Their definitions might vary, but clearly they contribute to this area. But most scholarly work on international human rights around the world has, traditionally, focused on C&P rights; thus, they have tended to overlook the work of development agencies as rights-promotion agents. This is starting to change, and Chapter 1 cited some work on development rights that is beginning to alter the landscape. But these efforts reflect a small minority of the rights literature. At a time when the indivisibility of rights is gaining greater acceptance both within and outside the UN and its member states, the literature on rights is slow to catch up.

Most significantly, as we have seen, many staff in UN development agencies most definitely *do* see themselves as integral to the UN human rights regime and responsible not just for ES&C rights but also for a broad range of rights issues. This is notable among the higher level staff at the UN, whose job is to see the "big picture," and who are aware of their organization-wide mission to pursue a rights-based agenda in the widest possible way. "Rights are our business" was a refrain heard many times. They often, but not always, view themselves as charged with rights implementation in a very broad sense.

UN agencies also, at least to some extent, work with the office of the UN High Commissioner for Human Rights and coordinate rights policies with that organization. In that respect, they are already part of the larger, more formal human rights framework. UN development agencies are also working with states to help with the preparation of documents for the Human Rights Council's UPR process. UNICEF in particular has been in the forefront of this effort. Here is the real promise of right implementation through development aid: the ability of UN agencies to work cooperatively, rather than in an adversarial way, with states to improve their rights records. This can't be emphasized too much: RBA represents a more *cooperative* way of pursuing rights, one that works with governments and inside countries rather than criticizing from Geneva or New York. And it comes with monetary incentives. It includes the incentives of continued aid, improved economic performance (presumably), and the approval of international bodies. Development aid can be a "carrot" (along with the stick of traditional naming and shaming) to lead states toward greater rights performance. And by working at the local and national level rather than just the international level, it is obviously more able to adapt to local conditions and consider the politics of implementation. It is cooperative, local-level, gradual, and based on consensus between host and agency.

The range of C&P rights spelled out in Chapter 1, which were examined in greater detail throughout the book, are obviously the place to start. Democratic participation, speech rights (and the related right to information), legal equality, access to justice, and other areas are central priorities. There is, clearly, a need to tie these rights to the development process. We can say that if development is defined as rights, then promoting rights is promoting development: but in reality, it is much more useful and persuasive to tie rights promotion to measurable development outcomes. In other words, these agencies are still largely limited by the need to connect their rights-promoting activity with more traditional development priorities. Promoting women's rights is largely (albeit not exclusively) done on the argument that it increases women's economic and social contributions; promoting a right to speech is justified because of its role in creating greater government accountability; and so forth.

UN agencies will be limited by the need to make these justifications until and unless they can fully convince states on the merits of their proposed redefinition of development. There are also simple, practical limits. No development agencies are well placed to do much to help political prisoners, for example. Issues that are entirely tangential to development, or that are central to government security priorities (or both), will almost certainly remain off limits. Even in a country as progressive as India, development agencies know there are issues they can't touch. The situation in Jammu and Kashmir, for example, might as well not exist to the UN agencies in India, at least publicly: there is simply no way to discuss it in a development context. It is not likely there ever will be, but this is largely true of *all* UN human rights mechanisms. They can complain about severe human rights abuses, but, short of Security Council action, there is not much that can be done to force states to act. There might be some advantage to agencies that understand their limitations and gently probe those limits. On the other hand, RBA has been applied in difficult, even dangerous, areas; for example, in peace-building situations in many countries (Action Aid, 2009; Bouris, 2007, pp. 26–33). It would be obviously wrong to imply that RBA could serve as a replacement for other, more confrontational means of pursuing rights, but it would be equally wrong to think it can serve only in states already open to rights talk that have a democratic (or at least open) political system.

The notion of using development work to leverage progress in human rights requires some further deep thinking by the UN. Most documents on RBA still adhere to the traditional formulation; that is, the promotion of rights is a way of furthering economic development. For political reasons, they tend to avoid the notion that these rights are goods in and of themselves. UN staff have different opinions about this: while they might say, in one interview, that as part of the UN system they have an obligation to support *all* the goals of the UN, they will just as often point out that an overt commitment to rights will take away their ability to do their core work or is simply not part of their "comparative advantage." Yet there is tremendous opportunity to move toward rights promotion through these agencies, over and above what they are already doing, if the proper methods were developed by staff.

Implications for International Relations Theory

Chapter 1 laid out some of the importance of this study for the field of international relations theory, and in particular our understanding of international organizations and their place in the international system. It was proposed that this study reinforces the image of IOs as "open systems," able to change and adapt as they interact with their environment, rather than seeing them as simple agents of states or as acting according to the simple logic of bureaucratic politics—the desire to maximize resources, influence, and so on. Still, to fully understand the open-system approach, one has to take into account the bureaucratic politics within the organization—how ideas are filtered through the lenses and preconceived notions of staff, and then interact with the incentives the staff receives through bureaucratic channels. Looking at IOs this way helps to see why they act as they do: their level of independence from state direction, their choice of priorities, and in particular their openness to outside ideas, and the way those ideas might be interpreted and implemented in unexpected ways by IOs. This fits into the general trend of academic work that tries to understand IOs as organizations that have their own way of operating, as "agents" who do not always do the bidding of their "principals" but also might not themselves have a single set of priorities or directives. From an IR theory standpoint, the lesson is clear: it is impossible to understand the work of IOs without looking at the local level and examining the ways that policies are filtered through the experiences of staff.

Understanding the *incentives* staff members face is particularly important here. These incentives and their implications have been studied extensively and have important ramifications in IR theory. The World Bank presents a good example to illustrate this. Issues like the environment, lending quality, and human development have had a hard time taking root in the Bank because of the incentive structures that reward "moving money out the door" rather than making sure that all Bank rules and policies are adhered to by borrowers (Darrow, 2003, p. 201). In the various agencies studied here, there is variation in how much the staff is given the appropriate incentives to follow a rights policy. Some agencies—UN Women is good case—have strong incentives to implement a fully rights-oriented policy, as they are free to essentially define success as merely working toward rights promotion. At UNICEF, recall, the Child Protection unit is judged fairly directly based on their adoption of RBA, while the Health unit is still beholden to traditional metrics: declining infant and child mortality rates, increased levels of immunization, and so forth. They tend to struggle more with the meaning and implications of RBA since their work is largely technical and easily measured by results-based management techniques. This is where Chapter 6, on assessment, provides particular insight: under a system that uses results-based management, showing the results of RBA can be particularly difficult. So adoption of RBA will vary and be uneven. It is important to know what you are assessing, and then to give staff appropriate incentives to pursue those outcomes. So, the variation in the ability of IOs to adopt new ideas depends significantly on internal factors.

Implementation of a rights-based approach to development also opens interesting questions about IOs as the conduits for new ideas in world politics. The role of ideas in shaping behavior is well established, and a diverse literature exists on how ideas are spread through IOs (Finnemore, 1994; Krook & True, 2012; O'Neill, Balsiger, & Vandeveer, 2004; Pevehouse, 2002; Sikkink, 1991).

IOs are obviously not perfect conduits; the preferences of staff and the circumstances they find themselves in shape the ideas they transmit. IOs also have preferences of their own. They don't simply embody these ideas and transmit ideas through example; they actively work to change state behavior and state interests. Elsewhere I have argued that the key element in understanding IO agency is their ability to shape state interests *against the wishes of states* (Oestreich, 2011); when IOs act but no one much cares, or when they do not challenge any core state interests, there is no theoretical interest because state control is not substantively challenged.

It was also suggested in Chapter 1 that the research here fills a gap in the understanding of IO independence. "Independence" in this context does not simply mean an organization making decisions; any organization of any size does that. And some discretion is always delegated to a bureaucracy. To be meaningful in international relations terms, independence refers to agencies acting in ways *not preferred by member states*, in particular powerful member states (Oestreich, 2011). The literature of norm diffusion, for example, is not just about the spread of ideas, it is about spreading ideas that change the way states define their rational self-interest, in ways they would not have changed otherwise. Why *not* use nuclear weapons when they will help you win wars (Price & Tannenwald, 1996); why not pollute the Mediterranean when it keeps industrial costs down (Haas, 1989); and so forth. The resistance of India and other states to the concept of RBA helps demonstrate that there is independence here. As discussed in Chapter 1, nearly every work on IO independence focuses on the process of the organization *taking on* new responsibilities or policies, but resistance also exists at the level of policy *implementation*, and this sort of resistance is vastly understudied. To fully understand the working of IOs, it is vital to see not just where their preferred policies come from but also how they can carry them out in the face of member-state opposition.

So how do IOs change state interests and behavior? While previous work has focused on things like idea diffusion (Park, 2006), the logic of appropriateness (Checkel, 2005), or the influence of larger state actors on smaller ones, this study examines the direct means of influence between IOs and states. In these examples IO staff follows specific strategies to change state behavior. It isn't through osmosis, but direct influence. Staff in international organizations working to change state behavior is not new in and of itself, of course, as any work on conditional lending (to use just one example) would show. And issues from nuclear weapons policies to environmental governance to development policy have been examined before. But the current study sheds some light on new strategies for doing so. It suggests that IOs can broaden the realm of topic where they can seek to influence state behavior. Also, we have seen that a focus purely on the national level is a mistake: in some cases IOs engage with subnational government bodies also. This has been another blind spot in IO literature, looking at the interaction of IOs with subnational actors. Yet it matters: the government of Rajasthan, for example, might be more open to influence than that of Uttar Pradesh. So not all local-level interactions can be grouped together or taken as subordinate to national-level influence.

Seeing these different levels adds nuance to the process of norm adoption and implementation, nuance that is useful both from an academic and a practical perspective. Finnemore and Sikkink (1998) have famously described the life cycle of norms, from "norm emergence" through a period of adoption by states, to "internalization" of the norm after a "norm cascade" in the international system. Norms are marked by ideas that initially seem at odds with state interests or practice but become internalized through socialization until they are accepted by states as the way business is done. This process is complex, of course. Amitav Acharya (2004) notes that domestic concerns matter; in particular, norms are interpreted through local eyes and adapted to fit local customs and ideas. Other scholars note the importance of local capacity (Vandeveer & Dabelko, 2001) in norm adoption and the complex "implementation game" played by states protecting their own interests while under pressure from international actors (Deere, 2009).

These elements of local culture, capacity, and interest all appear as IOs press on with a rights-based approach to development. In this case, the game of implementation, driven by UN agencies, is particularly complex: both state and local-level "players" have their own interests and agendas. UN agencies face the complex task of working at various levels of government and society simultaneously, using different tactics depending on their audience. The national and local levels are very different. There are even civil society actors outside government, for example, the local landowners who threatened to "beat up" NGO workers trying to empower Dalits in the countryside. Still, UN agencies have significant resources and advantages when helping adapt international norms to local situations. The results of this book add nuance to our understanding of the process of changing norms.

One nuance is more focus on implementation of ideas rather than just their adoption. Alexander Betts and Phil Orchard usefully divide norm "institutionalization" from norm "implementation." Institutionalization is the process of norms emerging in international law and organizations, and becoming part of the international system as preferred practice. Implementation is how the norms "play out in practice" within states (Betts & Orchard, 2014, p. 1). Once a norm becomes institutionalized, there remains the process of turning it into practice. This process is complex and often contested. In this case the norm itself is not especially well defined, neither to UN agencies nor to the Indian parties who have to carry things out in practice. So interpreting norms to be compatible with local language and custom, and making them more than rhetorical exercises, must recognize that norms do not always have fixed meanings but instead can evolve as the language used to describe them evolves (Krook & True, 2012; Wiener, 2007). This process is two-sided: both the state and the international organizations have their own preferences and agendas, and those interact in complex ways. UN agencies interpret norms to make them more palatable to the state (India, in this case), to make them more useful, or to make them more applicable to specific functions, such as improved health care or access to education. Government officials filter ideas and norms through their own lenses. This is not consistent but varies depending on who is doing it and what they want. The "rights-based approach to education" will seem different to a member of the Indian Supreme Court, or to a District Collector, or to a local Panchayat member; and each will have their own reasons to implement it or not, and to interpret what that implementation means. The process is simultaneously highly directed (norms don't just diffuse through some indefinable process—they are carefully thought out and promoted) and chaotic (with multiple games being played at multiple levels).

Norms, again, are really interesting when states resist them: their ability to change state behavior has greater meaning when it works against a state's perception of its own interests or preconceived identity. For the most part, the literature on norms in world affairs focuses on the various ways that resistance is overcome: through the pressure of epistemic communities, through adaptation to local conditions, through the force of legal restrictions, and so forth. As UN agencies press for the adoption of rights-based approaches to development, they show just how adaptable such agencies can be in pursuing the norms they consider central to their mission. The focus on resistance in this book—the myriad stories of Indian government officials, or even local people, fighting against outside interference—is a sign that something is happening: norms aren't just being ignored, and aren't simply diffusing through the international system, but are being picked up by IOs and made their own. This requires skill and patience, qualities not usually examined by scholars of international politics, yet qualities that are the sign of IO learning and adaptation.

Applicability to Other Cases

All of the above will mean very little if we determine that what has been happening in India is sui generis and not helpful for understanding other situations. Does the India case show that RBA represents a new, more adaptable way to promote human rights in other countries as well? This is, after all, a single case study, and while there were good reasons for choosing India for the study, it does represent a particular situation at a particular time in its history. There is value in presenting a single country with all the good and bad being done in the name of RBA rather than "cherry-picking" the best projects from various countries. India has a well-developed (although not always well-functioning) legal system so there are plenty of opportunities to see how new rights legislation can be enforced. And it is a large country with a diverse population and a very large UN office, so it presented many opportunities to see various types of projects in various conditions: indigenous areas, urban and rural, agricultural and industrial, and so forth.

Also, keep in mind that India is a democracy. There is no denying that it is often more open to human rights talk than many other countries. On the other hand, as a country with a strong sense of identity, and ancient and highly developed sense of its own culture, and an emerging role as a world power (Brewster, 2012; Paul & Nayar, 2003), it can be particularly sensitive to outside influence or any implication of "cultural imperialism" or ethnocentrism on the part of development agencies. Its relationship with both multilateral and bilateral development agencies is nuanced and complex. India's desire to emerge as a global power makes it want to be seen cooperating with international agencies and to be applying the very highest international standards to its legal and human rights systems. At the same time, that sense of power makes it all the more resistant to interference from UN agencies, bilateral donors, and other outsiders. Most bilateral donors have been asked to remove themselves from India or have done so themselves, as India no longer feels the need for help from most smaller programs. Their small resources are simply no longer needed or worth the effort involved. India is similarly unconvinced that it needs help from the UN, except perhaps from the World Bank (which, again, is included here under the UN umbrella). So there is some resistance, of various types, to UN rights efforts. Recall, too, India has demonstrated growing opposition to *all* development aid tied to social or political change, aligning itself instead with states pressing for greater commercial opportunities without strings attached.

The situation in Jammu and Kashmir makes an interesting point. As mentioned earlier, no UN agencies would discuss working on human rights in Jammu and Kashmir, and none of the organizations studied here have any real presence there. (There is, of course, a UN Peacekeeping mission along the border with Pakistan, and also an International Committee of the Red Cross presence.) For the most part, UN staff can't even discuss working in Jammu and Kashmir; the politics of getting involved in that area are just too complicated and sensitive. It is not likely that the government would allow any interference. This does not bode well, of course, for the applicability of RBA in many other countries that are repressive or are experiencing serious political violence. In the end, governments get to determine what can and can't be done within their borders.

Other states might be more repressive, less open to outside ideas, and less developed in terms of their political and legal systems than India. But many are also more dependent on foreign aid and more in need of the technical assistance and capacity building that is the bread and butter of most UN development agencies. This gives these agencies some extra leverage. And at least during my research in India and elsewhere, UN staff seem resolved that "rights are what we do." Conversations with staff at the very highest levels of UNDP, UNICEF, and other agencies revealed an organizational directive to pursue a rights-based approach in *every* country where they operate, not just those which seem most open to the idea. How successful this will be—how meaningful in terms of real results—will depend on the factors discussed throughout this book. Can resistance be overcome in every case? Certainly not. But how much RBA is truly institutionalized, how much staff learns to play the political game necessary to push for it effectively, how much it is truly changing in terms of policy, all matter. While Jammu and Kashmir might be off limits for much discussion, other zones where there is conflict—for example, in Chhattisgarh, where the Naxalite movement still controls some territory—is not, and there has been progress helping to protect the rights of children and civilians.

Using development to pursue human rights is not the answer to every rights question, nor is it the ultimate solution to economic development. However, there is no reason to think that a forceful—not rhetorical, but real and useful—policy of integrating *all* human rights with development assistance cannot be pursued in a wide variety of contexts. That is what is being done now, although in some cases more slowly and carefully than in others. To this end the main point of this project—that UN agencies are able to adapt themselves to local conditions and press for politically sensitive goals—is a key element. Developing the ability to work on rights and development in a variety of contexts is a real strength of UN agencies. Or at least a potential strength. This work ought to be encouraged.

References

Acharya, A. (2004). How Ideas Spread: Whose Norms Matter? Norm Localization and Institutional Change in Asian Regionalism. *International Organization*, 58(2), 239–275.

Action Aid. (2009). *Rights-based Approaches and Humanitarian Interventions in Conflict Situations*. London: Action Aid.

Anghie, A. (2004). *Imperialism, Sovereignty, and the Making of International Law.* New York: Cambridge University Press.

Betts, A., & Orchard, P. (2014). The Normative Institutionalization-Implementation Gap. In A. Betts & P. Orchard (Eds.), *Implementation and World Politics: How International Norms Change Practice* (pp. 1–26). New York: Oxford University Press.

Bouris, E. (2007). *Complex Political Victims.* Blomfield, CT: Kumarian Press.

Brewster, D. (2012). *India as an Asia Pacific Power.* New York: Routledge.

Charlesworth, H., & Larking, E. (Eds.). (2015). *Human Rights and the Universal Periodic Review.* Cambridge: Cambridge University Press.

Checkel, J. T. (2005). International Institutions and Socialization in Europe: Introduction and Framework. In J. T. Checkel (Ed.), *International Institutions and Socialization in Europe* (pp. 3–30). New York: Cambridge University Press.

Cowan, J. K., & Billaud, J. (2015). Between Learning and Schooling: The Politics of Human Rights Monitoring at the Universal Periodic Review. *Third World Quarterly, 36*(6), 1175–1190.

Cranston, M. (1962). *What Are Human Rights?* New York: Basic Books.

Darrow, M. (2003). *Between Light and Shadow: The World Bank, the International Monetary Fund and International Human Rights Law.* Portland, OR: Hart.

Deere, C. (2009). *The Implementation Game: The TRIPS Agreement and the Global Politics of Intellectual Property Reform in Developing Countries.* New York: Oxford Universty Press.

Doninguez-Redondo, E. (2012). The Universal Periodic Review—Is There Life Beyond Naming and Shaming in Human Rights Implementation? *New Zealand Law Review, 4,* 673–705.

Donnelly, J. (1985). *The Concept of Human Rights.* New York: St. Martin's Press.

Donnelly, J. (2003). *Universal Human Rights in Theory and Practice* (2nd ed.). Ithaca, NY: Cornell University Press.

Easterly, W. (2015). *The Tyranny of Experts: Economists, Dictators, and the Forgotten Rights of the Poor.* New York: Basic Books.

Feeney, P. (1998). *Accountable Aid: Local Participation in Major Projects.* Oxford, UK: Oxfam GB.

Ferguson, J. (1990). *The Anti-Politics Machine: "Development," Depoliticization, and Bureaucratic Power in Lesotho.* New York: Cambridge University Press.

Finnemore, M. (1994). International Organizations as Teachers of Norms: The United Nations Educational, Scientific, and Cultural Organization and Science Policy. *International Organization, 47*(4), 565–597.

Finnemore, M., & Sikkink, K. (1998). International Norm Dynamics and Political Change. *International Organization, 52*(4), 887–917.

Flood, J. P. (1998). *The Effectiveness of UN Human Rights Institutions.* New York: Greenwood Press.

Forsythe, D. P. (2000). *Human Rights in International Relations.* New York: Cambridge University Press.

Frost, M. (2002). *Constituting Human Rights: Global Civil Society and the Society of Democratic States*. London: Routledge.

Ghai, Y. (2000). Universalism and Relativism: Human Rights as a Framework for Negotiating Interethnic Claims. *Cardozo Law Review*, 21(4), 11131–11141.

Haas, P. M. (1989). Do Regimes Matter? Epistemic Communities and Mediterranean Pollution Control. *International Organization*, 43(Summer), 377–403.

Hafner-Burton, E. M., & Tsutsui, K. (2007). Justice Lost! The Failure of International Human Rights Law to Matter Where Needed Most. *Journal of Peace Research*, 44(4), 407–425.

Hathaway, O. (2002). Do Human Rights Treaties Make a Difference? *Yale Law Journal*, 111(8), 1935–2042.

Hayter, T. (1971). *Aid as Imperialism*. Harmondsworth, UK: Penguin.

Khang, D. B., & Moe, T. L. (2008). Success Criteria and Factors for International Development Projects: A Life-Cycle-Based Framework. *Project Management Journal*, 39(1), 72–84.

Krasner, S. (1999). *Sovereignty: Organized Hypocrisy*. Princeton, NJ: Princeton University Press.

Krook, M. L., & True, J. (2012). Rethinking the Life Cycles of International Norms: The United Nations and the Global Promotion of Gender Equality. *European Journal of International Relations*, 18(1), 103–127.

Kusek, J. Z., & Rist, R. (2004). *Ten Steps to a Results-based Monitoring and Evaluation System*. New York: World Bank.

Landman, T. (2005). *Protecting Human Rights: A Comparative Study*. Washington, DC: Georgetown University Press.

Mihivc, J. (1995). *The Market Tells Them So: The World Bank and Economic Fundamentalism in Africa*. Atlantic Highlands, NJ: Zed Books.

O'Neill, K., Balsiger, J., & Vandeveer, S. D. (2004). Actors, Norms, and Impactt: Recent International Cooperation Theory and the Influence of the Agent-Structure Debate. *Annual Review of Political Science*, 7, 149–175.

Oestreich, J. (2011). International Organizations in International Relations Theory. In B. Reinalda (Ed.), *The Ashgate Research Companion to Non-State Actors* (pp. 173–184). Burlington, VT: Ashgate Press.

Park, S. (2006). Theorizing Norm Diffusion Within International Organizations. *International Politics*, 43(3), 342–361.

Paul, T. V., & Nayar, B. R. (2003). *India in the World Order: Searchign for Major-Power Status*. Cambridge: Cambridge University Press.

Pevehouse, J. C. (2002). Democracy From the Outside In? International Organizations and Democratization. *International Organization*, 56(3), 515–549.

Price, R., & Tannenwald, N. (1996). Norms and Deterrence: The Nuclear and Chemical Weapons Taboos. In P. J. Katzenstein (Ed.), *The Culture of National Security: Norms and Identity in World Politics* (pp. 114–152). New York: Columbia University Press.

Sikkink, K. (1991). *Ideas and Institutions: Developmentalism in Brazil and Argentina.* Ithaca, NY: Cornell University Press.

Vandeveer, S. D., & Dabelko, G. D. (2001). It's Capacity, Stupid: International Assistance and National Implementation. *Global Environmental Politics*, *1*(2), 18–29.

Weiner, L. (2006). Accountability in International Development Aid. *Ethics & International Affairs*, *20*(1), 1–23.

Wiener, A. (2007). Contested Meanings of Norms: A Research Framework. *Comparative European Politics*, *5*(2), 1–17.

Woods, N. (2006). *The Globalizers.* Ithaca, NY: Cornell University Press.

Zvobgo, E. J. M. (1979). A Third World View. In D. Dummers & G. Loescher (Eds.), *Human Rights and American Foreign Policy* (pp. 90–108). Notre Dame, IN: University of Notre Dame Press.

Notes

CHAPTER 1

1. Anonymous interview 1.
2. Anonymous interview 2.
3. Anonymous interview 3.
4. Anonymous interview 4.
5. Anonymous interview 5.
6. Anonymous interview 6.

CHAPTER 2

1. Anonymous interview 7.
2. Anonymous interview 8.
3. Anonymous interview 9.
4. Anonymous interview 10.

CHAPTER 3

1. Anonymous interview 11.
2. Anonymous interview 12.
3. Anonymous interview 13.
4. Anonymous interview 14.
5. Anonymous interview 15.
6. Anonymous interview 16.
7. Anonymous interview 17.
8. Anonymous interview 18.

9. Anonymous interview 19.
10. Anonymous interview 20.
11. Anonymous interview 21.
12. Anonymous interview 22.
13. Anonymous interview 23.
14. Anonymous interview 24.
15. Anonymous interview 25.
16. Anonymous interview 26.
17. Anonymous interview 27.
18. Anonymous interview 28.
19. Anonymous interview 29.
20. Anonymous interview 30.
21. Anonymous interview 31.
22. Anonymous interview 32.
23. Anonymous interview 33.
24. Anonymous interview 34.
25. Anonymous interview 35.
26. Anonymous interview 36.
27. Anonymous interview 37.
28. Anonymous interview 38.
29. Anonymous interview 39.
30. Anonymous interview 40.
31. Anonymous interview 41.
32. Anonymous interview 42.

CHAPTER 4

1. Anonymous interview 43.
2. Anonymous interview 44.
3. Anonymous interview 45.
4. Anonymous interview 46.
5. Anonymous interview 47.
6. Anonymous interview 48.
7. Anonymous interview 49.
8. Anonymous interview 50.
9. Anonymous interview 51.
10. Anonymous interview 52.
11. Anonymous interview 53.
12. Anonymous interview 54.

13. Anonymous interview 55.
14. Anonymous interview 56.
15. Anonymous interview 57.
16. Anonymous interview 58.
17. Anonymous interview 59.
18. Anonymous interview 60.
19. Anonymous interview 61.
20. Anonymous interview 62.
21. Anonymous interview 63.
22. Anonymous interview 64.
23. Anonymous interview 65.
24. Anonymous interview 66.
25. Anonymous interview 67.
26. Anonymous interview 68.
27. Anonymous interview 69.
28. Anonymous interview 70.
29. Anonymous interview 71.
30. Anonymous interview 72.
31. Anonymous interview 73.
32. Anonymous interview 74.
33. Anonymous interview 75.
34. Anonymous interview 76.
35. Anonymous interview 77.
36. Anonymous interview 78.
37. Anonymous interview 79.
38. Anonymous interview 80.
39. Anonymous interview 81.
40. Anonymous interview 82.
41. Anonymous interview 83.
42. Anonymous interview 84.
43. Anonymous interview 85.
44. Anonymous interview 86.
45. Anonymous interview 87.
46. Anonymous interview 88.
47. Anonymous interview 89.
48. Anonymous interview 90.
49. Anonymous interview 91.
50. Anonymous interview 92.
51. Anonymous interview 93.

52. Anonymous interview 94.
53. Anonymous interview 95.
54. Anonymous interview 96.
55. Anonymous interview 97.
56. Anonymous interview 98.

CHAPTER 5

1. Anonymous interview 99.
2. Anonymous interview 100.
3. Anonymous interview 101.
4. Anonymous interview 102.
5. Anonymous interview 103.
6. Anonymous interview 104.
7. Anonymous interview 105.
8. Anonymous interview 106.
9. Anonymous interview 107.
10. Anonymous interview 108.
11. Anonymous interview 109.
12. Anonymous interview 110.
13. Anonymous interview 111.
14. Anonymous interview 112.
15. Anonymous interview 113.
16. Anonymous interview 114.
17. Anonymous interview 115.
18. Anonymous interview 116.
19. Anonymous interview 117.
20. Anonymous interview 118.
21. Anonymous interview 119.
22. Anonymous interview 120.
23. Anonymous interview 121.
24. Anonymous interview 122.
25. Anonymous interview 123.
26. Anonymous interview 124.
27. Anonymous interview 125.
28. Anonymous interview 126.
29. Anonymous interview 127.
30. Anonymous interview 128.
31. Anonymous interview 129.
32. Anonymous interview 130.

CHAPTER 6

1. Anonymous Interview 131
2. Anonymous Interview 132.
3. Anonymous Interview 133.
4. Anonymous Interview 134.
5. Anonymous Interview 135.
6. Anonymous Interview 136.
7. Anonymous Interview 137.
8. Anonymous Interview 138.
9. Anonymous Interview 139.
10. Anonymous Interview 140.
11. Anonymous Interview 141.
12. Anonymous Interview 142.
13. Anonymous Interview 143.
14. Anonymous Interview 144.

Index

abortion. *See* sex-selective abortion
"Access to Justice" programs, 60
    RBA in, 37, 46, 51–53
    rights included in, 51, 66
    UNDP use of, 51–52, 64–69, 161
Acharya, Amitav, 189
ADR. *See* "Assessments of Development Results"
advocacy, 7–8, 88, 91, 112, 130, 151, 168–69
"An Agenda For Development" (Annan), 32
Annan, Kofi, 23, 32
Armed Forces (Special Powers) Act, 43
"Assessments of Development Results" (ADR), 158, 162–65
Awami League, 2

Bangladesh National Party, 2
Barnett, M. N., 14, 15
Beigbeder, Y., 15
Beijing Declaration, 128
Betts, Alexander, 11, 189
"Bihar Rural Livelihoods Project" social exclusion study, 123–24
"block volunteers," 94–95
Brock, K., 8
Busan Fourth High Level Forum on Aid Effectiveness, 17

C4D. *See* Communication for Development program
Carriere, Rolf, 2
CEDAW. *See* Convention on the Elimination of All Forms of Discrimination Against Women
CEDC. *See* "children in especially difficult circumstances"
Center for Good Governance, 71
"child collectives," 94
Child Protection (CP), 52, 87–89, 97–102, 161, 187
children, 2, 94, 106. *See also* Convention on the Rights of the Child
    labor and trafficking issues of, 54, 101–2, 131
    violence against, in India, 43, 131
"children in especially difficult circumstances" (CEDC), 97–98
civil and political (C&P) rights, 185
    abuse by government agencies in India, 43
    advocacy difficulty of, 7–8
    conflict zone staff on, 105–6
    decentralization implications of, 81
    ES&C rights interdependence on, 5–6, 9, 19–20
    human rights scholarly work focus on, 183–84

civil and political (C&P) rights (Cont.)
  "naming and shaming" in, 16, 184
  no backlash directives on
    handling, 180–81
  in RBA, 8–9, 19, 179
  resistance to, 60
  RTD and RBA connections and
    differences on, 20–24
  UNDP involvement in, 60–61,
    65–68, 82–83, 86
  UNFPA use of, 135
  UN promotion of, 4, 179–80, 184
  women's rights promotion of, 54–55
civil society organizations (CSOs), 73,
  94, 106, 111, 127, 159
Cold War, 11, 20, 23
Committee on Human Rights, 4
Communication for Development
  (C4D) program, 51, 54–55, 110
conflict zone, 87, 103–7, 130
Convention on the Elimination of All
  Forms of Discrimination Against
  Women (CEDAW), 54–55,
  128, 131–32
Convention on the Rights of the
  Child (CRC), 2, 44, 94, 104,
  132, 161
  CP unit as guardian of, 88
  as rhetorical tool, 87
  UNICEF use of, 12, 32, 46–47,
    54–55, 86, 89, 97
Cornwall, A., 8
Country Programme Action Plan
  (CPAP), 62, 87, 90–91, 135
Covenant on Civil and Political
  Rights, 36, 48
  Article 19 on RTI in, 53
Cox, Robert, 149
CP. *See* Child Protection
C&P. *See* civil and political rights
CPAP. *See* Country Programme
  Action Plan

CRC. *See* Convention on the Rights of
  the Child
CSOs. *See* civil society organizations

decentralization
  C&P rights implications of, 81
  in India, 49
  and participation promotion in
    UNICEF, 113, 168
  strengthen from below in, 74
  UNDP agenda and technical support
    of, 49, 77
  as UN key development
    strategy, 48–50
Declaration on the Right to
  Development, main propositions
  of, 21–22
Democratic Governance (DG), 45, 60,
  66, 165
  caution and diplomacy in, 75–76
  CSOs use in, 73
  UNDP program evaluation
    of, 163–64
  UNDP staff on, 73–76
  women in, 74–75
  "working both sides" in, 75
Dey, N., 70
DG. *See* Democratic Governance
Dijkzeul, D., 15
discrimination, 35, 47, 135, 162
  disaggregating data to find, 95
  historical, 39, 43, 122
  HIV/AIDS regarding, 109
  against indigenous peoples, 50
  poverty as, 6, 43, 124
  problem in India, 43–44
  of Scheduled Castes and Tribes, 40,
    43–44, 50, 77, 79, 142
  of transgender community, 3, 52
  UNDP fighting of, 51
  against women and girls, 44, 50–51,
    79, 131, 139

Donnelly, Jack, 20, 183
"dowry murders," 44

economic, social, and cultural (ES&C)
    rights, 7, 40, 181
    C&P rights interdependence on, 5–6,
        9, 19–20
    different approach in, 19–20
    India violations of, 44
    as uncontroversial, 19
    UNFPA use of, 135
    UN promotion of, 4–6, 179–80, 184
education, 90–92, 94
    RBA implications in, 36–37
    UNICEF approach to, 95–97
empowerment, 6, 8, 76, 154
    four elements of, 35
    in RBA, 34–35
    of women, 129–30, 142–43
    World Bank statement on, 34–35
"equity agenda," 62–63, 117–18,
    121–22, 143–44
ES&C. *See* economic, social, and cultural
    (ES&C) rights
evaluation and assessment
    of RBA, 154–57
    of UNDP, 154, 159–61, 163–66
    of UNFPA, 169–70
    of UNICEF, 160, 167–68
    of UN Women, 160, 171–72
    of World Bank, 154, 172–73

"farmers' suicides," 18
Finnemore, M., 14, 15
"First Referral Units" (FRUs), 160
Forsythe, David, 183
FRUs. *See* "First Referral Units"

Gandhi, Mahatma, 49
Gauri, Varun, 6
gay rights, 82
gender-based violence (GBV), 137

gender responsive budgeting (GRB),
    130–31, 160, 171
General Assembly Resolution 59(1), 53
general strikes. *See hartals*
Gini coefficient, 121, 124
government capacity building, 60
    gap between rights rhetoric and reality
        in, 78–79
    MGNREGA in, 78–79
    nonelected officials in, 78
    Panchayats in, 49, 74–75
    Pathways for an Inclusive Indian
        Administration as, 51, 78
    positive change in, 79
    UNDP in, 70–71, 76–81
    UNICEF programs strength
        in, 167–68
    women's and caste issues in, 77–78
Grant, James P., 2, 97
GRB. *See* gender responsive budgeting
Gready, P., 7
Gruskin, Sofia, 121

Haftel, Y. Z., 15
Hamm, Brigitte, 6–7
hartals (general strikes), 2
hijra (transgender) community, 3, 52,
    64–65, 160
HIV/AIDS, 10, 61, 82, 109, 111, 173
Human Development Index, 61–62, 151
Human Development Report, 63, 151
human rights, 3, 33, 43, 133
    difficulty pushing for, 150
    equity and discrimination in, 47
    Human Rights Watch report on issues
        in, 41–42
    India monitoring of, 183
    indivisibility of, 7, 19
    RBA as alternative in
        promoting, 183–84
    RBA legal obligation of, 157
    RTI as, 72

human rights (*Cont.*)
  UN directive on, 32
  UNDP issues in, 16–17, 26
  UNFPA issues in, 138–41
  UN hidden work on, 4–5
  UNICEF promotion of, 16–17, 51, 54–55, 86
  Western influence on, 182
  WHO promotion of, 16–17
  World Bank on, 119
Human Rights in International Relations (Forsythe), 183
Human Rights Watch, 41–42, 44
HUNGaMA Survey Report, 112

ICPD. *See* International Conference on Population and Development
ICPS. *See* "Integrated Child Protection Scheme"
IDA. *See* International Development Agency
IFIs. *See* international financial institutions
Ikea, 98, 101
Ikea Foundation, 61
IMF. *See* International Monetary Fund
Independent Evaluation Group of World Bank, 154–55, 172
India, 16
  child labor and trafficking issues in, 43, 54, 88, 101–2, 131, 139, 171
  civil rights abuse by government agencies in, 43
  decentralization in, 49
  discrimination problem in, 43–44
  economy growth in, 40–41
  ES&C rights violations in, 44
  high growth and poverty rates in, 121
  human rights monitoring in, 183
  Human Rights Watch report on issues in, 41–42
  ICPS adoption by, 99
  implementation of rights lacking in, 38
  international agencies cooperation in, 191
  labor conditions in, 44
  legal system in, 41
  main political parties of, 2
  malnutrition in, 109–12, 121
  National Human Rights Commission issues in, 42–43
  Naxalite movements in, 103, 105, 192
  NCBF of, 77
  PRI in, 49, 77
  RBA resistance of, 15, 17, 191
  rights challenges in, 182
  rights implementation case study of, 24–25
  RTE in, 90
  RTI in, 53–54, 72
  sex selection and forced sterilization problem in, 139–41
  sex-selective abortion in, 98, 132, 137, 139–40
  UNDAF goals in, 44–45
  UNFPA history in, 134, 137–38, 169
  UNICEF influence in, 102–3
  violence against women and children in, 43, 131
  women disempowerment in, 129
  women's rights in, 54–55
Indian Constitution, 43, 94, 120
  equality in, 121
  justiciable and non-justiciable rights of, 39–40
  legal rights in, 40
  nondiscrimination in, 50
  PIL in, 40
Indian National Commission for Protection of Child Rights (NCPCR), 94
Indian Parliament, 39, 53, 72
Indian Supreme Court, 53, 72, 140

Index 207

"Integrated Child Protection Scheme" (ICPS), 99–100, 105
intergovernmental agencies, 2
International Committee of the Red Cross, 47
International Conference on Population and Development (ICPD), 139
International Development Agency (IDA), 118
international financial institutions (IFIs), 11
International Monetary Fund (IMF), 2
international organizations (IOs), 11
  bureaucratic politics of, 14–16, 186
  changing state behavior in, 187–88
  as conduits for new ideas, 187
  independence of, 4–5, 14, 188
  life cycle of norms in, 188–89
  norm institutionalization and implementation in, 189–90
  norm resistance overcome in, 190
  as "open systems," 186
  policy implementation resistance in, 188
  principle-agent problems in, 14
  pushback of, 16
  rights policy incentives in, 187
  sociological approach to internal working of, 15–16
  subnational government interaction of, 188
international relations theory (IR), 186–87
IOs. *See* international organizations
IR. *See* international relations theory

Jammu, India
  no UN agencies in, 185, 191–92
  terrorism in, 42–43, 47
Jan Jagriti Kendra (JJK), 64–66
JEEV. *See* Justice Equity Empowerment Volunteers

JJK. *See* Jan Jagriti Kendra
Joint UN Programme on HIV/AIDS (UNAIDS), 51, 61, 109
Jonsson, Urban, 47, 151, 156
Justice Equity Empowerment Volunteers (JEEV), 65

Kashmir, India
  no UN agencies in, 185, 191–92
  terrorism in, 42–43, 47
Kaufmann, Daniel, 37
Kirk, Jason, 126

Landman, Todd, 183
Langford, M., 7
LGBT, 82
local governing bodies. *See* Panchayats

Mahatma Gandhi National Rural Employment Guarantee Act (MGNREGA), 40, 80, 91, 120, 131, 165
  in government capacity building, 78–79
  problems in, 79
  as RBA example, 78–79
  rural poor employment guarantee of, 51, 78
Mawdsley, Emma, 17
Mazdoor Kisan Shakti Sangathan (MKSS), 69
M'baye, Keba, 21
MDGs. *See* Millennium Development Goals
MGNREGA. *See* Mahatma Gandhi National Rural Employment Guarantee Act
"The Millennium Development Declaration," 67
Millennium Development Goals (MDGs), 7, 18, 62, 80, 87–89, 90
Miller, Hannah, 8

208   *Index*

Ministry of Health and Family Welfare, 160
Ministry of Panchayati Raj, 74, 77
Ministry of Women and Children, 68
MKSS. *See* Mazdoor Kisan Shakti Sangathan

Naandi Foundation, 112
National Aids Control Organization, 109
National Campaign for People's Right to Information in India, 69
National Capability Building Framework (NCBF), 77
National Human Rights Commission of India, 42–43
National Rural Employment Guarantee Act (NREGA), 125
National Rural Health Mission, 111, 138
National Rural Livelihoods Mission, 124, 127
National Rural Livelihoods Project, 124
Naxalite movements, 103, 105, 192
NCBF. *See* National Capability Building Framework
NCPCR. *See* Indian National Commission for Protection of Child Rights
New Delhi, India, 12, 17, 41, 54, 61, 76, 91
New International Economic Order, 21
nongovernmental agencies, 2, 25
non-governmental organizations (NGOs), 23, 47–48, 52, 63, 82, 102
NREGA. *See* National Rural Employment Guarantee Act

Office of the United Nations High Commissioner for Human Rights (OHCHR), 34
Orchard, Phil, 189

PAHELI. *See* Peoples Assessment of Health, Education and Livelihood program
Panchayat Act, 81
Panchayati Raj Institution (PRI) system, 49, 77
  affirmative provisions for poor in, 123
  women's rights in, 54–55
  World Bank regarding, 126
Panchayats (local governing bodies), 94, 110, 130, 153, 162, 164, 170
  capacity development of, 49, 74–75
  DG in, 73
Pathways for an Inclusive Indian Administration, 51, 78
Peoples Assessment of Health, Education and Livelihood (PAHELI) program, 79–80
PIL. *See* public interest litigation
PIO. *See* public information officer
Positive Women's Network (PWN+), 171–72
poverty, 6, 43, 121, 124–25
Prenatal Diagnostic Techniques (Regulation and Prevention of Misuse) Act, 140
PRI. *See* Panchayati Raj Institution system
Protecting Human Rights (Landman), 183
Protection of Women from Domestic Violence Act, 132
public information officer (PIO), 53, 70–71, 165
public interest litigation (PIL), 40
PWN+. *See* Positive Women's Network

RBA. *See* "rights-based approach to development"
RBA strategies
  government disaggregated data use as, 151–52

Human Development Report use in, 151
media use to ensure transparency as, 152
rights issues not using "rights" terms as, 152–53
rights language acceptance by government as, 152–53
UN "convening power" and goodwill as, 153
RBM. *See* results-based management systems
Reinalda, B., 14
resistance, 31, 56, 190
   C&P rights, 60
   government, to language of RBA, 151
   India's towards RBA, 15, 17, 191
   policy implementation, of IOs, 188
   RTI governmental, 72–73
   towards UNDP, 60–61, 80–81
results-based management (RBM) systems, 89, 108–9, 179, 187
Right of Children to Free and Compulsory Education Act (RTE), 90–92, 94
"rights-based approach to development" (RBA), 3–5, 167. *See also* RBA strategies
   "Access to Justice" programs in, 37, 46, 51–53
   "accountability" in, 36
   as alternative in promoting human rights, 183–84
   central argument for, 174
   conflict zone political implications of, 103–7
   as *cooperative* way of pursuing rights, 184–85
   counterfactual analysis in, 158–59
   C&P rights in, 8–9, 19, 179
   CP use of, 98–100
   definition unclear of, 152, 179, 181
   different approaches coexist in, 155
   duties creation in, 38
   empowerment of people in, 6, 8, 34–35
   "entitlements" as key element of, 7
   equity in, 45
   evaluation of, 154–57
   government resistance to language of, 151
   health sector staff on, 110
   HIV/AIDS program use of, 82, 109
   "hold governments to account" in, 37–38
   human rights legal obligation of, 157
   implementation results of, 175
   India's resistance to, 15, 17, 191
   inequality and inequity link in, 122
   MGNREGA as example of, 78–79
   as moral imperative, 156–57, 161
   "negative" rights in, 35
   nondiscrimination as central component to, 50–51
   nonmeasurable results of, 178–79
   as normative framework, 156, 174
   Nutrition staff on, 109–10, 112
   other cases applicability of, 190–92
   "participation" as strategy in, 36, 47
   policy development and service delivery in, 7
   political and moral elements of, 33–34, 174
   "positive" rights in, 34
   pressuring governments into action by, 38–39
   as producing development, 156
   project-level evaluation inconsistencies in, 155
   question and challenge existing structures in, 149
   RBM versus, 108–9, 187
   respect for all rights in, 37
   results hard to measure in, 175

"rights-based approach to development"
(*Cont.*)
  as rhetorical exercise, 8, 13, 55, 144
  rhetoric and reality of, 144, 178
  right to education implications
    in, 36–37
  right to information in, 53–54
  root causes in, 6
  RTD connections and differences
    of, 20–24
  as set of policies, 23
  spotty compliance in, 161
  strategies of, 151–54
  technical areas lag in, 179, 181
  theory of change in, 158
  UN agencies staff on, 17–18
  UN before, 10
  "UN Common Understanding of the
    Human Rights-based Approach
    to Development Cooperation"
    statement on, 33
  UN definition of, 32
  underserved populations in, 35–36
  UNDP disaster relief and mitigation
    use of, 81–82
  UNDP use of, 60, 75, 78, 81–82, 161
  UNFPA use of, 136–37, 141, 179
  UNICEF approach to education
    using, 95–97
  UNICEF use of, 87–89, 90, 94–97,
    112–13, 161, 180
  UN organizational directive of, 192
  UN rights-development link study
    of, 157–58
  UN terminology inconsistent
    use in, 14
  UN traditional formulation
    of, 185–86
  "voice" and "participation" in, 110
  whether it works central issue
    of, 154–55
  women's rights in, 54–55

  World Bank use of, 118–20, 122, 127,
    143, 172–73
rights language, 152–53
  UNFPA use of, 140–41, 143
  UN use of, 10–11
  World Bank use of, 122–23
right to development (RTD), 17
  RBA connections and differences
    to, 20–24
  as rhetorical concept, 23
Right to Education Act, 40, 91, 163, 179
Right to Education Campaign. *See*
  Shiksha Ka Haq Abhiyan
right to information (RTI), 60, 91, 99, 120
  Covenant on Civil and Political Rights
    Article 19 on, 53
  General Assembly Resolution
    59(1) on, 53
  goal of, 70
  government officials hostility and
    resistance towards, 72–73
  in India, 53–54, 72
  as indigenous movement, 70, 71
  MKSS in, 69
  political spin on, 71
  roots of, 69–70
  UNDP public awareness promotion
    of, 71–72
  UNDP use and support of, 53, 70–71,
    73, 165
  UN Special Rapporteur on Freedom
    of Opinion and Expression on, 53
  World Bank support of, 53, 122, 127
Right to Information Act, 40, 53
  anecdote about, 69
  purpose of, 70
Roberts, Alasdair, 72
Roy, A., 70
RTD. *See* right to development
RTE. *See* Right of Children to Free and
  Compulsory Education Act
RTI. *See* right to information

Sano, Hans-Otto, 7
Sarfaty, G. A., 15
Scheduled Castes, 46–47, 73, 119–20, 126
  discrimination against, 40, 43–44, 50, 77, 79, 142
  economic marginalization of, 151
Scheduled Tribes, 46–47, 68–69, 103, 119–20, 126
  discrimination against, 40, 43–44, 50, 77, 79, 142
  economic marginalization of, 151
  empowerment of, 76
Schmitz, Hans-Peter, 6
school management committees (SMCs), 49, 93–94, 96
Second High Level Forum on Aid Effectiveness, 61
Sen, Amartya, 7, 36, 121, 122, 124
Sengupta, A., 21
sex selection and forced sterilization, 139–41
sex-selective abortion, 98, 132, 137, 139–40
sexual and reproductive health (SRH), 135
Shetty, Satish, 72
Shiksha Ka Haq Abhiyan (Right to Education Campaign), 93, 99
Shue, Henry, 19, 38
Singh, Shekhar, 69, 72
SMCs. *See* school management committees
SRH. *See* sexual and reproductive health
Sumner, A., 7

Tamil Nadu Chief Justice, 68
Tehran World Conference on Human Rights, 20
theory of change, 158–60
Thomas, Caroline, 8
Thompson, A., 15

trafficking, 43, 139, 171
  CP handling of, 88, 101–2
  of women and girls, 54, 101–2, 131
transgender. *See hijra*

UN. *See* United Nations
UNAIDS. *See* Joint UN Programme on HIV/AIDS
UN Charter, 11, 23, 119
  Article 2(7) of, 12–13, 151
"UN Common Understanding of the Human Rights-based Approach to Development Cooperation," 33
UN Country Directors, 12
UNDAF. *See* United Nations Development Assistance Framework
UNDG. *See* United Nations Development Group
UNDP. *See* United Nations Development Program
UN Entity for Gender Equality and the Empowerment of Women. *See* UN Women
UNFPA. *See* United Nations Population Fund
UN-Government of India Joint Programme on Convergence, 50
UN High Commissioner for Human Rights, 24, 38, 108, 184
UNICEF. *See* United Nations Children's Fund
United Nations (UN), 53
  "community-level engagement" instead of rights talk in, 9
  "convening power" and goodwill as RBA strategy of, 153
  C&P and ES&C promotion in, 4–6, 179–80, 184
  decentralization as key development strategy in, 48, 50
  development priorities of, 3

United Nations (*Cont.*)
  development programming questions of, 178
  effectiveness of policies in, 26–27
  "equity agenda" of, 62–63
  ES&C rights emphasis of, 5–6
  human rights directive of, 32
  human rights hidden work of, 4–5
  human rights scholarly work ignoring of, 183–84
  Jammu and Kashmir off limits to, 185, 191–92
  MDGs and RBM complaints in, 89
  MDGs as key goal of, 88
  national ownership promotion in, 61
  as "neutral" agency, 182
  new diplomatic skills in, 26
  non-interference in host state politics of, 2
  no political backlash directives in, 180–81
  norm institutionalization and implementation in, 189–90
  norm resistance overcome in, 190
  politics avoidance in, 150
  RBA definition of, 32
  before RBA in, 10
  RBA of, 3–4
  RBA organizational directive of, 192
  RBA terminology inconsistent use in, 14
  RBA traditional formulation of, 185–86
  replacing "mobilization" with "participation anecdote of, 150
  rhetoric and reality of rights in, 13
  rights as rhetorical exercise of, 8
  rights-development link study of, 157–58
  rights language use in, 10–11
  rights promotion through development assistance in, 14, 55–56
  rights promotion to measurable development outcomes limited in, 185
  service-based programming as rights promotion in, 180
  staff definition of "rights" in, 46–47
  staff rights promotion conflict in, 13
  as strategic actors, 153–54
United Nations Children's Fund (UNICEF), 9, 11, 15, 23, 25–26, 60, 192
  action plan program areas of, 88
  analysis of development outcomes in, 166
  bilingual education promotion of, 95
  "block volunteers" training in, 94–95
  C4D program of, 51, 54–55, 110
  capacity-development programs strength of, 167–68
  CEDC interest of, 97–98
  "changing gears" in, 166
  "child collectives" of, 94
  Child Protection program of, 52
  conflict area access of, 106–7
  conflict zone as politically sensitive area of, 103–4
  conflict zone political implications of RBA, 103–7
  conflict zone staff cautiousness in, 104–5
  conflict zone staff on C&P rights, 105–6
  country evaluation terms of, 167
  CPAP education sectors of, 90–91
  CPAP goals of, 87
  CP as "the rights unit" of, 87–89, 97, 161, 187
  CP handling of child labor and trafficking issues in, 88, 101–2
  CP objective in, 97–98
  CP staff on RBA in, 100
  CP use of RBA in, 98–99

CRC use in, 12, 32, 46–47, 54–55, 86, 89, 97
decentralization and participation promotion in, 113, 168
disaggregating data importance in, 95, 113, 168
equity importance to staff in, 45
evaluation difficulty in, 160
evaluation report criticism of, 168
"every child, everywhere" principle of, 106
health sector staff in, 110
high-impact child survival strategies promotion of, 2
HIV/AIDS program in, 82, 109, 111
human rights promotion role of, 16–17, 51, 54–55, 86
ICPS support of, 99–100
influence in India of, 102–3
key parts of evaluation in, 167
legal system training of, 94
local communities organizing by, 3
MDGs in, 87
Nutrition sector work in, 109–12
planning document of, 45
political involvement of, 182
RBA approach to education of, 95–97
RBA conflict zones work of, 87
RBA integration in, 87–89, 90, 94–97, 112–13, 161, 180
RBA understanding by staff in, 167
RBM versus RBA in, 108–9, 187
replacing "mobilization" with "participation anecdote of, 150
rights implementation of, 86–87
RTE legislation behind the scenes work of, 91–92, 96
school quality improvement concern of, 92–93
schools as "zones of peace" creation by, 106
Shiksha Ka Haq Abhiyan work with, 93

SMCs creation of, 49, 93–94
staff on education advancement politics in, 96–97
staff on rights importance in, 107–8
theory of change in, 158
violence against women and children problem in, 43, 131
Water and Sanitation work of, 110–11
women's rights work of, 54
United Nations Development Assistance Framework (UNDAF), 55, 63, 121
improved governance outcome in, 45
India goals of, 44–45
United Nations Development Group (UNDG), 134
United Nations Development Program (UNDP), 9, 15, 23, 25, 55, 134, 181
"Access to Justice" programs use of, 51–52, 64–69, 161
activities of, 3
ADR on governance portfolio of, 164–65
ADR report critiques on, 162–63
ADR report on human development outcomes in, 158, 162
capacity building of, 70–71, 76–81
contribution sources of, 61
CPAP of, 62
C&P rights involvement of, 60–61, 65–68, 82–83, 86
decentralization agenda of, 77
decentralization technical support of, 49
development as rights achievement in, 67
DG in, 73–76
DG program evaluation of, 163–64
discrimination fight in, 51
empowerment in, 35
evaluation data sources of, 159
evaluation difficulty in, 160–61, 165–66

United Nations Development Program (*Cont.*)
　hijra community work of, 52
　Human Development Index use of, 61
　human rights promotion role of, 16–17, 26
　"Integrating Human Rights with Sustainable Development" guidelines of, 32
　JJK work with, 64–66
　local self-help group support of, 49
　measurable progress in, 163
　MGNREGA work of, 78–79
　"national implementation" use in, 63
　number of programs and lack of focus in, 163
　PAHELI program and staff description of, 79–80
　Panchayats capacity building of, 49, 74–75
　Pathways for an Inclusive Indian Administration project of, 51, 78
　PIO training in, 71
　program areas of, 62
　program evaluation report of, 154
　RBA use in, 60, 75, 78, 81–82, 161
　resistance towards, 60–61, 80–81
　rights discussion with staff of, 12
　RTI public awareness promotion by, 71–72
　RTI use and support in, 53, 70–71, 73, 165
　"Scheduled Tribes and Other Traditional Forest Dwellers Act" implementation by, 68–69
　"sensitization" training for judges in, 68
　staff on C&P rights in, 67–68
　staff on working with *hijra* community, 65
　structural adjustment in, 22
　successes in, 164–65
　theory of change caveats of, 159–60
　transgender rights training program and goals of, 64–65
United Nations Entity for Gender Equality and the Empowerment of Women, 128
United Nations Human Rights Council, 4, 24, 43, 183–84
United Nations Population Fund (UNFPA), 18, 25–26, 117, 132, 160
　agency collaborations of, 134
　assessment failures of, 170
　assessment national-level achievement goals for, 169
　assessment successes in, 169–70
　budget problem regarding goals for, 169
　country strategic plan outputs of, 136
　C&P and ES&C rights use in, 135
　discrimination against women and girls fought in, 50–51
　empowerment of women in, 142–43
　GBV awareness promotion of, 137
　human rights issues of, 138–41
　India government history with, 134, 137–38, 169
　information and knowledge as human right issue of, 138–39
　priority issues of, 135–36
　progressive programming in, 138
　RBA use in, 136–37, 141, 179
　rhetoric and reality of rights promotion in, 144
　rights language use in, 140–41, 143
　rural committees promotion of, 142
　sex selection and forced sterilization as human right issue of, 139–41
　SRH focus of, 135
　staff on rights implications in, 136–37
　strategic plan outcomes focus of, 134–35
　technical nature of work in, 143

top staff key priorities in, 138
women's rights work of, 54
United Nations University, 34
United States Agency for International Development (USAID), 67
Universal Declaration of Human Rights, 11–12, 33–34, 36, 48, 50, 122
Universal Human Rights in Theory and Practice (Donnelly), 183
Universal Periodic Review (UPR), 18, 43, 44, 183–84
UN Security Council, 16, 119, 185
UN Special Rapporteur on Freedom of Opinion and Expression, 53
UN Women, 3, 25–26, 55, 117, 142–43, 181
  assessment operations of, 170–71
  CEDAW as human rights document of, 133
  conflict zone work of, 130
  Dalit women empowering program evaluation of, 172
  empowerment of women by, 129–30
  evaluation difficulty in, 160
  goal of, 128
  GRB in, 130–31, 160, 171
  human trafficking program assessment of, 171
  mandate of, 128
  priority areas of, 128–29
  programming partners of, 130
  PWN+ program evaluation of, 171–72
  revolutionary nature of work in, 133–34
  rights policy incentive structures of, 187
  social change promotion of, 131–32
  social structure transformation of, 132–33
  violence against women work of, 131
  women's political participation and leadership promotion of, 130
  women's rights work of, 54

UN Women Fund for Gender Equality, 172
UPR. *See* Universal Periodic Review
USAID. *See* United States Agency for International Development
Uvin, Peter, 8, 20, 34

Vandenhole, W., 7
Verbeek, B., 14
Vienna Declaration of 1993, 20

Wade, Robert, 16
Weaver, C., 15
WFP. *See* World Food Programme
WHO. *See* World Health Organization
WLHA. *See* Women Living with HIV/AIDS
women, 77–78, 128. *See also* Convention on the Elimination of All Forms of Discrimination Against Women
  in DG, 74–75
  discrimination against, 44, 50–51, 79, 131, 139
  empowerment of, 129–30, 142–43, 172
  rights in India of, 54–55
  violence against, in India, 43, 131
Women Living with HIV/AIDS (WLHA), 171–72
World Bank, 2–3, 9, 12, 25–26, 40–41, 191
  antipoverty program of, 124–25
  assessment of, as mixed, 173
  "Bihar Rural Livelihoods Project" social exclusion study of, 123–24
  country strategy of, 118
  decentralization technical support of, 49
  empowerment statement of, 34–35
  equality and equity difference in, 120–21
  "equity agenda" of, 117–18, 121–22, 143–44

World Bank (*Cont.*)
  equity in, 62–63, 120–22
  evaluation mixed results of, 172–73
  growth and equity promotion in, 125–26
  HIV/AIDS sector work assessment of, 173
  human rights regarding, 119
  incentive structures of, 187
  inequality and inequity link in, 122
  political activity prohibited in, 11
  poverty reduction political side in, 124
  priority areas of, 119–20
  PRI regarding, 126
  RBA use in, 118–20, 122, 127, 143, 172–73
  reproductive and child health empowerment project evaluation of, 154
  rights implementation frustration of, 126–27
  "rights" word use in, 46
  as risk-averse, 181
  RTI support in, 53, 122, 127
  safeguard policies and criticism of, 127–28
  staff on RBA, 118–20
  staff on rights language use in, 122–23
  underserved groups targeting of, 126
  women's rights in, 128
World Food Programme (WFP), 19, 23
World Health Organization (WHO), 11, 15, 25, 134
  discrimination fighting as development tool in, 51
  HIV policy change sought by, 10
  human rights promotion role of, 16–17
  RBA and technical work of, 143

Yamin, A. E., 7
Yashwantrao Chavan Academy of Development Administration (YASHADA), 71

www.ingramcontent.com/pod-product-compliance
Ingram Content Group UK Ltd.
Pitfield, Milton Keynes, MK11 3LW, UK
UKHW021329180426
11947UKWH00017B/1529